EVERYBODY
IS SITTING ON
THE CURB

EVERYBODY IS SITTING ON THE CURB

How and Why America's Heroes Disappeared

ALAN EDELSTEIN

Westport, Connecticut
London

Library of Congress Cataloging-in-Publication Data

Edelstein, Alan.
    Everybody is sitting on the curb : how and why America's heroes
disappeared / by Alan Edelstein.
       p. cm.
    Includes bibliographical references and index.
    ISBN 0-275-95364-5 (alk. paper)
    1. Heroes—United States. 2. United States—Civilization—
Philosophy. I. Title.
    E169.1.E28 1996
    973—dc20   95–50897

British Library Cataloguing in Publication Data is available.

Library of Congress Catalog Card Number: 95–50897
ISBN: 0-275-95364-5

First published in 1996

Praeger Publishers, 88 Post Road West, Westport, CT 06881
An imprint of Greenwood Publishing Group, Inc.

Printed in the United States of America

The paper used in this book complies with the
Permanent Paper Standard issued by the National
Information Standards Organization (Z39.48–1984).

10 9 8 7 6 5 4 3 2 1

Andrea: *Unglücklich das Land, das keine Helden hat!*
Galileo: *Nein, unglücklich das Land, das Helden nötig hat!*

Andrea: Unhappy the land that has no heroes.
Galileo: No, unhappy the land that needs heroes.

Bertold Brecht, *Leber des Galilei*

The chief business of the nation, as a nation, is the setting up of
heroes, mainly bogus.

H. L. Mencken

We can't all be heroes because somebody has to sit on the curb and
clap as they go by.

Will Rogers

Contents

Acknowledgments

This book could not have been written without the friendship, support, and guidance of a number of people. Ed Falick was always there when needed; it's been like this forever. Linda Martinez is bright and talented and unfailing in her encouragement and support. Holly L. Dietor, Glenn and Linda Marston, and Regina M. Tabackman provided me with insights, a sense of proportion, and substantial amounts of humor. Anyone who has written a book knows how important these are and how hard they are to find. Ginny and Alan Busch and Denzel and Jennifer Stoops supplied encouragement and support. So did Sadie Edelstein; mothers often do that.

Several people read various portions of this work. My colleagues at Towson State University in Maryland—Marion Cockey, Victor Fisher, Irwin Goldberg, M. Barbara Leons, R. Guy Sedlack, and Jay Stanley—suggested substantive changes in the text. MaryKay Mulligan and Gordon Herbster suggested significant structural revisions in the text. The book is better for the imagination, wisdom, and efforts of all of these people.

It is impossible to overstate my debt to my wife, Carole Ann Sharp, for her efforts in seeing this book reach its conclusion. Without her support and enthusiasm it wouldn't have been completed; without her suggestions and insights it would have been a lesser work.

Part I

The Problem

Chapter 1

No More Heroes

INTRODUCTION

The United States has run out of heroes. "Hero" refers to a national hero, a Universal American around whom we all would rally if called. The hero is the man—rarely the woman, a point to be considered later—who inspires children and adults, who reflects the finest qualities of the American people, and who is recognized by the American people as an inspiration and as someone who reflects those qualities. It is not just that the hero represents most if not all Americans; it is that most if not all Americans are happy to have him as their representative. That is the man who is gone from our lives—and permanently.

Nor are there any arenas from which a modern American hero can arise. Quite the contrary, many of the fields from which Americans drew their past heroes are gone, and the structures of other fields that were once sources of American heroes have been altered to the point of obstructing the creation of new heroes.

The argument here is not that there aren't heroic people in the United States anymore. Americans perform heroic acts every day. A glance at any local newspaper testifies to that assertion. "Ordinary" men and women in this country regularly perform extraordinary feats of courage and self-sacrifice. As a matter of course members of local police and fire departments save lives while risking their own. Federal agents who place themselves in danger combatting drug traffickers, the men and women of our armed forces, and the people who work in emergency rooms of big city hospitals are only some of the Americans who routinely perform actions that can only be called heroic.

But these heroic actions do not necessarily make them heroes. They are performed as a function of the job and in that sense they are not extraordinary. More important, these heroic actions, brave and self-sacrificing as they may be, are generally acknowledged locally, not nationally. To be a hero is to be a national hero, and to be a national hero is to have national recognition. If this were not the case the "American hero" would be defined by a small number of people, by a few individuals living within a limited geographical area. The American hero would be reduced to idiosyncratic and compartmentalized whim.

To avoid this possibility, the respect and admiration of people throughout the United States is a requisite for status as an American hero. The only way to become a national hero is to accomplish something that demands and receives national recognition. But that doesn't seem to happen anymore. It is difficult to recall the last ticker-tape parade for an individual American hero. Ticker-tape parades these days celebrate groups: freed hostages, winning ball teams, returning service personnel. Even those who courageously helped in the rescue of the people trapped after the explosion of the Federal Building in Oklahoma City were admired collectively. The individual American hero has vanished.

Americans generally agree that we no longer have any heroes, that the giants that once dominated our history in various arenas no longer exist, and that no new heroes have risen in their place. That is one reason why Americans today look backward for their heroes. Tales of politicians and military men, gunfighters and sports figures, gangsters and adventurers, idols and celebrities of not so recent history, are constantly relived in movies and on television, and the images of past heroes are regularly shown on calendars and posters. We recall our past heroes with great enthusiasm because there aren't any contemporary heroes of equal stature to take their place.

So uncertain is the status of hero in the United States today that even some of our traditional heroes have come into question. In part this is because of "political correctness," but in part it is because of a diminishing reverence for and increasing cynicism toward heroes generally. A list of America's heroes who are under attack include Columbus, perhaps the easiest example, who has gone from being "the discoverer of America" to being a butcher of innocents, a cruel and inept conqueror, a symbol of genocide. Since his assassination John Kennedy has been idolized, but he has also been vilified to the point where Douglas Brinkley regards some of the attacks on his memory as approaching a "vendetta." Albert Einstein, the twentieth century's symbol of intellectual greatness, has been accused of being "an adulterous, egomaniacal misogynist." And Walt Disney, who made his reputation by making wholesome films for the whole family to enjoy, was, according to a biography—an "unauthorized" one, obviously—impotent, anti-Semitic, and an alcoholic. Further, he "never actually drew Mickey Mouse." [1]

There have been attacks on George Washington, a slave owner; on Thomas Jefferson, a racist and slave owner (Washington freed his slaves, Jefferson didn't); on Paul Revere, who never did reach Concord (and the celebrated midnight ride may have been a sham); on Abraham Lincoln, who, in addition to telling stories that were racist, knowingly dealt with dishonest politicians; and on the defenders of the Alamo, who were at best liars and at worst cowardly.

None of the efforts at demythifying the heroes of America's past has succeeded as of yet, and it is unlikely that the images of idols such as Washington, Jefferson, or Lincoln, to select the most obvious examples, will be destroyed. Still, the efforts to harm their memories do exist, and there can be no doubt that the legends of some of America's past icons will suffer. Future generations will have fewer traditional heroes to admire, if they have any at all.

There is ample proof, both anecdotal and substantive, that the United States no longer has any heroes, nor has the ability to produce new ones. Numerous people have gone on record suggesting that the American hero has vanished. Both historian Arthur Schlesinger, Jr., and political scientist Larry Nachman, for example, argue that we live in an era that is void of heroes. Our lives are no longer filled with and controlled by great men. Kenneth Clark, the noted psychologist, argues that regardless of the field, the time of the national hero is past. Others agree that we no longer create heroes in the United States. Daniel Boorstin dislikes those who today are feted but who are simply "manufactured" heroes of our time, and Kim McQuaid calls his study of the Vietnam/Watergate Era a "history without heroes." [2]

People as diverse in attitudes and personality as Tom Wolfe and Jimmy Carter, Norman Mailer and Mike Royko concur: there is today a paucity of heroes in the United States—virtually none. Royko argues that today's role models are no match for those of America's past and Mailer suggests that there's no one left to "capture the secret imagination of a people and so be good for the vitality of his nation." Jimmy Carter has noted that ours is "an age of few heroes." Tom Wolfe agrees, adding that the situation is not going to improve in the foreseeable future. Russell Baker in his *New York Times* column has suggested that "heroes are pretty well all washed up in America these days," while Walter Turett Anderson, writing in the *UTNE Reader*, asked have we "outgrown the age of heroes?" A *Newsweek* magazine article is titled "In Search of Heroes." The author of the article, Peter H. Gibbon, is not optimistic about the success of the search. Writing in *The New Yorker*, Bill Buford notes that "ours is not a time of heroes," and a play by Sam Shepard has one character noting the rapid death of our heroes; the reason: "it's a sign a' the times." [3]

Another indication that people are aware that the American hero has vanished is discernible from contemporary literature. An amazing number of books and articles published in the United States, both fiction and nonfiction, are titled or subtitled "the last hero," an obvious indication that the authors believe that there are no heroes left in the country, that the subject of the book or article was or is America's final hero. An equally impressive number of books and articles wonder where America's heroes have gone. Some call attention to individuals the authors believe should be regarded as national heroes but who are unknown to most people. There are writers who come right to the point. Edward Hoagland, Joshua Meyrowitz, Don Wycliff, and Daniel Walden all ask the same question: What has happened? Where did America's heroes go? [4]

Most important of all, the American people do not think that the United States has any heroes. This attitude on the part of the people is of special significance because a hero, and especially an American hero, is a social creation. The American hero is, and can only be, a consequence of the attitudes of the American people: a hero is a hero only because the people say he is. The denial of the existence of an American hero by the American people, then, is critical because their denial is the final statement about the subject.

And they do deny the hero. A survey published in *Time* magazine pointed out that only two men were regarded as heroes to people between the ages of 18 and 44, Robert Kennedy and Martin Luther King, Jr., both dead more than twenty years at the time the survey was taken. That may be why President Clinton evoked their memories in a speech in May 1994. They were the last people who could be celebrated by the nation. In the years since the *Time* survey was taken no one has been elevated to the status of Kennedy or King in the eyes of the American people. A more recent *Time*/CNN poll indicated that younger Americans cannot agree upon a hero. On a broader level, one study revealed that fully 70 percent of the people—seven out of every ten Americans—believe that we no longer have any living heroes. That percentage is unlikely to improve in time. If anything, the number of Americans who believe in an American hero will diminish. Because the American hero is a product of the beliefs of the American people, and as Americans believe that we no longer have any American heroes, ipso facto, we no longer have any American heroes.[5]

YOU CAN SEEK BUT YOU WILL NOT FIND

Arthur Schlesinger, Jr., is incorrect in suggesting that our age "objects" to heroes (as well as to hero worship). It doesn't object to heroes, it just can't find any. The United States still searches for heroes, still seeks them out. On occasion the search borders on the frenetic. In fact, the public demand for heroes is so extensive that there are advertisements for them. *Parade* magazine asked people to nominate an unsung hero so that he might receive national recognition, and *Newsweek* magazine ran an advertisement from *America's Awards* asking people to "send us a story of your hero." The cover of an earlier issue of *Parade* magazine featured a picture of John F. Kennedy's children; the accompanying article had them asking the public to "Help Us Find A Hero." [6]

The Carnegie Hero Fund located in Pittsburgh, Pennsylvania, is dedicated to identifying, locating, and rewarding individuals throughout the country who have performed heroic deeds. The fund has specific criteria to determine who qualifies as a hero and stipulates that those whose "vocations require them to perform [heroic] acts" are ineligible to receive the award. There are exceptions to the rule however: those who perform acts of courage that are "clearly beyond the line of duty" may be regarded as heroes. A second organization, The Giraffe Project based in Washington, D.C., also recognizes heroes, specifically "local heroes who stick their necks out to make the world a better place." Although more subjective in its judgment than the Carnegie Hero Fund and limited geographically because it looks for local heroes, the idea is the same: seek out and recognize heroes. [7]

The media are doing their part to find contemporary American heroes. One television program (on the Arts & Entertainment network) was in fact called "Heroes" and ABC has its "Person of the Week," a weekly segment of ABC's national news broadcast designed to demonstrate to us that we still are capable of producing heroes, people of consequence. It is not at all unusual for a "Movie of the Week" or for television magazine shows (or print magazines, for that matter) to tell the story of an unheralded individual who accomplished something praiseworthy. Newspapers also contribute to the effort to find and to call attention to potential national heroes. Sunday supplements regularly include stories detailing the exploits of an unknown individual who risked life and limb for a significant purpose. This is all fine and the individuals considered here surely deserve their place in the sun. But as heroic as their efforts are, and as noble as the efforts of the media are to celebrate those efforts, they cannot hide the fact that the United States no longer has any heroes.

HERO SUBSTITUTES, HEROES MANQUÉ, AND CELEBRITY-HEROES

The general realization that we no longer have any heroes, coupled with a need—occasionally a desperate need—for a hero, explains several recent phenomena, including the extraordinary degree of celebration over Desert Storm and the labeling of anyone even remotely associated with it as a hero. Public demand is what creates heroes, even if, as Gerald White Johnson has noted, that creation is occasionally made "out of the scantiest materials."

When this is carried to an extreme virtually anything becomes praise-worthy. Barbara Tuchman commented that, at a conference on heroes she attended, "the . . . hero [that they were talking about] was [a] little girl who'd fallen down a well." Tuchman's point was exactly the problem with the desperate search for a hero: That little girl was courageous, but she "didn't do anything to make herself a hero—she was just in the news."[8]

Because nations need heroes, when there are no true ones available false ones are created. That is why the United States today enjoys temporary heroes and hero substitutes. The United States cannot let the idea of the American hero fade away and so Americans anoint heroes regardless of their qualifications for that once esteemed status. For years polls have reported that the people Americans admire the most are from the world of popular entertainment, people of considerable fame within society but who make limited contributions to society. Our "heroes" are almost exclusively sports stars, actors and actresses, and representatives of popular culture. For example, the leading representatives of the "Heroes of Young America" from 1980 through 1990 consisted of ten entertainers and one athlete. (General Schwarzkopf was the leading hero of young America in 1991.) In 1993 the top female heroes were, in order of popularity, Connie Chung (a newscaster most celebrated then for having interviewed Tonya Harding), Monica Seles (a professional tennis player), and Tori Spelling (an actress). That year the top male hero by far was basketball star Michael Jordan. Some children (all boys) have reported their heroes to be Rambo, Arnold Schwarzenegger, and Freddy Krueger (the killer from the *Nightmare on Elm Street* films). In the mid-1990s the Mighty Morphin Power Rangers were the heroes of America's girls and boys.[9]

For Daniel Boorstin one problem is that even if we do derive our culture heroes from the world of entertainment, they are not from the classical portion of that world. We take our culture heroes from the entertainment world's more popular forms. One assumes that Boorstin prefers classical music to rock, ballet to the "Tush Push," and Broadway to daytime soaps. But there is no reason why practitioners of the classical arts are more qualified to be American heroes than those from the more popular arts. Whether one sings an aria from Puccini or the current pop, country, or rap hit, whether one stars in *Death of a Salesman* or *Guiding Light*, whether one performs in *Swan Lake* or on an MTV dance show, one is still a singer, an actor, or a dancer, respectively, and none of these professions demand a heroic persona. Creative ability is indicative of imagination and talent, not heroism.

The more significant point is that cultural celebrities, the heroes of popular culture and occasionally high culture, the practitioners of the lesser or serious arts, have during the past few decades become the representative voices of Americans. Culture artists are now the voices of reason—or lunacy—within the United States. For years "serious" magazines and journals have published articles about movie, television, and sports stars, analyzing their opinions on everything from politics to religion, from international relations to the nation's economy. Currently fashion designers and models speak the truth to the masses. Calvin Klein is interviewed by Larry King, and Ralph Lauren and Karl Lagerfeld by Charlie Rose; Cindy Crawford (among other celebrity models) is a regular on cable television.

Of course much of this is not new. Sports stars and entertainment celebrities have always been included among America's folk heroes. There were a substantial number of movie stars and sports heroes during the decades preceding World War II: Chaplin, Pickford, and Fairbanks; Cooper, Lombard, and Gable; Ruth, Wills, and Dempsey; Louis, Zaharias, and Gehrig. And most were anything but reticent about offering their views on a number of subjects. But among these celebrity heroes were other, more substantial representatives of the United States: military men and scientists, politicians and businessmen, adventurers and moral leaders. Recently, because there are no other national heroes and because culture heroes have instant access to the media, they have become our only heroes and on occasion advocates for causes, many of them inane, some of them contro- versial. Their right to speak out for what they believe in is guaranteed by the Constitution. Their right to do so as American heroes is guaranteed by a lack of other American heroes.

Celebrities, Boorstin points out, are people who are famous for being famous. Their accomplishment (singular) lies in the fact that they are known to the masses and, the masses would like to think, by the masses. The cause for their being known is, of course, irrelevant. The modern celebrity lives as did Antonio Salieri in Peter Shaffer's *Amadeus*: forced to endure "being called 'Distinguished' by people incapable of distinguishing." But Salieri recognized the foolishness of it all and hated the circumstance, while at least some of our "distinguished" citizens cannot see the fatuity of the situation, and virtually all of them enjoy their celebrity status. They capitalize on the fifteen minutes of fame allotted to them by Andy Warhol, and become temporary heroes in the process. Because there are no longer any true heroes left, ersatz heroes will have to do.[10]

The contemporary American hero, then, is in effect a hero manqué, a celebrity for whatever reason—for athletic ability, for audience appeal, for the fact of being a celebrity. Herb Greer correctly argues that the majority of America's current heroes receive honors that "tend to be onetime, ephemeral moments and sentiments." The reason is that America's current heroes are themselves onetime, ephemeral heroes, celebrities of the mo- ment. [11]

Some caution is advised here, however. While celebrity status by no means makes one a hero, celebrity status is necessary for the existence of the hero. To be a national hero is to be admired by a considerable number of people, which means that one must be known by a considerable part of the American public. That is, without "minstrels to sing of them or scribblers to set them down" acts that are heroic will simply disappear; they will vanish. Yet the efforts of minstrels and scribblers also define the celebrity. With the advent of mass communications—the mass media— and the relative ease with which one can become famous, it becomes easy to confuse the hero and the celebrity. Clearly Boorstin is correct in his assessment regarding the fatuity of celebrity, but fame is a part of the deal and consequently a celebrity catch-22 exists.[12]

A second facet of this paradox is that while the hero can only be a national hero if he is known to the public, the public cannot inquire too deeply into the private life of the hero. For a hero to exist in the United States, the media must insure that while the hero's exploits are being celebrated by the public, his peccadilloes, failings, and errors of action and judgment are kept hidden from them.

In the past this was often done. Perhaps the (now) most famous instance here is the media's willingness to refrain from discussing President Franklin D. Roosevelt's physical handicap. All of this will be considered in some detail below. For the moment it is worth noting that in the media both supporters and detractors of FDR kept their silence. But that was then. Today members of the media seem willing—anxious—to expose and exploit any weakness, real or perceived, that they detect. Journalists have ambitions too, and today journalists can become the story; witness Woodward and Bernstein. And one doesn't become famous because of what one does not write.

LOCAL HEROES AND JUST ABOUT EVERYONE ELSE

Another consequence of America's desire for a hero is a willingness to accept as a hero those who are known only to a few people. Increasingly there are celebrations of the local hero, the hero of the street, community, town, village, or city. Not to be misunderstood, there can be no doubt that these people are worthy of the accolades offered them; they are celebrated because they have performed courageous acts, and they deserve the recognition and praise they receive. But the very fact that they are local heroes and that the attention they receive is limited (unless for one reason or another the national news media pick up their story), underscores both the need for and the lack of a national hero.

A while ago the *Ladies Home Journal* cited fifty American heroines. More recently, Peter Goldman listed "100 New American Heroes." Both lists consisted of people who were unknown to the nation at large. They were local people doing significant things but in a limited area. Still more recently, *The Washington Post Magazine* did a feature on "Unsung Heroes"—"people who made a difference," and *Modern Maturity* ran an article entitled "Everyday heroes" [sic]. The article told of "ten people who made a difference day in, day out." *Newsweek* ran a similar story in its May 29, 1995 issue. [13]

There are also books devoted to celebrating the local hero, for example, by Bill Berkowitz and Nat Hentoff. But the individuals celebrated within these works, again, are unknown to all but a few Americans. It is precisely because there are no longer any national American heroes that these local heroes are needed. Berkowitz recognizes this: our lack of (national) heroes requires that we get a "new heroic model for our time." And because all we have left are celebrities and they "don't do the job," we need a "local hero working at a community level." Further broadening the use of the term "hero" and offering a still greater indication that the United States has run out of heroes (and also indicating that the nation is desperate for them) is the claim that almost everyone is a hero. Elizabeth Stark, for example, calls "Mom and Dad: The Great American Heroes," and if that level of inclusion were not wide enough, Phyllis McGinley argues that "the masses of men live lives of quiet heroism." [14]

But there is a problem here. Ralph Waldo Emerson correctly noted that the heroic cannot be what is common, the common cannot be heroic. The hero must be different from the masses in order to be a hero; if he isn't then the term "hero" is meaningless. "Attractive" exists only because "unattractive" exists and the hero exists only because most people are unheroic. To claim that most people are heroes is, in effect, to claim that there aren't any heroes.

A final consequence of the vanished American hero might be noted in passing: the assignment of heroic status for the sake of cause or purpose or just because someone is liked or has survived a difficult time. Increasingly, people have applied the term "hero" to individuals who take up causes that they endorse or whose actions they approve, or just because they are personable or because they lived through an unfortunate experience. One book, for example, describes environmentalists as "eco-heroes," and Daniel Boorstin's *The Creators* is subtitled "A History of Heroes of the Imagination." *MS.* magazine named "40 Male Heroes of the Past Decade." William Goldman points out that the American theater has "culture heroes," actors and actresses celebrated in the extreme. There are heroes specific to professional gamblers, as Anthony Holden points out. Articles have described Lawrence Welk as a "Heartland Hero." Bernard Goetz was proclaimed to be the "subway hero" and George Holliday was a "folk hero." Holliday, you may recall, took the video of the Rodney King beating. Timely perhaps, but heroic? [15]

Also described as heroes have been such figures of consequence as Keron Thomas, who drove off in a subway; Owen J. Quinn, who parachuted off the North Tower of the World Trade Center; and Philippe Petit, who walked along a wire stretched between the two buildings of the World Trade Center in New York City. These men may reasonably be described as eccentric or colorful or interesting, but not as heroic. And reminiscent of the little girl trapped in the well to whom Barbara Tuchman referred, President Clinton termed those who survived the summer flood of 1993 as "heroes."

Should we tire of our fleetingly famed celebrity-heroes, we can rely on pseudoscience to provide us with someone like Caryl Chessman who was, to at least some people, a "Reichian hero." Chessman was a Reichian hero because he "escaped repression," he broke "free into humanity." He did this by kidnapping a young woman and forcing her to fellate him. He was tried, convicted, and executed for kidnapping some years ago. But apparently, somehow, he was a hero.[16]

HEROES OF AMERICA'S PAST

Perhaps the most painful part of the lack of American heroes today is that America has traditionally been a nation of heroes. Norman Mailer only slightly exaggerates when he suggests that "America is a country which has grown by the leap of one hero past another." From the soldiers at Valley Forge to those who fought at Gettysburg, from Pickett's Charge to Belleau Wood to Normandy to Bastogne, the American soldier has worn an aura of heroism. That aura was dimmed—unjustly—at places like Heartbreak Ridge and the Mekong Delta.[17]

American pioneers were also surrounded by an aura of heroism, both during and after the time that they crossed the wilderness in covered wagons, on horseback, and on foot. They were preceded by earlier American heroes, men of unusual courage, like Jim Bridger and Jim Beckwourth, mountain men and fur trappers, men who lived peacefully with the Native Americans they met. Later other settlers and explorers battled Native Americans in fearsome, internecine conflicts, which produced nationally recognized heroes on both sides of these conflicts.

Surely the original cowboys, "America's first continental citizens," who ranged from the Midwest to California, were regarded as national heroes, as were the cowboys who came after them. There can be little doubt that were one required to choose a single figure to represent the American hero, the cowboy would be the choice of most Americans.[18]

The gunfighters and the bandits came later, after the bloodiest of the battles with the Native Americans had been won by the settlers and the army, after the pioneers had started to farm the land, after the wilderness had been controlled. Yet it is these gunfighters and bandits, rather than the pioneers and settlers, who make up much of the folklore of the American

West and who have traditionally been regarded as heroes. Heroes need an element of glamor, and reaching for a gun is more glamorous than reaching for a plow.

The celebration of outlaws as heroes is only a memory recalled within American folklore. Most of the gunfighters of the past would today be involved in drive-by shootings, and the bad men and women of the 1920s and 1930s, who, less in fact than in imagination, continued the legacy of the outlaws of the post–Civil War West, are gone now for more than half a century. No one has taken their place within the national legend, nor could anyone take their place today. Today we would not be enthralled by their violence; they would not be glamorized in the 1990s.

People who stood on principle when that principle coincided with the ideals expressed by the Constitution—and on occasion when it didn't—are also counted among America's heroes, although not all that frequently, just as American heroes have included artists and poets, scientists and scholars, but not very many. America is a nation of action, and it is action that usually defines American heroism, not the conceptions that stimulated the deed. The Wright Brothers may be respected by the American people because they invented the airplane, but Charles Lindbergh and Amelia Earhart were glorified by the American people because of the excitement they generated when they flew their planes.

In the past some national and (nationally known) regional politicians were given genuine, heartfelt tributes, and some inspired awe and respect. Men as different as Franklin D. Roosevelt and Huey Long certainly had impassioned detractors, but they were truly loved too. The glamor that was associated with nationally known politicians was assassinated on November 22, 1963, however, and interred by means of a presidential resignation on August 9, 1974.

Some heroes have disappeared because our needs have changed. When there were unexplored areas we needed heroic figures to brave that unknown, both within and without the United States. But there are few areas left on earth to be explored and so we have no explorer-heroes. The mountain man cannot return. Besides, there is every possibility that the adventurer and explorer of the past would today be regarded as psychologically unstable and a danger to himself or to others. If he was married and had children when he left home to pursue his adventures (and many did), and left them behind when he set off into the wilderness (and many did), he would today be castigated for deserting his family.

WHEN THE DECLINE OF AMERICAN HEROES STARTED

The United States saw the beginning of the end of its nationally recognized heroes at the conclusion of World War II. After the Second World War the structure and culture of American society so changed that the hero was increasingly denied a place within it. That may seem to be a relatively trivial consequence of so colossal an event, but the gradual departure of the hero from the United States is a significant reflection of the changes that the war brought to American society.

Perhaps the best example here is the military. Modris Eksteins has argued that the existence of individual military heroism was eradicated on the battlefields of the First World War. Wave upon wave of men rushing into machine gun fire demonstrated insanity, not heroism. Modern warfare had eliminated both the need for and the possibility of individual heroism under fire. William Pfaff agrees with Eksteins. Before the First World War one could "plan to become a hero," but the Great War ended the notion of not only the plan but of the fact of the individual hero. Before that conflict one could demonstrate his courage and daring, he could show how a man ought to act while in combat. But during World War I technology and sophisticated weaponry proved that individual heroism was no longer necessary and only occasionally commendable.[19]

Yet Eksteins and Pfaff may be overstating their case. The invention of modern warfare is generally credited to Ulysses S. Grant at the Battle of Vicksburg during the War Between the States, and even if modern warfare was not invented by Grant, it was certainly used by him. There can be no doubting the mass struggles, mass armies, and mass slaughters that were a part of the American Civil War. The wholesale killing that was made possible by the Gatling gun and, more important, by the movement by train of large numbers of troops, was first seen in this conflict. The individual soldier was just an indistinct blur within an indistinct mass of combatants.

Yet in the Civil War and in World War I—and in those excursions to Cuba and the Philippines at the turn of the century—as well as in World War II, wars of indistinct masses of people, combatants and noncombatants, the United States produced true and well recognized heroes. Grant and Lee, Farragut and Jackson, among others in the Civil War; Pershing, Eddie Rickenbacker, and Alvin York in World War I; MacArthur, Eisenhower, and Audie Murphy, among numerous others in World War II, all qualified and were recognized as national heroes. But that's where it ends. It is hard to name a nationally recognized hero of the Korean "Police

Action" or of the war in Vietnam, two bloody conflicts in which American combat forces fought with valor and honor. Neither the brief skirmish in Grenada nor the invasion of Panama allowed for a nationally celebrated hero, and the conflict in the Persian Gulf celebrated everyone and therefore no individual hero. U.S. involvements in Somalia and Haiti again saw American military personnel act bravely and again saw the nation generally ignore that bravery.

The military is just the most obvious area in which to make the point of the vanished American hero; other areas will be examined below. For the moment consider just one more. Businessmen were well regarded in the United States from the 1940s through the early 1960s. The Great Depression had shaken America's confidence in the acumen of America's business leaders, but during World War II and continuing for some time thereafter, top businesspeople in the United States were often regarded as heroes. This regard was due in part to their contributions to the war effort and in part to America's affluence after the war. America's businessmen were often thought of as brilliant and self-sacrificing; on occasion they were thought of as noble. Especially noteworthy here were the men who headed the three giant American automobile companies.

All of this changed in the ensuing decades. By the 1980s it was difficult to find a public figure in any other field with a worse reputation. The hero-businessman had evolved into the villain-businessman, and again especially noteworthy here were the heads of the three giant American automobile companies. Perhaps Ralph Nader's book *Unsafe at Any Speed*, published in the early 1960s, started the questioning of the motives of businessmen generally and those in the automobile industry specifically. In any event, the tendency to question the integrity of businesspeople grew. By the 1980s Americans were not concerned with the acumen of businessmen; Americans were concerned with their lack of ethics, their avarice, their disregard for anyone and anything save their own incomes. Their successes may have made some businessmen wealthy; it did not make them heroes.

Military men and businessmen, once regarded as heroes in the United States, are just two examples here. Beginning in the late 1940s and continuing throughout the rest of the century, American heroes within a variety of areas gradually, consistently disappeared. In the early and mid-1960s we had Kennedy and King, the last two American heroes. By the 1970s America's heroes were creatures "with magic powers—laboratory creations or people from outer space." By the 1990s, save the triviality of the celebrity in whatever field, and the local (and generally transitory) hero, the American hero had ceased to exist.[20]

THE ANTI-HERO

For a brief period of time, when the nation first realized that heroism was no longer in style and the idealism necessary for the existence of a hero began to evolve into cynicism, the anti-hero appeared in the imagination of the American public. If one could not enjoy an individual-as-symbol to represent the nation, the society, and the culture, then one could enjoy an individual-as-symbol to repudiate the nation, the society, and the culture. The United States could occasionally accept someone who repudiated everything and everyone but himself.

Some see the development of the anti-hero arising more than a century ago. Marshall McLuhan, for example, dates the anti-hero to William Makepeace Thackeray's *Vanity Fair*. That "novel without a hero" was written in 1848. Perhaps McLuhan is right, but it is generally agreed that the anti-hero made his appearance in the 1920s, in large measure because so many people thought that the devastation of the First World War required a revision of the traditional hero. For example, Paul Johnson argues that the anti-hero made his appearance in the early decades of this century: "*A La Recherche* and *Ulysses* [written from 1913 to 1927 and 1914 to 1921, respectively] marked . . . the entrance of the anti-hero." Harold Lubin agrees; it wasn't until the 1920s that the anti-hero reached a high level of consequence in some social circles. [21]

The anti-hero generally disappeared during the Great Depression and World War II. He made a comeback almost immediately after that war, as if in recognition of the fatal wounding of the genuine national hero during the conflict. As he had appeared after and as a consequence of the First World War, he reappeared after and as a consequence of the Second World War. Confused about his own existence and about the reason for that existence, the anti-hero saw all causes, ideals, and meanings as subterfuge on the one hand and futile on the other. The anti-hero stood apart from the mob. For a time that was enough to attract followers.

The anti-hero is European in origin. And while he has the literary forebear noted, as well as several others—Fyodor Dostoyevski, Søren Kierkegaard, and Friedrich Nietzsche, for example—he reached full maturity in the writings of the French existentialist philosopher Jean-Paul Sartre, and most celebrated of all, in Albert Camus's essay "The Myth of Sisyphus."

As Europe tried to rebuild after World War II, the dissatisfaction with the powers that be caused many to question anyone's right to have any power. Walter Laqueur notes that "the post-war period [in Europe] . . . witnessed a steady erosion of authority." The intellectual class in Europe in general and in France in particular rebelled by creating new art forms, film *noir*, for example, and the theater of the absurd. The working classes rebelled in violence, by forming youth gangs such as the Teddy Boys in England and the *Bloussons* in France. All of this was reflected in the contemporary philosophy in Europe, one based on existence "without reason, without cause, without necessity." This was an outlook that seemed almost inevitably to lead to the creation of a morose, existential anti-hero.[22]

When America took hold of the existential anti-hero, he was transformed from the brooding, confused intellectual—of, say, Albert Camus's *The Stranger*—to an individual with values informed by American traditions: singularity of purpose, physical presence, a willingness to take risks. The angst-ridden European anti-hero may have remained an anti-hero when he moved to the United States, but the qualities that he demonstrated were American. He was changed intellectually by American writers—Hemingway and Mailer, and even by Mickey Spillane—and he was changed emotionally by Hollywood and American television.

The angst or confusion that was the mark of the European anti-hero was celebrated in the United States as individualism, the sine qua non of any admired American. The American anti-hero may be a loner, but he was neither isolated in the world nor despondent. World-weary pessimism is not America's style. Moreover, while the European anti-hero in his depression was avoiding authority, the American anti-hero was angrily challenging authority; he was too busy to be morose. The brooding European stranger became an American traveler in Jack Kerouac's *On the Road*. The despondent and dejected European became the "beat" and antiestablishment American.

The anti-hero has always been a central figure within the popular arts, especially in the 1950s among folksingers and writers. Marshall Fishwick credits Jack Kerouac, but especially Woody Guthrie and Norman Mailer, with drawing the nation's attention to the anti-hero. Through their music and writings they helped to create the age of the anti–hero in America, the rebellious post World War II era of beatniks and the first rumblings of the counterculture.[23]

For a time in the 1950s and 1960s the counterculture people were successful in the United States. For a time anti-heroes became America's true heroes, easily outshining all of the nation's traditional heroes. But the individual anti-hero didn't last. Edward Hoagland correctly notes that the anti-heroes, "even the classy existential variety," vanished and fairly quickly. When the youth culture took over the United States in the mid-1960s, the challenge to authority became collective, not individual, and challenge to authority for purpose was replaced with challenge to authority for the sake of challenge to authority. Rebelliousness became pop culture and the American anti-hero became "the absurd hero." Finally he just disappeared. [24]

More important, perhaps, American culture couldn't take the anti-hero for too long. Quin Martin, a television executive, has noted that anti-heroic television shows—he uses "East Side, West Side" as an example—never stay around long. The problem is that anti-heroes tend to lose, things don't often go their way, and Americans enjoy winning and elation, not losing and frustration. One can be an anti-hero, but in the United States one has to be a successful anti-hero. [25]

American anti-heroes still appear in American literature and movies on occasion, usually in the guise of fictional American iconoclasts of the past and present, cowboys and private eyes. By and large, however, Americans are left with neither hero nor anti-hero—neither the first, who is able to represent us, nor the second, whose individuality and rebelliousness enchant us.

EXPLANATIONS

We are not lacking for explanations as to the disappearance of the American hero. These range from the psychological to the existential to the spiritual. Some have suggested that technology has eliminated the need for the hero, while others have suggested that the nature of what constitutes a hero—at least in the popular imagination—has changed. It has been suggested by some that the world is no longer as heroic as it once was, while others, in a tone reminiscent of Allan Bloom, claim that the villain is moral relativism. Some suggest that the cause is homicide, that we've murdered our heroes. Others suggest that the problem is cynicism: we no longer have any heroes because the few beliefs we have kept are so dispassionate that we are no longer capable of standing in awe of anyone or anything.

Some blame the 1960s and others see it as a failure of the system—whichever system is currently in disfavor—while some say the collapse of the family structure is the cause. Others simply suggest that heroism "is out of style," which does little more than beg the question: why, then, is it out of style? And, of course, blame has been placed on television and the computer, nuclear power and relativity, Freud, Marx, Nixon, Watergate, and the Kennedy assassination. Some people simply shrug and quote Emerson: "Every hero becomes a bore at last," which may be true but still leaves a key question unanswered. Even if our heroes of the past disappeared because they became boring, why haven't new heroes, in whatever form, arisen to take their place?

Perhaps the clearest statement of the cause for the lack of heroes comes from Joe McGinniss. McGinniss went looking for an American hero and couldn't find one. The reason that he couldn't find one, he says, is that there aren't any more heroes, and the reason that there aren't any more heroes is that there are no more heroic deeds to be done. [26]

But that is untrue. There are numerous heroic deeds to be done. The problem is that there is no one to do them and the source of the problem is American society, the nation's social structure and the culture. The United States, in effect, refuses to allow the hero to exist.

American social structure and culture (in sociological jargon, our group characteristics, the things that guide our behaviors; and the behaviors themselves, including our attitudes and beliefs, respectively) have changed since World War II. As they did, American values changed, and the quality and characteristics that people sought in their heroes changed. People do not rapidly evolve physically or intellectually. They do not in and of themselves change dramatically within the brief span of a few decades. What does change dramatically in so brief a period are social conditions and social systems. When this happens people's values, aspirations, and expectations are altered.

From the end of World War II through the end of the century, the United States changed—and dramatically. One consequence of these changes was that within American society the meaning of "hero" also changed. A second consequence was that within American society the hero slowly vanished. The American hero, as people once understood that term and the qualities it represented, no longer exists. And Americans miss him deeply. Consider, for a moment, the Gulf War and the nation's response to it. Perhaps these will illustrate both the lack of contemporary American heroes and our need for them.

Chapter 2

The Gulf War and Its Aftermath

THE WAR

On August 2, 1990, Saddam Hussein's Iraqi Republican Guard invaded Kuwait. Five days later President George Bush sent American troops to the Middle East to protect Saudi Arabia from a possible Iraqi attack. In September the president ordered over 150,000 additional American land, sea, and air personnel to the Persian Gulf, and in early November he announced a second reinforcement of the troops already stationed in the Middle East. There were now more than half a million members of America's armed forces in the area, apparently preparing to do battle with Saddam. The president, it seemed, had decided to fight.

Negotiations in Washington and in the United Nations Security Council secured permission for President Bush from, respectively, the Congress of the United States and that often disorganized international organization to use force to free Kuwait if Iraqi forces had not been withdrawn by January 15, 1991 (midnight, Eastern Standard Time). The Iraqi Republican Guard stayed in Kuwait, and on the night of January 17, American planes stationed at bases in Saudi Arabia, together with those from six United States carriers stationed in the Persian Gulf, and joined by planes from six other nations, attacked selected targets in Kuwait and Iraq.

The bombing was relentless; by February 27, the allies had flown over 100,000 sorties. By way of comparison, during the final fourteen months of the Second World War fewer than 25,000 missions were flown against the Japanese. In less than six weeks the allies had flown four times the number of missions against Iraqi forces than had been sent against the Japanese

Empire in over a year. Not surprisingly, the damage to Iraq's military was devastating.

Given this softening up of the Iraqi defenses, it cannot be surprising that the ensuing ground war was brief. It began on February 24 and ended on February 28, one hundred hours later. One consequence of the brevity of the land war was the relatively small number of American combat casualties: 146 killed and fewer than 400 wounded. (There were 159 U.S. noncombat deaths and 244 allied troops killed in action.) These figures are slight when compared to the number of people who might have been killed or wounded or, indeed, the number of casualties reportedly anticipated by the Pentagon. The number of Iraqi military personnel and civilians killed will probably never be known for certain. Initial estimates placed the figures at perhaps 100,000 Iraqi soldiers killed and over 100,000 Iraqi civilians killed both during and immediately after the war. [1]

The astonishing speed with which the allies in general and the Americans in particular conquered the Iraqi forces had other effects. It established beyond question the military power of the United States. After all, the United States had engaged in combat with—and crushed—the fourth largest army on earth; the Iraqi army wasn't a Stone-Age military force. Iraq had biochemical capabilities and had already demonstrated its willingness to use them. Saddam was trying to develop a nuclear weapons system, and who knew for certain the progress he had made? The Iraqi threat seemed quite real, at least on paper.

Yet in the end that threat was in fact limited, weak in the extreme. The battles were over virtually before they started because of America's technical superiority, because of effective American military preparation, and because of the abilities of those relatively few members of America's military forces who did battle with the Iraqis.

In terms of military leadership, too, it is clear that Iraq was outclassed, that the war was over before it started. General H. Norman Schwarzkopf, the commander-in-chief of the United States Central Command, regarded Saddam as an execrable military commander. Saddam Hussein, in Schwarzkopf's well-publicized words, "is neither a strategist, nor is he schooled in the operational arts, nor is he a tactician, nor is he a general, nor is he a soldier. Other than that," Schwarzkopf added, "he's a great military man." And this judgment is verified by the way the war went, by the weakness of the Iraqi military. While the United States had prepared to do battle with a formidable enemy, the enemy turned out to be feeble. The enemy was overwhelmed at the onset of hostilities and provided the United States with a clean, quick military success.

THE PUBLIC RESPONSE

One wag commented that the parades celebrating America's victory in Desert Storm lasted longer than the war itself. An exaggeration perhaps, but the fact is that the hundred-hour land war in the Persian Gulf would have been not much more than a battle—and a brief one at that—in World War I, World War II, the Korean "Police Action," or the Vietnam conflict. To illustrate this point: the Battle of Verdun in World War I lasted ten horrible months, and the Battle of the Bulge in World War II lasted nearly two months and cost 77,000 American casualties. "Pork Chop Hill" was fought over during the Korean conflict from mid-April 1953 to mid-July 1953, and the struggle for "Hamburger Hill" during the war in Vietnam lasted a full and bloody month. This is why Malcolm W. Browne regards one of the most celebrated confrontations to take place during the Gulf War, the fight at Khafji, as pretty much "a minor skirmish" when compared with those he had seen in other wars, and why Earl Tilford, a historian, comments that in time Desert Storm will be regarded as little more than "a footnote" in history.[2]

Clearly, none of this diminishes in any way the efforts of those who engaged in combat in the Gulf. They did what they were supposed to do. But the brevity of the battles does suggest that from the point of view of other conflicts, the Gulf War was a modest one.

Given this, how did America respond to the Gulf War and to the men and the women, combatants and noncombatants, who served in the United States military? Given America's military might and technological advantages, given Iraq's military failings and inept leadership, given the limited nature of Desert Storm, what was the response of the nation to the Gulf War? The answer to these questions, of course, is that initially and for several months immediately following the war the nation responded to both American military personnel and to the war itself with a furor bordering on ecstasy. Parades were everywhere, flags were everywhere, and yellow ribbons—now the symbol of Americans gone from home—were attached to cars, trees, and lampposts. Home Box Office (HBO) celebrated "America's Proudest Moment"—Live * One Night Only * Sunday, March 31st—with Whitney Houston.

Those expressing "a great deal" or "quite a lot" of confidence in the military grew from 50 percent in 1981 to 88 percent in March 1991, exceeding by 30 percentage points confidence in America's religious institutions. Several months later close to nine out of ten Americans thought that we should take pride in the accomplishments of our military forces in Desert Storm. As if there were a contest, Washington, D.C., and New York City argued over which would throw the more grandiose parade dedicated to celebrating Desert Storm. Television ran a four-part series on the conflict in the Persian Gulf (on the Arts & Entertainment network), and T-shirts, flags, bumper stickers, pins, and anything else that could be embossed with symbols of America's victory and that could be dreamed up by vendors, went on sale and sold well. Everyone wanted to be a part of Desert Storm, to celebrate the moment.[3]

Memorial Day 1991 was filled with invocations thanking the powers that be for the safe return of so many of America's brave soldiers, sailors, pilots, and support personnel and celebrating the one hundred-hour victory. The wisdom and the courage of the nation's political and military leaders were endlessly praised. American politicians had come a long way from responsibility for the 241 American servicemen killed in Lebanon by a terrorist bomb in 1983. The American military had come a long way from responsibility for the massacre at My Lai in Vietnam. The top brass in particular had come a long way from the furor surrounding General William Westmoreland, commander of U.S. combat forces in Vietnam from 1964 to 1968, who, justly or not, was vilified by both the public and the media, and who was involved in a lawsuit with CBS because of a dispute as to the legitimacy of that vilification.

In dramatic contrast to the treatment received by Westmoreland, General Colin Powell, the chairman of the Joint Chiefs of Staff, and General H. Norman Schwarzkopf, the commander of U.S. forces in the Persian Gulf, were almost deified by the public and the press. (Throughout the war the American press sounded more like local sportscasters broadcasting the home game than like journalists explaining an international military confrontation.)[4]

Congress authorized a gold medal for General Powell, the medal to be sculpted by the United States Mint. The chairman's face appeared on the cover of a seemingly endless number of magazines; and he was in great demand as a speaker, his fees initially ranging from $17,000 to $28,000 and, in time, reportedly reaching $60,000 per speech. The 1993 contract for his autobiography reportedly brought him $6.5 million—a favorable biography of General Powell had been published immediately after the Gulf War ended—and there was talk of his getting the fifth star. He didn't.

As soon as the conflict reached its conclusion, Powell was spoken of as a potential candidate for the vice-presidency although his political views, as he said himself, were unknown. By the time he retired from the military in 1993 Powell was spoken of as a presidential candidate; by 1995 the talk of his potential as a presidential candidate had increased. His political future seemed even brighter after the publication of his memoirs and the accompanying media hype attached to the promotion of the book. "Powell for President" committees were formed and there appeared to be a solid groundswell of support for his candidacy. Again, all of this occurred without Powell declaring his political allegiances; indeed, throughout his book promotion he carefully avoided stating his political opinions. Finally, in the fall Powell proclaimed that he was a Republican and announced that he would not seek the office of the presidency. That ended speculation about his political career, at least for a while. (If you were listening closely, a collective sigh of relief from the Republican front-runners for the office could be heard. President Clinton's sigh of relief could also be heard.)

General Schwarzkopf, too, was inundated with honors. Instantly dubbed "the world's most popular general," he also received a Congress-approved gold medal coined by the mint, his face also appeared on magazine covers everywhere, and he also was considered for political office. He was offered up as a potential candidate for the 1992 Democratic presidential nominee (again, without anyone being burdened by the knowledge of his political views). This all ended here, however. Schwarzkopf early on averred that he was not at all interested in a political career. But he did seem to enjoy his newfound celebrity, public appearances, and public speaking. And he took full advantage of these.

General Schwarzkopf's numerous speaking engagements brought initial fees ranging from $20,000 to $30,000. In addition to being (gently) interviewed by Barbara Walters, Schwarzkopf was knighted by the queen of England and led the Kentucky Derby parade. He also signed a book deal with Bantam for an estimated $5 million, the book presciently titled *It Doesn't Take a Hero*—a favorable biography of the general appeared within six months of the victory in the Gulf War—and there was talk of his getting the fifth star. He didn't.

The response celebrating America's fighting men was less focused but no less enthusiastic. Everyone associated with Desert Storm was honored by the public. Troops who not only never fired a shot but who never heard a shot fired were hailed as heroes. Men and women who were never at all in any danger were celebrated as heroes as were men and women who were under fire. Little distinction was made between those who risked—and those who lost—their lives in Desert Storm and those who were merely inconvenienced by Desert Storm (or not inconvenienced at all). Few distinctions were made by the American public as to what were truly heroic behaviors and what were merely good intentions.

Just being an American in uniform in the Persian Gulf in 1991—or just being in the service during the crisis—guaranteed more accolades than being in battle in Korea in 1951 did and certainly brought more accolades than fighting in Vietnam in 1971 did. Americans, George F. Will said, "have not been so happy since V-J Day" in 1945. Everyone was a hero, from President Bush to the foot soldier.[5]

This suggests a problem. Harry S Truman wasn't considered a hero during the Korean "Police Action," nor was Ronald Reagan celebrated as a hero during the confrontations in Grenada or Libya. Vietnam certainly did not make heroes of Presidents Eisenhower, Kennedy, Johnson, or Nixon. These presidents may have been respected and admired, even idolized at different times in their lives, but they weren't regarded as heroes when they led the nation during the conflicts noted. The heroes were the men who did heroic deeds, not the men who directed the deeds to be done. It is odd that President Bush was regarded as a hero and odd that everyone involved with the conflict in the Gulf was assumed to have acted heroically.

In Desert Storm the United States and its allies had defeated a militarily inept third-world country, a country with a gross national product equal to that of Kentucky. The "national praise" for the returning Gulf War veterans was, as Jay Stanley comments in the *Army Times*, "dramatically disproportionate" to the war itself. Why, then, the national hysteria? Why in June of 1991 did about two-thirds of the American people not only still endorse the war, but feel that we should have continued fighting until Saddam was toppled from power? Why the almost unstinting devotion to the war (once it had started, for as Tom Wicker points out, enthusiasm was limited before the conflict had begun)? Why the celebration—indeed, adulation—of Powell and Schwarzkopf? Why the eagerness to regard virtually all military personnel involved with Desert Storm as heroes? [6]

THE EXPLANATION

Americans fight, they say, not for national purpose but for morality. Americans claim to have rejected Carl von Clausewitz's argument that war is merely politics by other means. Americans choose to see evil, not politics, as a cause for war. It is certain that President Bush played upon this theme. He discounted political reasons for going to war as well as economic ones (Kuwaiti and Saudi oil). The president spoke of a "new world order" in his speech to a joint session of Congress at the conclusion of the war. In his 1991 State of the Union address the president spoke of a national effort to halt aggression and suggested that the United States alone was able to bring power and "moral standing" to that effort.

In his claim to the moral high ground during the Gulf War, the president was fortunate. The leader of Iraq, Saddam Hussein, a man whose malevolence President Bush hyped up by comparisons with Hitler, proved a marvelous foil; he was almost out of central casting. Arrogant, cruel, ruthless, a man who ordered poison gas to be used upon his own people, Saddam was—and as of this writing still is—everything a president could want in an international foe. This being the case, and even opponents of the war acknowledge that it was, the need for a moral justification for the war was satisfied. America's military could be and were justly praised for having the moral high ground. The righteousness that sustained America's military and policy makers lent encouragement to the celebration of America's victory.

But even if moral justifications for Desert Storm are left aside for the moment, there were other reasons, reasons embedded within American culture, that prompted the overwhelmingly favorable reception the war and its participants received back home. The most obvious of them was the memory of Vietnam, the decade-long political and military nightmare that scarred the nation in general and the military in particular. Many thought that the battles in Kuwait, however brief and however one sided, at last relegated Vietnam to the history books, and that may have been one of the reasons for entering into combat with Iraq. At the conclusion of the Gulf War the president said that Vietnam was finally behind us and the nation cheered in agreement.

The national enthusiasm for the Gulf War and for the military was also enhanced by the war's unambiguous outcome. The armed forces of the United States (and their allies) won the war decisively. They didn't in Korea—even though American combatants there weren't asked to win, just to maintain the status quo, which they did; nor did they win in Vietnam—even though American combatants there did not lose a single major battle. In Korea and in Vietnam, America's combat soldiers did what was asked of them by the top brass and by the politicians, but in both Korea and Vietnam there was some confusion, some questions as to the outcome. In the Persian Gulf there could be no ambivalence. The good guys won and won quickly. There was little time during the war to muse over its implications or consider any ensuing negative consequences.

There was morality on the side of the United States and the villainous Saddam on the other side, and there was the memory of Vietnam to be erased and the reinstatement of the military to a position of respect. There was the limited number of allied casualties and the speed with which the conflict was settled to celebrate as well. And finally there were the heroes.

And there were a lot of them, as suggested earlier. Every soldier, sailor, pilot, everyone even remotely connected with Desert Storm, was regarded as a hero. And they were necessary: "A hero is a hero," Susan Baer wrote, "and we haven't had a good hero in a long time. America needed him." Baer was speaking here of Schwarzkopf, but he was only the most celebrated of the heroes at the time. Bush and Powell, Richard B. Cheney (the secretary of defense) and James A. Baker (the secretary of state) and General Thomas P. X. Kelly (the spokesman for the army) were heroes too. Everyone was a hero and this is not good.[7]

There are problems with assigning the label of "hero" to everyone associated with a conflict in which few were, in fact, heroic. It not only demeans the efforts of all who were exceptionally courageous, the usual military criterion for being a hero, it also renders the term itself meaningless. It equates the Medal of Honor winner with the soldier who did his job and nothing more.

More than denigrating those who were truly heroic, the rush to label everyone a hero tells something of a nation desperate for heroes, and therein lies a problem. *Time* magazine put it this way: "Though its feelings are understandable, there is something scary about a country that aches for heroes and leaders in this way."[8]

Clearly, General Schwarzkopf did well in the Gulf, but could other generals have done as well? Was Schwarzkopf that exceptional as a military commander? Can one compare Desert Storm with, for example, the invasion of Europe, with D-Day? Is General Schwarzkopf to be compared with General Eisenhower?

Most wars produce nationally recognized heroes (there are no other kind). This was certainly true throughout American military history—excepting the four engagements preceding Desert Storm and the two (thus far) proceeding it: Korea, Vietnam, Grenada, and Panama, and Somalia and Haiti. In these cases the lack of heroes was due to lack of public recognition of extant bravery, not a want of courage on the part of American combat forces. Until the conflict in the Gulf, we hadn't had a military hero for forty-five years—not since World War II, since Ike and MacArthur and Audie Murphy, despite numerous actions by America's military during those years. America has certainly had heroic individuals in its armed forces since World War II, but they didn't receive national recognition, they weren't national heroes. The wars in which they fought were unpopular, misunderstood, or unglamorous, the issues they defended were muddled, and the reasons for their sacrifices were questioned. The conflicts did not produce heroes and the efforts of the troops were unappreciated, their bravery went unrecognized.

Desert Storm gave the United States the chance to acknowledge again our national heroes, and the nation jumped at the opportunity. We celebrated everyone involved as a national hero. But this adulation reflects not upon the actions of those whom we called heroes, but upon the nation's search for someone upon whom to place that appellation. This does not suggest that the men and the women who participated in Desert Storm didn't do their job; obviously they did. It does suggest that the nation was looking for someone to call hero, and that the response was excessive. That excess suggests more than a nation's search for a hero: it suggests an unfulfilled need.

The United States needs a genuine hero, but that need cannot be fulfilled. America can no longer produce heroes as it did in the past. Nor is this a question of degree; it is a question of kind. Americans have and will continue to enjoy trivialities as heroes, as well as transitory and local heroes, but the true American hero, the national hero, has vanished and will not reappear. American society will not allow it.

Chapter 3

Understanding the American Hero

THE USUAL EXPLANATIONS OF HEROES

The primary arena for the examination and explanation of heroes is mythology, which explains why tales of giants, ogres, and the demigods of a mysterious past so often come to mind when one thinks of heroes. Mythological tales celebrate people who may or may not have lived—rarely the former—and tell of their glorious and improbable deeds. Dragons are slain and maidens are rescued, fierce creatures are defeated and mystical forces are challenged. Valiant men and beautiful women—or on rare occasion valiant women and, well, attractive men—are the subjects of these tales. The hero surmounts impossible odds, wages noble war, fights ferocious and cunning villains. Theseus enters the Labyrinth to slay the Minotaur, Aeneas survives the trials to find his way home, Sir Galahad seeks the Holy Grail, Robin Hood defeats the Sheriff of Nottingham.

Mythical heroes can fail. For example, Lancelot, among the greatest of the mythical heroes, never did see the Holy Grail. Mythical figures may be tragic as well. The heroes of Greek mythology almost always were. Oedipus and Ajax, Antigone and Electra, for example, were tragic in perhaps the most shattering of ways: they did not know who or what they were. Many of the heroes of Greek mythology lacked sufficient self-knowledge, *sophrosyne*, and even more suffered the sin of pride, *hubris*. Tragedy awaited the hero who ignored his limitations, as when Icarus's wings melted when he flew too close to the sun. Indeed, Greek mythology seems to stress the heavy cost of *hubris*.

Of course all of the tales of Greek mythology weren't tragedies or warnings; sometimes things worked out for the heroes. Perseus, with the help of a god and a goddess, Hermes and Athena, killed Medusa. Prometheus, often regarded as the first hero, took fire from the heavens and presented it to man. In punishment, Zeus had him chained to a rock while an eagle gnawed at his liver, but Hercules rescued him.

In the United States the man most celebrated for examining and explaining the purpose of the mythical hero is Joseph Campbell. Campbell's hero generally follows a specific route: he leaves, he is involved in an adventure, he returns home. Yet Campbell's mythical hero is not often the one who achieves greatness; he is the one who evokes others to achieve it. In this Campbell's mythic hero has a purpose: to guide and save society, to bestow "boons" by inspiring others. [1]

Traditional mythical heroes, then, have several social purposes. At minimum they both warn us and press us to achieve greatness, depending upon who is examining the reason for the hero.

The contemporary version of mythical heroes of the past is found in literature, in both popular and erudite writings. In classical literature, heroes strive to represent the loftier elements of human existence; in popular literature, heroes more or less represent the escapist fantasies of human existence. In both cases, of course, they must meet with the approval of the society before they will be accepted as heroes. The Byronic hero as one example and the hard-drinking private eye as another must both reflect their society's view of itself.

Within classical literature some heroes suffer inner conflict, a failure perhaps of excessive desires, which sounds very much like the problems facing many of the heroes of Greek mythology. Indeed, there can be little doubt that classical literature was influenced by Greek mythology. Other heroes of classical literature are consumed by passion, by ambition, as is Byron's *Childe Harold*. More modern literary heroes, such as those found in the writings of Franz Kafka and Albert Camus, face confusing and meaningless worlds and are thereby tormented. Kafka's hero may face a strange and confusing world as in, for example, *The Trial*, while Camus's existentialist hero confronts a meaningless universe.[2]

Americans are less existentially oriented than Europeans. Consequently, classical American literary heroes are more likely to have to deal with real entities. James Fenimore Cooper, Herman Melville, and Ernest Hemingway had their heroes battle substantial opponents. Natty Bumppo confronts the wilderness, Captain Ahab goes up against Moby Dick, and the Old Man challenges the sea. Little of the Kafkaesque confusion or of

Camus's sense of isolation, little of the European angst here. However pride—hubris—is often a problem for American literary heroes.

The modern (popular) American literary hero is probably best represented by one of two characters, the cowboy or the private eye. Following the tradition of classical American literature, the heroes within these genres are not especially concerned with the metaphysical, the mystical, or the existential. In this Shane and the Continental Op aren't far apart. A stranger, a good and moral man, faces a corrupt system. That is the ideal of the modern American literary hero. He is pragmatic and tough, and he deals with the world as it is given to him.

Both mythology and literature, traditional and contemporary, classical and popular, deal with imaginary heroes. Other areas have a more tangible focus and, consequently, a more analytical approach to the subject. History has examined and explained the hero, but here real people, not mythological ones, are of concern. The most significant position in historical analysis as regards heroes is that of the "great man" theory, a view that appeared off and on within historical writings for well over a hundred years.

The great man theory is a nineteenth-century European creation, inspired in all likelihood by Napoleon Bonaparte. Certainly Georg Hegel was awed by the French emperor's power and his conquests, and perhaps Friedrich Nietzsche was following Hegel's lead when he too supported a theory of the great man in history. Henri Bergson argued against historical determinism—the antithesis of the great man view—and for the vitality of the individual. In the United States, William James argued a weaker form of this theory, acknowledging the power of social forces but retaining the view that the individual has the power to shape, in whatever degree, his own fate.

The most forceful of the early statements concerning the great man was given by Thomas Carlyle. For Carlyle, history *is* the hero. In the 1840 publication *On Heroes and Hero-Worship*, Carlyle writes: "The history of the world is but the biography of great men." The hero directs, controls, determines the way in which the world goes. Its fate is in his hands. The hero, to Carlyle, determines the direction of the masses. Further, these great men are quite literally a godsend. They are our heroes because we require their guidance. Freedom, according to Carlyle, "is the right of the masses to be guided by the wiser."

Yet even Carlyle, for all of his hero worship, seemed to acknowledge that there are social forces acting upon the great man. In *The Hero as Poet* he writes: "The Hero can be Poet, Prophet, King, Priest or what you will, according to the kind of world he finds himself born into." This seems to limit the hero's choices and seems to make the society into which the hero is born—the culture and the social structure—critical to his being a hero.

A more contemporary view that parallels that of Carlyle is offered by Sidney Hook. In *The Hero in History*, Hook argues that specific individuals formed history. His most detailed example is the significance of Lenin for human history: "The thesis of this chapter is that had it not been for the work of [Lenin] we should be living in a vastly different world today." The world would have been a different place had he not led the Russian Revolution. Hook argues that events in the years after 1917 were shaped because of Lenin's existence.

To many people the hero is "good." Kent Ladd Steckmesser argues exactly that: "The basic appeal of the legendary heroes is that they served good causes." Hook disagrees. The "goodness" of the individual is irrelevant, the effect of his life is what matters. The consequences of the hero's actions determine his status, not the hero's beneficence or malevolence. The success of the 1917 Bolshevik Revolution was due not to goodness or badness but to Lenin's planning and policies, the execution of his strategies. This makes him an "event-making" man who has "redetermined the course of history " and influenced "the life of the great majority of men, women, and children on the face of the globe." [3]

The idea of a hero in history determining the fates of the masses is not currently in vogue. For many people, there are simply too many factors shaping human existence to argue that a single individual, hero though he may be, can direct the fortunes of the world and its peoples. Still and all, the theory is not dead. Henry Kissinger recently offered a view, more intricate than that of Carlyle's great man theory, that shares some of its premises. Robin Wright, too, argues a similar position regarding Pope John Paul II. Edward Rothstein says that Jascha Heifetz personifies a "great man" theory within the arts.[4]

Two additional areas consider the hero, albeit only tangentially: philosophy/religion and psychology. The question of the place of the hero has been briefly examined in philosophy, usually in conjunction with religious studies. Philosophy and religion are here concerned with the significance of heroes for the interpretations of life the heroes offer their followers. The heroes may also reveal much about past societies whose philosophies are significant to scholars today, for example, the relationship between the heroes of the Greek myths and the philosophies of ancient Greece and how an understanding of those heroes can help us interpret those philosophies.

Biblical heroes within the Judeo-Christian tradition define the qualities that God wishes us to have or at least wishes that we would strive to attain. Heroes within the Judeo-Christian tradition set standards we use to measure our own worth.

Although they haven't generally pursued the subject in great detail, psychologists have considered the question of the significance of the hero. Carl Jung, Erik Erikson, Sigmund Freud, and Otto Rank, among others, have directly or indirectly examined the phenomenon of the hero, however briefly. More often than not, psychological considerations of the hero deal with conflicts within the hero as an individual. As Dorothy Norman has it, these conflicts are concerned with "our most essential struggle with ourselves." For Jung, as for most analysts, the hero's movement is toward "self-growth and psychological maturity."[5]

According to Norman, Jung and others argue for a "single heroic archetype . . . [whose] subpatterns, or stages, are repeated in the various disciplines that deal with human experience—anthropology, history, philosophy, psychology, literature, and art." Absent from this list is sociology, which is not surprising. Viewed sociologically, there is no single archetypical hero. Each society has a specific culture to reflect and each may have several possible heroic types, and the more complex the society the greater the number of heroic types it is likely to have. In a society as complex as the United States there can never be a single heroic form, a single archetype.[6]

A QUESTION OF SOCIAL RECOGNITION

The meaning of "hero" in the United States is often inexact, partly because the United States doesn't have a heroic tradition dating back several hundred centuries as in, for example, the legends of King Arthur or Robin Hood, and partly because the American hero is an achieved status. Stephen Jay Gould considers the first point: "Older nations can convert the heroes of their antiquity into true gods, fully freed from the quotidian reality of their actual lives. Newcomers like the United States must construct their legends from recent historical figures—and mythology must then compete with memory and documentation." It is harder, that is, to be a hero of recent memory than a hero of millenia past. And it is impossible today.[7]

The second point is of considerable interest here. It means that the American hero is chosen by the people. There is a subjective quality to the use of the term "hero" and often an emotional quality as well. Generally, to be regarded as a hero in the United States one must have done something daring and gallant and, critically, one must be recognized by the nation at large as having done something daring and gallant. And that recognition must be sustained.

The American hero comes from the collective, from the American people. An unspecified but substantial number of people must assert that a given individual is a hero and they must maintain that assertion for an unspecified but significant period of time. That is, having performed a heroic act does not automatically confer the status of "hero" on an actor. As will be discussed momentarily, there must also be recognition of the actor as a hero, ideally unofficial and unstructured (unorganized) recognition. In time, of course, publicity and official (organized) recognition of the hero as a hero will follow and a symbiotic relationship will evolve. Increasing publicity increases the likelihood of official recognition and official recognition enhances one's status as a national hero, which naturally increases the publicity one receives.

Under the best of circumstances there is spontaneous support for a given individual as a hero. With only a little knowledge of the person or precipitating event(s), the people just appear to recognize and support the hero as a hero. The media then helps to sustain that recognition and support.

The ideal situation—when the nation seems spontaneously to claim an individual as a hero—is quite rare, but it has occurred. Custer's Last Stand at the Battle of Little Big Horn led to Custer being annointed an American hero almost spontaneously. Of course even here it was necessary for the newspapers of the time to exaggerate the account of the battle and Custer's bravery. Equally important, Libby Custer—the colonel's wife—worked tirelessly to ensure that her husband's heroism would be instantly respected and then worked to ensure that it would not fade from the national memory. She was eminently successful at both of these tasks.

Similarly, the feats of various sports figures (Red Grange) and outlaws (John Dillinger), adventurers (Robert Peary) and military leaders (Ulysses S. Grant), have resulted in their almost spontaneously being regarded as heroes by the nation, although in these cases too the services of a favorable press were appreciated, not to say imperative. A national hero requires national recognition which, in turn, requires national awareness of the hero and of the heroic deed(s).

As applied to the American hero, then, it is not enough to assert, as Daniel Boorstin does, that the hero is an individual of substantial accomplishment, one who achieved "greatness." And Sidney Hook is mistaken in considering as heroes both "historical figures who are famous . . . and individuals who have influenced events without achieving great popular fame." [8]

In the United States the hero becomes a hero because he is known to the public. One cannot be a hero if no one knows that one has done something heroic and deserves to be called a hero. To be a hero is to assume a specific status, and a status exists only because others recognize and accept one's claim to a status. If one claims a status but no one acknowledges the claim—say the status of hero—then one is a lunatic, not a hero. The queen of England is queen of England exactly because she is so recognized in Great Britain. The American hero is an American hero exactly because he is so recognized by the nation.

Peter Berger has argued that each society creates the people that it needs to keep going. In no sense is this statement more accurate than in consideration of society's heroes, and nowhere is it truer than in the United States. As Americans need heroes, Americans create heroes. In the United States heroes are literally and exclusively a social creation, a product of the American people's needs and creations, their public admiration and adulation.[9]

THE HERO AND THE HEROIC ACT

The significance of social recognition for the hero may be shown by considering that a heroic act, even a celebrated heroic act, will not necessarily produce a hero. One cannot become a hero to the nation if the nation doesn't know that one exists, but recognition is not enough. Even if the heroic act is known and even if the heroic actor is respected, he may be only a heroic actor and not a hero. Fame, respect, and admiration are necessary for the hero to exist, but they are not sufficient.

The public makes a distinction between the hero and the heroic figure, a distinction that is not as fine as one might imagine. The former is an American inspiration and is beloved by the nation; the latter may be admired and respected, but for one of several possible reasons, he is not regarded as a national hero by a sufficient number of people for a sufficient period of time. Proof of this assertion may be found in two examples.

Obviously many people contributed to the Allied victory in World War II and many of those involved in the battles—enlisted men, noncommissioned officers, and officers—were properly regarded as heroes. Several men were promoted to the highest rank attainable in the United States Army, five-star general. Even within this select group two stand out, for more than any of these highest ranking soldiers (save, perhaps, General George Catlett Marshall), Generals Dwight D. Eisenhower and Douglas Mac-Arthur were directly involved with the course, actions, and demands of the war.

Eisenhower and MacArthur made the most difficult and immediate decisions, and the lives of more American military personnel were in their hands than in the hands of other officers. Both were brilliant military commanders and both were admired, even adored, by many Americans. Each in his own way was a heroic figure, but unlike Douglas MacArthur, Dwight David Eisenhower became an American hero. After the war he served first as chief of staff and then as president of Columbia University, and in time commanded the armed forces of the NATO alliance. Eventually, of course, he won election and reelection to the presidency, both times by substantial majorities. In 1959, according to a Gallup poll, he was the most "admired man in the world"—for the seventh year in a row.

Douglas MacArthur was commander of the occupying forces in Japan following World War II, and led the United Nations' forces in the Korean "Peace Action." He fought a dubious battle with President Harry S Truman over his conduct and outspokenness during that conflict, was relieved of his command, and after a ticker-tape parade and after addressing the Congress, faded into history. Certainly his stature in the eyes of most Americans was (and is) less than that of Eisenhower. Eisenhower was a hero to the nation, he was a national hero; MacArthur was a hero to some Americans, in effect, a local hero.

MacArthur's military brilliance and his celebrity could not compensate for a confidence that bordered on arrogance and a demeanor that suggested rigidity. His fault, of course, was not his arrogance but his inability to control the impression of that arrogance. He did not mix well with the troops under his command. His confrontations with people of power and influence received a great deal of national attention, especially the confrontation with President Truman, the final battle of MacArthur's career. MacArthur's forthrightness when there were disagreements with powerful men led to resentment on the part of those men. This led to negative publicity, which, clichés notwithstanding, is not better than no publicity at all. It cost MacArthur a great deal of public support and possibly the Republican nomination for the presidency in 1952.

Eisenhower, on the other hand, also a brilliant strategist and, as historians are lately discovering, an effective president, was wise enough to conceal his arrogance if indeed he was arrogant. That he was ambitious and had, in kinder phrases than those usually used for MacArthur, a strong ego and a healthy sense of self, is obvious. Anyone who suggests that he should be president of the United States, that he should lead the most formidable economic and military power in history, that he ought to direct the fate of what was then called the "free world," is hardly humble and self-effacing. Yet Eisenhower was well-liked, heroic in person as well as deed. He was a public figure who did not seem to seek publicity. He shared the glory of military victories with his subordinates, seemed to have an easy and casual manner in dealing with his troops, and was accepted by the American people as an extraordinary military leader who was likable, as someone of exceptional ability yet one who was decent, even emollient. He seemed the hero, and he was.

Both Ike and Mac performed heroically, but only one was an American hero.[10]

An argument can be made that the greatest baseball player of all time was an exceptionally nasty, unusually gifted outfielder for the Detroit Tigers named Tyrus Raymond Cobb. Babe Ruth called Cobb the best natural hitter to ever play the game. According to Ruth no one has ever equalled Cobb's hitting ability and no one ever will. And Ruth said this even though he did not get along with Cobb. No one did. And that is one reason why the finest hitter ever to play the game—he has the highest lifetime batting average in the history of baseball (.367), until recently held the record for the most total hits by any player, and his career strike-out total is 357 (and he played for nearly a quarter of a century)—is rarely talked about, except perhaps snidely as in *Field of Dreams* or off-handedly as when he's referred to as "a mean-spirited psycho" or when he's described as "barely human." [11]

Occasionally someone—George F. Will, for example—will point to the astonishing accomplishments cited above and throw in a few more impressive statistics (Cobb stole home more than any other player in history) and even apologize for him, if only half-heartedly. He was not, Will points out, the only man for whom "viciousness was a normal part of the game," although Will does allow that Cobb "may have set the major league record for concentrated meanness." But by and large Cobb is mentioned favorably only when his record-setting feats are cited as they are broken. Thus, when Tom Seaver was elected to the Baseball Hall of Fame he received 98.8 percent of the votes, "breaking a record set by Ty Cobb." And usually whenever his name is mentioned so is his irascibility.[12]

The 1994 movie of Cobb's life did little to help him become an American hero. In fact, it may have made that possibility even more remote, if indeed it could be more remote. Terrance Rafferty, reviewing the film for *The New*

Yorker, notes that it didn't "glorify its protagonist," and that "there wouldn't be much point" in trying. Janet Maslin, reviewing the same movie, worries about America's desperate search for heroes. "So how badly, *Cobb* wonders, does America need its heroes? Badly enough to play by new rules when the star athlete is a miserable man?" Maslin need not be concerned. The fact is that, notwithstanding all of those accomplishments on the baseball field—including that astonishing .367 lifetime average—Ty Cobb is no American hero.[13]

Babe Ruth, on the other hand, is so much an American hero, so indelibly a part of America, as to be literally associated not only with baseball but with the nation itself. Everyone knows the tales of Japanese soldiers during World War II yelling out at American troops: "To hell with Babe Ruth," not "To hell with President Roosevelt" and certainly not "To hell with Ty Cobb." An endless stream of motion pictures about Ruth's life—many awful pictures to be sure, but they keep on coming—indicate a continuing interest in the Babe by Americans. Another indication of that interest is the $200,000 paid for the baseball Ruth supposedly hit for his 60th home run during that sensational 1927 season.

One explanation of the heroic status of the Babe comes from Bob Feller. With two weeks left to go in the 1938 season, Hank Greenberg of the Detroit Tigers had hit 58 home runs (still a major league record for a right-handed hitter). Some have argued that pitchers avoided pitching to Greenberg during those final two weeks, and that they did so because they didn't want to see a Jewish ballplayer break Ruth's record. Feller has a different explanation: "Many of the players . . . remembered Ruth fondly . . . and . . . didn't want Greenberg to break his record . . . with no offense to Hank." [14]

There's probably some truth to the anti-Semitic argument and some to the story of the players' hero worship of Ruth. Feller argues that for professional baseball players, Ruth "singlehandedly" restored "public confidence in their sport after the 'Black Sox' scandal erupted in 1920." [15]

But while all of this explains the admiration Ruth received from other baseball players, it does not explain why he, and not Cobb, for example, was the idol of millions of fans. Of course there is the possibility that Cobb might have come along too soon; his career was ending just when the American mania for athletes was taking off. But there is more to it than this. Ruth gave a bit back. Greenberg, who regards Ruth as the "greatest ballplayer who ever lived," noted that "he was a hero and despite his sexual appetite and drinking too much and eating too much, he also used to go to a lot of hospitals and visit kids who were sick, and the photographers would go with him. He did a lot of good in that respect." [16]

One sure sign of Ruth as hero, if that has to be documented here, is that the public's adulation for Ruth has remained undiminished. It has been nearly seventy years since he hit his sixty home runs in a single season, but seventy years or not, newspaper articles still recount the glory days of Ruth, and books about his life are still regularly published. Decades after his death and decades after he played his last game, he is still idolized. It is for this reason that John Steadman can write about Ruth that "Baseball never had such a hero; nor has any other sport." [17]

Ruth and Cobb. Again, two men who accomplished heroic deeds within their field, but only one was a hero because only one was regarded as a hero.

To be a hero, then, one has to be a hero to the public. The heroic feat is necessary, of course, as is public recognition of the feat, but it is the man who is the hero and not just the individual who did a heroic deed. He must have the necessary qualities of a hero, or, more precisely, the public must perceive him as having those qualities. This is the difference between Eisenhower and MacArthur, Ruth and Cobb, and, to continue the comparisons, between two celebrated sex bombshells, Marilyn Monroe and Jean Harlow.

Both Monroe and Harlow were the sex symbols of their generations, both were blonds who exuded sensuality, both died prematurely. There were differences, of course—for example, the mysterious circumstances surrounding Monroe's death, her marriage to a baseball hero, and her alleged affairs with the Kennedys. Yet these cannot account for the fact that thirty years after her death Jean Harlow was remembered as an early version of Marilyn Monroe, while thirty years after her death Marilyn Monroe remains an American obsession. Similarly, Tom Horn is recalled in the main only by students of western folklore while Jesse James is still celebrated by the public—the movies about his life, some wonderfully inaccurate, keep coming, and there is a museum named in his honor. Willie Sutton robbed banks, and daringly, but is hardly remembered today whereas John Dillinger robbed banks, and daringly, and has remained a folk hero for more than sixty years. Eleanor Roosevelt's death evoked considerable sadness throughout the nation but nothing like the national mourning evoked by the death of Jacqueline Kennedy Onassis, "the last of the idols." Every boy (and more than a few girls) in America wanted to be Michael Jordan—remember "I wanna be like Mike"?—while few admired or said they "wanna be like" Wilt Chamberlain. But compare Jordan's and Chamberlain's stats some day. It is not their accomplishments on the basketball court that defined Jordan as a hero or failed to define Chamberlain as a hero. Jordan was a hero to the American public because Jordan the man was defined as a hero by that public; Chamberlain wasn't a hero to the American public because Chamberlain the man wasn't defined as a hero.[18]

The deed itself is not sufficient to create the hero; to be a hero one must possess the ability to win public acclaim as a hero, whether by a grin that seems to embrace the public, by a personality that exudes excitement or charm, or by extraordinary athletic abilities coupled with an outgoing personality. The point, then, is this: one can be a heroic figure, a momentary giant to one's friends and acquaintances, and still not emerge a hero to society. People of consequence within their own arenas have failed to emerge as heroes and have simply faded from the memories of their contemporaries during the course of their lifetime.

To be a hero is to receive broad social recognition as a hero and to do so for a long period of time. The people define their heroes.

A SOCIOLOGICAL LOOK AT HEROES

In his *Journals*, Nathaniel Hawthorne says that "A hero cannot be a hero unless in an heroic world." Hawthorne has the right idea, but the arena should be narrowed a bit. One cannot become and remain a hero unless society defines, accepts, and continues over time to recognize the idea of a hero. The culture and the social structure must permit and accept the heroic ideal for the hero to exist. Specifically, the culture and the social structure must allow the development and the recognition of a hero.

The national hero is a social creation, a cultural reflection shored up by structural ballast. Put another way, the national hero reflects the values of the culture as sustained by society's institutions, its structure. This is the basis of Sean O'Faolian's argument that the hero is a hero because he is able to represent an acceptable social norm. The hero on occasion may create the values of the culture; more often than not he sustains and clarifies them. In any culture, Erich Fromm points out, "there are widely shared traits that make up the social character." The most important of these traits, as determined by the society, are conspicuously manifested by the hero. It is the public recognition of this that makes the hero. This is one reason why Sidney Hook, ever the supporter of the individual hero, of the Great Man theory, recognizes that the hero only influences events because he meets "some social and group interests." The hero, again, is necessarily of and within society.[19]

Because social recognition creates and sustains the hero, the hero is before all else a sociological phenomenon. Oddly, however, sociologists seem not to have paid a great deal of attention to the phenomenon of the hero. The closest thing to a sociological theory of heroes is Max Weber's concept of charisma. That term, not the theory, is generally used casually to refer to a quality possessed by both true heroes and celebrity-heroes. The theory is often ignored although it is informative, even if imperfect, as applied to the modern American hero.

"Charisma," literally "gift of grace," suggests that an individual is empowered because of his extraordinary qualities, qualities that cannot be quantified but that demand that he be elevated to an exalted position, to a position of leadership. The charismatic leader "must perform miracles," the charismatic leader "must perform heroic deeds." Prophets, warriors, and heroes have been charismatic leaders. "Genuine charisma," Weber writes, "rests upon the legitimation of personal heroism," and the people do legitimate their hero. Indeed, it is their obligation to do so. In a statement reminiscent of Thomas Carlyle, Weber writes that "it is the *duty* of those to whom [the charismatic individual] addresses his mission to recognize him as their charismatically qualified leader." People, that is, have a responsibility to see and to follow the hero when and if he exists among them.

But Weber was thinking of religious and mythical figures when he created the charismatic ideal, not mortal human beings. That, of course, explains why this model is inapplicable in any way other than as an ideal type, a fiction against which to measure reality. Nor did Weber pretend otherwise.

There are at least three other reasons why Weber's charismatic theory falters when applied to modern American heroes. To begin with, in the United States, a nation of some 260 million people consisting of virtually every religion found on the planet, and containing among its citizens literally every possible shape, size, and complexion found within the human species, and with a plethora of ethnic groups, not to speak of an apparently endless number of cults, lifestyles, and socioeconomic categories, achieving unanimity on anything is just about impossible. Americans have traditionally recognized in broad terms—albeit generally with some dissent—who is and who is not an American hero. America was a nation defined by its first settlers, white Anglo-Saxon Protestants. Their traditions are still the foundations upon which the nation rests, but America has evolved and America's structure and culture have changed. In recent decades some changes have occurred quite rapidly and have been dramatic. The traditions and definitions of the past are losing their powers.

One of Weber's assumptions regarding conditions within society that permit acceptance of the charismatic figure, the hero, is the homogeneity of the society. Given the heterogeneity of and the consequent contentiousness among at least some segments of American society, it is certain that anyone who claims directly or indirectly to possess charisma, or to be so designated by his followers, will be challenged by at least one social group, and probably more than one.

A second problem is that for Weber the charismatic hero must repeatedly demonstrate his charismatic qualities. "[P]ure charisma," Weber argues, "does not know any 'legitimacy' other than that flowing from personal strength, that is, one which is constantly being proved." When one task is completed a new one will arise. And this new task will have to be handled with dispatch, just as the old one was, and it obviously is impossible to continue this indefinitely. The charismatic leader cannot long remain a charismatic leader, a hero, within American society; no one can be perpetually victorious.

This is why a great many of those whom Americans call heroes have met untimely deaths and why living heroes are so frequently replaced. Those who have died gallantly and unexpectedly (preferably while they were still young) often remain in America's memory as gallant and youthful, heroes in perpetuity. Those who live eventually fail.

In general, then, the only living heroes that the United States can enjoy are transitory ones. American heroes who live a long life will be celebrated for a while and then fade into obscurity. This is the fate of celebrity, entertainment, and most sports heroes. American heroes who die prematurely remain within our historical memory, their promise becomes a part of American folklore. This was the case with heroes as disparate as Billy the Kid and Martin Luther King, Jr. Perhaps Menander was right, those whom the gods love die young; certainly America's heroes do. More to the point here, they are the only ones who can remain American heroes.

The third reason why Weber's charismatic model fails in the United States today is economic. According to Weber, the charismatic figure should discount any financial rewards that might come his way. He is not interested in "pecuniary gain." This not only goes against the American grain, it ignores the reality of life in the United States today.

That it goes against the American grain to avoid financial reward was recognized by Alexis de Tocqueville over one hundred fifty years ago. De Tocqueville had this to say about Americans: "I know of no country . . . where the love of money has taken a stronger hold on the affections of men." And indeed, it is difficult to find a contemporary American hero who did not profit financially from his status, and equally difficult to find anyone who faults him for this. It is, for example, usually forgotten or conveniently ignored that Charles Lindbergh, regarded by some as the quintessential American hero (before his alleged Nazi sympathies became known), undertook that difficult and dangerous task, the first solo flight across the Atlantic Ocean, for what was at the time a sizable amount of money.

This tradition of a strong connection between wealth and heroism continues unabated; consider the incomes of athletes and rock and movie stars, America's current charismatic figures. It is, in fact, virtually impossible today for anyone who enjoys any form of social recognition not to receive financial rewards, usually substantial ones. Even in the unlikely event that one's interest in wealth is limited, the fact of being famous almost automatically results in economic rewards. The fame that comes with being a hero virtually assures offerings of the publication of one's autobiography (with a sizable advance) as well as talk-show appearances and posters and a made-for-television movie. There is a great deal of money to be made from these ventures, and it would be foolish if the hero of the hour, the subject of all of this attention, did not accept some of it. After all, the money will be made anyway; surely the hero deserves his share. And his newly acquired agent and manager will see to it that he (and they) get it. Weber could never have foreseen all of this.

There is difficulty, then, in asserting that the American hero possesses classical Weberian charisma. But the theory of charisma does suggest where to look for the social hero in that it suggests that people choose their heroes. The society assigns the status and selects the task(s) to be (successfully) performed. All of this indicates that the way to determine the American hero is sociologically, that is, through empirical investigation. By using sociological empiricism to examine and explain America's heroes it is possible to understand the fact of the American hero while avoiding the mists of mythological heroes, the grand theories of historicism, the soul-searching of philosophy and religion, and the mental probings of psychology. That is, an understanding of the hero—especially the American hero—should be based upon the fact of who America's heroes were and why.[20]

When Larry D. Nachman searches for a definition of heroism he doesn't look in a dictionary, he looks to the world. He wants the definition to be "cultural." He wants "a philosophical explanation of the place of heroism in human affairs." It follows that the definition of "hero" is also cultural and not derived from a dictionary. But as these definitions are cultural, a "philosophical explanation" of the phenomena of heroism and of human heroes is less called for than is a sociological one. An understanding of the American hero can only be based upon examinations of who, in fact, American heroes were, why they were chosen to be American heroes, and how they became heroes. And an examination of America's past heroes is critical to an understanding of the current lack of American heroes and to an understanding of the social conditions that once permitted the existence and adulation of heroes by the nation but no longer does.[21]

From an examination of our past heroes we can learn the qualities that Americans used to see in their heroes and no longer see; from past heroes we can learn of the social conditions—both cultural and structural—that once allowed Americans to admire some of their own, a situation that no longer exists. From past heroes we can understand the changes that have occurred in American society, changes that once allowed the hero to exist and then allowed the hero to disappear.

The heroes who lived in the pantheon of American history are idealized. Americans often wore (and for a chosen few still wear) blinders, allowing that their heroes possessed critical qualities—whether or not they actually possessed these qualities—and decided that these were their salient characteristics. Americans also ignored their heroes' failings, often gladly.

Nearly a century ago Max Weber argued that specific social conditions had to exist before capitalism could develop as an established economic system. More recently, Robert K. Merton argued that the growth and development of science as a specific, organized discipline—that is, as something other than a sporadically practiced, hit-or-miss affair—required a receptive social structure and culture. In other words, a social system conducive to capitalism, one that fostered a strong work ethic, had to precede capitalism; a system that supported and sustained scientific inquiry was necessary before a scientific community could exist. By the same reasoning, the hero is a consequence of social conditions. The culture and the social structure must permit both the development of the hero and the continued existence of the hero. In the United States today neither one does either.

But the United States has not suddenly stopped producing brave and daring individuals; Americans of the past were not less intelligent and imaginative than Americans today. Then as today they knew full well that in creating heroes they were creating idealized individuals. Part of the reason for the existence of American heroes of the past was a willingness on the part of the public to concentrate on the better qualities of their idols, and to ignore their idols' other, unpleasant qualities.

People have not evolved greatly within the past two centuries. If they are no longer willing to acclaim a national hero, if they permitted the American hero to disappear, the cause cannot lie within them. If the attitudes of the American people have changed so dramatically within recent years, the cause must lie within the recently altered social structure and culture of American society. People haven't changed; consequently, if America no longer has heroes, then the social system must have changed to prevent their existence.

We ought to try to understand those changes. We ought to try to understand the changes within the society whereby Americans who were once willing to allow heroes no longer are.

Part II

America's Past Heroes

Introduction

Generally, the more homogeneous the society—in social, political, ethnic, religious, and economic terms—the more singular the heroic type. Conversely, the more complex the society, the more disparate its citizens, the greater the variety of its heroes. Indeed, not only do complex societies have a variety of heroes, there may be variations "even within a single hero style."[1]

Because the United States is an enormously complex and diverse society, the American hero has traditionally taken several forms. The varying forms American heroes have taken does not imply that there are consistent and permanent groupings of heroes within American society. The frequency with which people within these forms are regarded as heroes changes as do the forms themselves. At different times in the history of the nation different arenas were more likely, others less likely, to produce national heroes. Varying social circumstances determined that the heroic nature of some activities were noticed while the heroic nature of other activities, which may have been well established earlier, were lost for the moment.

The hero, then, is a direct consequence of society, that is, the hero is determined by social structure and culture, both of which change over time. Therefore, definitions and determinations of who and why an American hero is an American hero cannot simply reflect a single ideal-typical conception of a hero. Quite the contrary. Following Weber, we can create an ideal-typical American hero(es) only after we have examined who in fact Americans have designated as their heroes, and how these designations have changed over time.

It is necessary to consider empirically and in some detail who Americans chose to celebrate as their heroes throughout the changing history of the nation. Empirical analysis will also explain why there has not been a single hero or heroic type in the United States, one ideal-typical hero. Most important here, it will allow us to understand why—save the local hero, the temporary hero, and the celebrity-hero—there can no longer be an American hero.

The several forms the American hero has taken can be placed in one of three categories: greater heroes, intermediate heroes, and lesser heroes. The categories have been stable throughout American history although the forms within them have not. Some of the forms have existed only briefly, some have remained a permanent part of American history, and some have fluctuated—that is, they have come and gone and returned (and may leave and return again). The longevity, brevity, or variations of a particular form of American hero has been a consequence of the times, of the attitudes of the generation of people sanctioning the hero. Those attitudes, of course, depend upon social circumstances.

The forms of those who fall within the category of greater American heroes are, in no particular order of importance, military heroes, sports figures, celebrities from the world of entertainment, political leaders, and heroes of the Old West. These forms have produced the most American heroes in terms of quantity and, measuring quality by longevity, the best of America's heroes. They constitute the most admired and widely recognized groups of American heroes.

Intermediate heroes are less frequently found within the pantheon of American heroes and are more likely to be inconsistently placed there. They are more likely than the greater heroes to be subject to social whim and caprice, their reputations more likely to be victims of social variations and fortunes. America's intermediate heroes, again in no particular order, are made up of people from the world of business, the criminal world, and people who were adventurers.

Finally, there are the lesser heroes among America's idols. These are the men and women who belong to forms we all feel we should admire and do admire; but we admire them as heroes because we feel that we should, that it is fitting to do so. We feel this obligation because we recognize that they contribute to society; but they do not contribute dramatically, with élan, and a bit of flash in a hero is admirable if not necessary. The lesser heroes within American society have come from intellectual and creative worlds such as the sciences and the arts. Included here are some of our moral leaders.

Some of these heroic forms are universal. Rare is the society that hasn't accepted some of its military as heroes, for example. Similarly, many societies regard their political leaders, their sports stars, and their entertainment celebrities as heroes. Even here, of course, there are cultural differences. A number of societies seem particularly drawn to memories of courageous, although defeated, commanders and their armies; Americans—with rare exception, for example, Custer—do not celebrate defeated military leaders. Other societies acknowledge the contributions of their successful business leaders, but few have done so with the enthusiasm of the United States. On the other hand, and unlike the people of some other nations, Americans only reluctantly have recognized their intellectual heroes, whether that hero was an artist, scientist, or moralist.

In other areas the forms are themselves culturally specific. Most obviously, the heroes of the frontier and of the West are uniquely American. This is the case even though other countries—Canada and Australia, for example—have had frontiers to settle and pioneers to do the settling.

While some heroic forms have disappeared and for obvious reasons, other heroic forms have been altered to suit the changing times. The key questions remain, however: who were selected to be American heroes and why?

Chapter 4

Military Heroes

Soldiers have traditionally been heroes to Americans. They have been honored because they risk their lives for their country and the principles that their country represents. Military heroes tend to become a permanent part of the nation's folklore, which is to say that the exploits of America's military heroes live in the memory of the nation. The American Revolution (Washington), the War of 1812 (Jackson), the Mexican War (Taylor), and the Civil War (Grant), the Indian campaigns (Custer), World War I, (Pershing and Alvin York), and World War II (Audie Murphy along with, and especially, MacArthur and Eisenhower) all produced heroes. Their individual feats cannot be improved upon, nor can these men ever be replaced in the national memory. One can't do "better" than Gettysburg or Belleau Wood or Normandy. And one can't separate these men from the history of the nation. They are and shall remain a vital part of that history.

Traditionally the military has produced more American heroes than any other arena of American life. A great number of political leaders are former military leaders. (Close to half of all American presidents served in the military, most of them saw combat, and a number were military heroes.) In the years immediately following a war, it is virtually impossible to get elected to office without having at least served in the military. This was the case after the War of 1812, the Mexican War, the Civil War, and World Wars I and II. Theodore Roosevelt's self-celebration—a skill at which he was most accomplished—during and after the Spanish-American War, if a war it was, made him a military hero to the nation.

Social recognition of the soldier as hero is obvious. The parades and the ceremonies, the medals and monuments, all contribute to and sustain the image of the soldier as hero. American popular culture, from comic books and toys to novels and movies, celebrates the military man, especially in times of war, and it does so despite the fact that war is horrible. Popular culture can celebrate the hero because it is the illusion and glorification of war that makes heroes. In the past we accepted the illusion and glorification. We are disillusioned today; today in war we see at best a limited glory.

The United States kept its illusions and glories and its heroes during World War II. But the illusions and glories diminished, and the heroes vanished, during the Korean conflict, despite the valor of the American soldier and the commanders of America's fighting men. General Matthew Ridgway, for example, exhibited exemplary leadership during the Korean War, according to Defense Secretary George C. Marshall, a man quite able to recognize leadership. Ridgway was largely, if not wholly, responsible for turning a weakened and defeated Eighth Army into a powerful and victorious one. But his death in 1993 received only passing attention at best.[1]

The war in Vietnam was brought into American living rooms, and that helped to complete our disillusion with and ended the glory of the whole business of war. When the Vietnam War ended, so did the American military hero. There can be no doubting the sad accuracy of Lawrence M. Baskir and William A. Strauss's statement: During the conflict in Vietnam the POWs were the "only real heroes." The actions of the courageous and valorous grunts, including here those truly heroic grunts, were not considered heroic. It appears that things will continue this way. Baskir and Strauss correctly reason that the deep and unyielding bitterness associated with the war precludes the creation of heroes of the Vietnam conflict.[2]

The ventures into Grenada, Lebanon, and Panama did not revive the American military hero. The happy response to the Gulf War heroes evaporated after just a few years, as sincere as that response was at the time. America's involvement in Somalia and Haiti did not produce any military heroes. Indeed, many Americans questioned both ventures, especially the effort in Somalia because of both the dubious outcome of the effort and, much more important, the lives of the forty-four American soldiers lost there.[3]

Further proof that the American military hero is to all intents and purposes nonexistent today is the fact that, while politicians had to be veterans to be elected to major office after World War II (and in some instances after the Korean "Police Action"), that requirement has passed into history. Avoiding duty in Vietnam did not stop Dan Quayle from the vice-presidency in 1988 and avoiding military service altogether did not prevent Bill Clinton from being elected to the presidency in 1992.

The usual explanation for this phenomenon, for the recent absence of the glory that has traditionally accompanied the American soldier and for the loss of stature of the military within the American pantheon of heroes, is that the unpopularity of the war in Vietnam both diminished the honor associated with the military and tarnished the image of the American soldier. America tolerated the war in Korea, and besides, no one really saw it. But television brought the Vietnam War home, and American popular culture in the 1960s and 1970s was often antimilitary. There were a number of antiwar and antimilitary plays, movies, and television shows as well as an apparently endless supply of antimilitary, anti–Vietnam War books.

The Vietnam protest marches received a great deal of attention, so much so that a great many people forget that initially, and until the Tet Offensive in 1968, the majority of Americans supported the war, some with considerable enthusiasm. In time, and after Tet, the unhappy images seen on television, growing distrust of government officials and military commanders, and the massacre at My Lai, all contributed to the country's eventual disillusion with the war. This is the most obvious reason why, despite the bravery of the soldiers, the war did not produce a single military hero, that is, a nationally recognized hero.

But the war in Vietnam was not the only unpopular war that this nation has fought. The Mexican War (1846–1848) was at least as unpopular as the war in Vietnam. People argued and debated and protested against it, and that war produced numerous American military heroes, two future presidents (Zachary Taylor and Franklin Pierce) among them. Throughout the conflict in Mexico, war managed to maintain its glamor and illusions in the United States despite the protests and denunciations of the engagement. And war surely maintained its glamor and illusions in the Civil War, the Spanish-American War, and World Wars I and II. It wasn't until the early 1950s, during the Korean "Police Action," that the United States failed to produce a war hero. The Korean War, an international conflict that failed to produce an American military hero, predates Vietnam; perhaps that war was an indication of our future attitude toward war, perhaps that is why it is often called "America's forgotten war."

Individual soldiers, sailors, marines, and airmen of World War II were the last American military heroes until the 1990s, when, during the Gulf War, Americans praised just about everyone who wore a uniform. Indeed, between World War II and the Gulf War and Somalia, and especially in the post–Vietnam era, the military as an institution was not celebrated. Memorial Day, which should commemorate the sacrifices that American service personnel have made, is today noted simply as the beginning of the summer. Fawcett and Thomas point out that the celebrations on the Fourth of July, traditionally a time of military parades, have evolved into "town pageants." They also note that "war is muffled in comedy by reruns of *Hogan's Heroes* and . . . M*A*S*H." From Korea through Vietnam, from Grenada and Panama, the military has failed to produce a nationally recognized hero. And in the Persian Gulf it produced too many.[4]

Why, then, has the American military hero disappeared? It cannot simply be that recent wars have been unpopular. As noted, the war with Mexico produced American military heroes despite harsh criticism of the conflict.

Part of the reason that the American military hero stopped being celebrated has to do with both the purpose and intent of the Korean and the Vietnam conflicts. By its nature, the military seeks victory in battle and victory for a just reason. But the two major conflicts in which the United States was engaged after World War II had these problems: the reasons for the engagements were somewhat obscure, and victory was not realized in the traditional sense of that term. As will be discussed momentarily, both Korea and Vietnam were at some distance physically and emotionally from the United States. Indeed, it is unlikely that many Americans had heard of either country before we became involved with them militarily. The fate of either nation did not seem to pose a threat to American security.

If there was, in time, intense interest in the war in Vietnam—in large degree because young Americans protested that war so vociferously—the Korean War almost evoked ennui back home. There was limited television coverage of the "Police Action," and life on the home front was, in the main, unaffected by it.

One reason for this is that the goal of the military in Korea was to maintain the status quo, and that happened. In Vietnam the goal was to establish the permanence of South Vietnam, and although the soldiers won their battles, the purpose was not realized. However, maintaining the status quo cannot produce heroes and neither can military defeat, even if the defeat is caused not by the combatants but by questionable political decisions.[5]

More than this, things changed after World War II, not just the question of maintaining the status quo rather than winning as in Korea or of withdrawing our forces as in Vietnam. Reality therapy, something that always damages the hero, was a factor in the disappearance of the American military hero. The military had always tried to conceal its errors, and as a rule they had the support of politicians in this attempt at subterfuge. Especially during the conflict in Vietnam, some members of the military were openly faulting the establishment itself (as opposed to blaming one or two members of that establishment for its errors), and a number of politicians had abandoned the military cause. The media, especially, refused to protect the military elite, and at times pointed out their failings with undiminished alacrity.

Historically, attacks on the military are unusual. Certainly during most wars and generally extending for a period of time after most wars—including here the Korean War—there were no such public attacks on the military establishment excepting the usual grumblings about the armed forces by, in the main, draftees. The attacks on the morality and efficacy of the United States military during the war in Vietnam, especially after the Tet Offensive, were in a different category altogether.

Before the end of the Tet Offensive, American folklore—the nation's traditional regard for military heroes—and the Cold War all contributed to a protective atmosphere, a national rallying around the flag and defense of America's military institutions. After Vietnam disillusion set in. We learned, for example, that not all American soldiers behaved selflessly. There were frequent reports of drug use, low morale, and insubordination, even of fragging officers. The actions of military leaders came to appear to be self-serving. Officers were seen less as soldiers and more like bureaucrats, less concerned with the men under their command than with ensuring that their own careers were protected. Clearly this limits the potential of the military hero. While it is true that military heroes are almost inherently concerned with "personal honor and glory," the ideal of self-sacrifice is inherently a part of those qualities. By definition, a military man who is known "as being exclusively concerned with his own aggrandizement" cannot be viewed as a military hero. [6]

Studs Turkel reluctantly called World War II "The Good War." It was good because everyone knew who was right and who was wrong. However, Paul Fussell's writings deglamorize war and argue that, purity of purpose aside, in the foxholes there wasn't a lot that was good about "The Good War." Fussell acknowledges that during World War II we had to simplify things, we had to create an ideology that would motivate a diverse, even disparate group of people. For Fussell it was necessary to glorify the reason for the war, but that did not diminish its horror.[7]

It is also true that our involvement in World War II was necessary and involuntary. Japan bombed Pearl Harbor and Germany declared war on the United States; the United States declared war on Japan and Germany in response to the bombing and to the declaration of war, respectively. That necessity was never obvious during the Korean War, but the good guys and the bad guys were still clearly defined; North Korea had invaded South Korea, and monolithic communism was a threat to Western civilization. However, Korea was a long way from home and the policy of containment, in full force in the early 1950s, was at best imperfectly understood by most Americans. The threat of North Korea to the United States proper was difficult to understand, as was the fate of South Korea (especially with Syngman Rhee as the leader of South Korea).

Our purpose in Vietnam was even less clear. A powerful, modern force, year by year decimated a small, technologically limited, independence-seeking nation that had once appealed to the United States for assistance. The justification for our involvement there was not obvious, and it became harder and harder to perpetuate the view that Hanoi (North Vietnam) threatened the United States in any way. In time it was increasingly believed by a large number of people that the struggle in Vietnam was unwinnable (recall that in 1968 presidential candidate Richard M. Nixon had a plan to end the war).

While it was simply unheard of to protest government actions during the Korean conflict, it became acceptable—even fashionable—to do so during the conflict in Vietnam, at least for a portion of the American population. Thousands of young people attacked the war, both for noble and for selfish purposes. Protests against the war grew in both size and volume and affected the nation at large. Surveys taken after the Tet Offensive of January 1968 indicated that a great many people believed that the government had lied about the progress of the war. The course of the war and its purpose—the point of the whole thing—increasingly were seen as muddled by more and more Americans. Confusion as to the purpose of the war increased in direct proportion to the number of American casualties.

After the conflict in Vietnam, war lost whatever glamor it had retained after the Korean conflict for a great many Americans (although some of that glamor was regained during the Gulf War, especially during the air combat missions). Of course if Fussell is correct, and there can be little doubt but that he is, what was truly lost during and after the conflict in

Vietnam was the illusion of glamor. But again, the status of heroes often rests upon illusion.

As suggested earlier, the traditional bravery of the individual soldier lost a great deal of its meaning in recent wars. Wars during the twentieth century used mass armies and long distance weapons and increasingly sophisticated technologies. Long distance weapons—rockets and missiles, for example—mean that a commander's presence in a combat zone is perhaps more dangerous than it once was. At the same time technology in the form of state-of-the-art-communications equipment makes the commander's presence in a combat zone unnecessary. General Schwarzkopf, it may be recalled, directed the Gulf War from a rear bunker, as was quite proper. It is foolish to risk the life of a field commander. Troops could be and were directed from a distance.

This is not a new fact of war. As noted earlier, Ecksteins argued that this was the case in World War I, and others have suggested that the U.S. Civil War saw the first mass armies. William J. Goode takes this view back still further: "The wars of mass movement that began in the Napoleonic era made it much more difficult for all the participants to know who had been conspicuously brave, quite unlike the small-scale raids or battles of previous centuries." In modern wars—that is, in the post–Napoleonic era—it has not been especially important to know who was "conspicuously brave," because individual bravery was "far less important militarily than in the battles that occurred prior to the nineteenth century."[8]

Still and all, individual bravery has always been esteemed within the military. Traditionally and currently, "heroic behavior elicits great admiration" within the military culture. That is why the Civil War, World War I, and World War II, for all of their mass destruction, did produce American heroes. As noted above, Sergeant Alvin York, arguably the best known Medal of Honor winner came out of World War I. York received a hero's welcome in New York City, and in 1941 a motion picture of his life story was released. The Second World War produced First Lieutenant Audie Murphy, the most decorated American combat soldier in that war. He also had his life portrayed by Hollywood. But by the time of the Korean War and during the years of the war in Vietnam, and despite the fact that both conflicts produced their share of courageous American combatants, the era of noting military heroes had passed. And Hollywood certainly wasn't making movies about their lives. Indeed, there were few movies made about the Korean conflict, and the movies that were made about the conflict in Vietnam did not at all celebrate either that war or the military.[9]

In their time York and Murphy were household names, but this was not because of the motion pictures about their lives. The motion pictures followed their fame, they didn't lead it. Both Korea and Vietnam produced men of unquestioned and institutionally recognized bravery. There were 131 Medals of Honor awarded to American service personnel during the Korean "Police Action" and 238 Medals of Honor awarded to American service personnel in Vietnam. But how many Americans know the names of any of them? Clearly, the winners of these medals were among the bravest of the brave. But they weren't national heroes. Their recognition came only from the military; the nation did not know of them.

One might wonder whether or not the salvaged image of the military, insofar as it has been salvaged by events in the Persian Gulf, would have remained unscathed if that war had dragged on for days, weeks, or years, and if more and more Americans saw family members and friends killed and wounded. Heroic illusions were reestablished in the Gulf War because of its brevity, because relatively few American soldiers were in immediate danger and in direct combat, and because of the relatively few casualties the United States suffered (along with our allies). Today it seems unlikely that the illusion could be maintained if other, less favorable, conditions prevailed. Not too long after the conflict in the Gulf, the situation seemed to return to normal; that is, only a few years after all of the hoopla and all of the celebrations, the Desert Storm heroes were pretty much forgotten and there was a noticeable lack of enthusiasm on the part of Americans for the military.[10]

The military hero is gone from America's wars—and has been gone for more than a quarter of a century. It is very important to stress that the disappearance of the military hero has nothing to do with the valor of America's combat forces. It has everything to do with the social admiration those combat forces receive. Disillusion with war, brought on in part by having wars brought into American living rooms—during the "invasion" of Somalia there were as many reporters on the shore as invading forces—undoubtedly contributed to the disillusion with the military hero.

Of course there wasn't any television coverage of the war in Korea, but there wasn't a clear reason for our being there either. The vague sense of purpose of the Korean "Police Action" also weakened American's regard for military heroism. Obviously, the rejection of the war in Vietnam by the youth culture contributed to a repudiation of the military as heroic, and the negative publicity surrounding the military commanders' concerns with body counts could not have done anything but harm their image.

The lack of clear reason for recent wars and a disenchantment with military bureaucracy has harmed the military, and modern technology (along with the mass armies) has diminished the significance of the individual soldier. All of these factors helped vanquish, as America's military enemies could not, the American military hero.

Yet there may be hope for the military hero. In June 1995, Air Force Captain Scott O'Grady was shot down over Bosnia. The captain survived on his own for nearly a week until he was saved by two well-trained and efficient rescue teams. O'Grady was regarded as a hero—albeit briefly, and even though it has been suggested that all he did was "survive an ordeal." If the United States gets involved with limited combat missions on a regular basis, the nation may see the return of military heroes, but in a modern form—that is, we may have transitory military heroes just as we have transitory civilian (celebrity) heroes.[11]

Chapter 5

Sports Heroes

In the United States today only a single business consistently produces heroes, the business of entertainment in its various forms. The hero-entertainment connection is symbiotic. Entertainment produces "stars," the current substitute for traditional heroes. The publicity surrounding a star feeds in part on his celebrity, the fact of his being a star, which in turn generates increased publicity. This increases the star's economic value, which again feeds his celebrity, which again feeds his publicity, which continues until he is replaced by a new star. Thus, throughout his tenure, the star gets wealthier and more celebrated. There appears to be an endless cycle here, although any individual celebrity-hero, including here the sports hero, even the unusually talented sports hero, has a limited lifespan.

Part of the appeal of both sports and show business, the two dominant entertainment fields, is that those who are successful in these areas are exceptionally well paid and afforded opportunities exclusive to members of celebrity circles. The advantages of being able to sing, dance, act, or hit or throw a ball, places some entertainment heroes above the masses, and being above the masses means being above many of society's rules. On a business level, contracts that bind most people are "renegotiated" at the convenience of the star; fans may be ignored and regarded with contempt; temper tantrums are a normal part of adult behavior. Some feel that they should be able to get away with criminal behavior. When notoriety accompanies these episodes, as it invariably does, the celebrity is further celebrated. Greater celebrity naturally increases the star's value which permits another renegotiation, increased contempt for the fan, and additional temper tantrums.

Probably nothing in recent memory demonstrated the power of celebrity as did the O. J. Simpson trial. A national obsession throughout 1995, the trial turned a former football star turned sports commentator into a pseudo-sports hero and celebrity-hero.

Simpson was a fine running back, but so were many others, including Walter Payton, John Riggins, and Franco Harris. The fact is that almost every professional football team has at least one talented running back on its roster. Simpson was well-known and popular during and after his playing days, but no more a sports hero than any other gifted running back. (Quarterbacks are football's sports heroes.) It was during the trial that Simpson, who in recent years was best known as a spokesman for a rent-a-car service, became a "sports hero." His accomplishments on the field didn't bring about this changed status. The media did, by their relentless coverage of the trial and, more importantly, by labeling him a sports hero.

The media made him a celebrity-hero, too. In consequence Simpson published a book, made a post-trial video, and saw the value of his memorabilia increase dramatically. O. J. T-shirts and posters sold very well.

The trial also made celebrity-heroes of virtually everyone associated with it. It turned unknowns into (instantly forgotten) television personalities, and turned some of the more prominent people associated with the trial into authors (who received substantial advances for their literary efforts). Most importantly, perhaps, the trial made clear many of the weaknesses of the American criminal justice system. If nothing else, it pointed to the markedly different attitudes of white and black Americans toward that system.

In order to flourish, the business of entertainment requires a number of people who have both leisure time and fairly sizable disposable incomes. The national per capita income was $95 in 1859. Sixty-eight years later, at the end of World War I, it was $586, "a rate of progress which far outruns any inflation of the currency." During those nearly seven decades the country went through a Civil War and the abolition of slavery, the Gilded Age, the closing of the frontier, unprecedented immigration, and an enormous growth of industry. And during that period the nation became interested in and then hypnotized by sports, by games. Beginning before the Civil War—baseball began in the 1840s—and increasing steadily after it, sports became a regular feature of American life.[1]

America's deep love of sports and sports heroes, however, really started in the 1920s. That period is often called "the Golden Age of Sports." George Mowry notes that the decade saw the "rise of mass spectator sports, and the virtual, if temporary, enshrinement in the national pantheon of the sporting heroes of the day." But it wasn't a temporary enshrinement—not even close: it was permanent, and Mowry might have understood this because he recognized that the media had a great deal to do with this rise of spectator sports. But when Mowry wrote, television was first coming into its own and few could foresee satellite dishes. No one could have imagined the effects of these on sports, athletes, and the fans.[2]

It hardly needs to be pointed out that in the United States today athletes are our heroes. We seek their autographs, pay absurd prices to watch them at work (or play), assume that we have the right to inquire into their private lives (we don't), and enjoy their successes, failures, excesses, and notoriety. Obviously, it is because of their extraordinary athletic abilities that we so admire them. Yet Grantland Rice thought that their talent was only a part of it. No doubt they have extraordinary athletic skills, but they also have an abundant amount of "that indescribable asset known as color, personality, crowd appeal, or whatever you may care to call it."[3]

And whatever you may choose to call it, it is the reason they are not only national heroes but often international heroes. It is the reason why millions of people adore them. In the past the extent of one's celebrity was limited because of technology, but, as implied, there are few such limits anymore. One is no longer restricted to glancing at a headline or reading a story about Babe Ruth or eating a candy bar supposedly named for him (it wasn't). Now one watches Michael Jordan on television. Now, to acknowledge the obvious, America's star athletes (with the help of television) come into homes everywhere in the world. And this helps to make them heroes and helps them sustain their position as heroes, especially the athlete-heroes who regularly speak with newscasters. By engaging in public discussions the athlete-hero permits the fan to get to know him, or at least he allows the fan to think so.

There is a fairly simple way to determine who the public—not only but especially the American public—accepts as their athlete-heroes: how much people buy the products the athlete-hero endorses. Mark Spitz, the swimming star of the 1972 Olympics, didn't do especially well in commercials, nor did Carl Lewis, the track and field sensation, nor many of the other athletes whose areas include swimming, skiing, track and field, and—with rare exceptions—gymnastics. But other athletes do well, often very well. [4]

There seems to be a specific type of athlete-hero in the United States to whom the public responds, a specific sport in which he participates. Basketball, baseball, football, and golf—and occasionally the nonsporting athletic event, wrestling—seem to produce athlete-heroes with consistency, at least to judge from the number of times they are used in commercials. An occasional hockey star (Gretzky), a tennis player (Agassi), and perhaps (following an Olympic year) a gymnast (Retton) endorse products on television. Boxers, on the other hand, generally do not. Even "Sugar" Ray Leonard, immensely popular, articulate, and charming, only sporadically was seen extolling the virtues of a cereal, beer, or athletic shoe. The exception to this rule is George Foreman, the once, current (and future?) heavyweight champion, who often is seen in television commercials. Oddly enough, "Big George"—now perhaps "Old George"—is popular because of his substantial size and power, yet he manages to come across as cuddly, an amazing feat to anyone who has seen him in the ring. One might think that he would be among the last men on earth who would be considered cute and adorable. But then, it always has been difficult to judge the reactions of the American public.

If it is true of athlete-heroes, as Gerald O'Connor says, that in some way "each . . . defines his age, personifies the spirit of his times," what is there to say about today's athlete-hero? What value does he represent?[5]

That value is, in a word, finance, for few illusions can exist any longer that the "game" of baseball or football or any other sport is just a game played for enjoyment. Perhaps it is still argued that "baseball is a game" that a great many children and their parents "play in one form or another"; and maybe people still write letters to the editors of newspapers around the country proclaiming that the sport of baseball is still a game, a sport. But the baseball strike of 1994–95, the masses of lawyers, and the squabbling between the players' union and the owners (as well as the lockout of professional hockey players at the beginning of the 1994–95 season and, as of this writing, the potential strike or lockout within the National Basketball Association [NBA]) should have disabused everyone of that notion once and for all. Sports is a business concerned as are all businesses with economic rewards. To some degree the athletes themselves are (extremely well-paid) commodities. Indeed, as suggested above, the commodities have become businesses, in large part because of the adulation they receive from their fans.[6]

Of course professional sports always was a business, a big business, as was the "amateur" world of college sports and the Olympics. None of this is new. Babe Ruth was well known for his business involvements and Joe Namath and Jack Dempsey, among other athletes, lent their names to Broadway restaurants. Sugar Ray Robinson owned businesses that capitalized on his name recognition.

Perhaps the passage of time has allowed the current images of the past athlete-heroes to become idealized, or perhaps because of limited technology and the cooperation of the press those images were permitted to be manufactured, distributed, and sustained by the team owners. In any event, the image of our past athlete-heroes is of sportsmen who were considerably less avaricious than our current athlete-heroes. On the occasions when they appeared too concerned with their salaries, the public ignored them, as will be noted below. Or perhaps at least one difference between current athlete-heroes and the athlete-heroes of the past is that the latter seemed to have had a sense of proportion.

The salaries of professional athletes are, according to most people, too high. Survey after survey indicates that a substantial majority of those questioned believe that ballplayers' incomes are excessive. (Similar surveys indicate that people feel the same way about incomes of the ball club owners.) Everyone except the ballplayers themselves seems to agree that the salaries of professional athletes are out of hand, and increasingly so. In 1991 the average (mean) salary for a professional baseball player was $890,844. In 1994 it was over $1,000,000. In 1986 the average salary for a National Football League (NFL) player was under $200,000; in 1994 it was $737,000. The average yearly salary in 1994 for an NBA player was about $5.5 million.[7]

These figures are not secrets. Quite the contrary, the salaries of professional athletes are so much a part of professional sports that newspapers regularly list that information. It should also be noted that even if the fans think that professional athletes are overpaid, it doesn't keep them from going to the games and thereby contributing to their astonishing salaries.

Parenthetically, it might be noted that Babe Ruth made a lifetime salary of $925,900 from baseball, slightly higher than the yearly salary of a mediocre professional baseball player today. His 1930 salary in current dollars would be $700,000. In their prime, in current dollars, DiMaggio, Williams, Mays, and Cobb would have earned significantly less than that. Even granting that standards were different then, there can be little doubt that today's salaries are excessive.[8]

Of course one might argue that top skills demand top salaries, but that doesn't work. When Jon Koncak, a seven-foot tall center, signed a six-year contract with the Atlanta Hawks, his career average at the time that he signed the contract was 6.2 points and 6.0 rebounds per game. But if his athletic statistics weren't sensational, his financial statistics were: more than $13 million for that six-year period. His salary, viewed from another perspective, is greater than the combined salaries paid over twenty years to the faculty of an inner-city high school. Koncak is, of course, just one of numerous examples of average players receiving anything but average salaries. For example, Chris Dudley, "with career averages of 4.6 points and 6.3 rebounds" got a "six-year, $24 million deal."[9]

Is this the fault of Koncak or Dudley or of anyone else who is offered that kind of money? Hardly. How many people offered a seven-figure salary to play ball would refuse it? The current system seems to dictate that immense salaries are as much a part of the game as athletic ability. And one part of the system is the publicity that attends salary negotiations. It wasn't always like this. In 1938 Joe DiMaggio held out for a higher salary. (DiMaggio did this with some consistency.) And even though it was DiMaggio, and even though there were only sixteen major league teams then, and even though it was the City of New York, the heart of the media industry, the Yankees simply ignored him; they wouldn't negotiate. The media barely noticed the story and the public didn't care, and during the third week of the season DiMaggio capitulated. And life and baseball went on.[10]

Because of competition as to who is the more valuable athlete, salaries are more than merely salaries today: they represent status. In the current world of professional sports, conspicuous consumption has lost all subtlety. Salary is one of the ways, indeed one of the most important ways, that athletes compete with one another. This is especially so because, as noted, athletes' salaries are published; everyone who follows sports knows that Jock A is getting more (or less) than Jock B.

That competition extends to the current practice of athletes selling their autographs. And it might also be noted that the values of the autographs are, like the salaries of the athletes, public knowledge. "Autographs," as *Time* magazine notes, "are no longer a hobby; they're an industry." For example, Mickey Mantle made as much as $30,000 during a single weekend of signing autographs. But that's pocket change. According to *Forbes* magazine, Nolan Ryan "signed 90,000 baseballs, photos and posters at $20 a scribble, for $1.8 million."[11]

The negative response to all of this, to what appears to many as unabashed greed, suggests a distaste on the part of the public for the excessive commercialization of sports and for the athlete-hero who sells his autograph. That works for adults. But how do you explain his hero's avariciousness to an eight-year-old? Suzanne W. Stout recalls wanting to ask the athlete-hero, please, at least make some eye contact with my child when you sign that $10 autograph.[12]

It might be noted that the selling of autographs appears to be a baseball players' enterprise, at least as of this writing. As late as 1995 tennis players at the U.S. Open actually signed autographs for nothing. But you did have to bring your own pen and paper.

Salaries and autograph sales are by no means the only way to wealth for some professional athletes. A few are indeed quite imaginative in pandering to the interests of their fans. For example, the *New York Times* has it that José Canseco once set up a 900-number hot line to enable him to keep his fans informed as to his activities. The fee was $2 for the first minute and $1 for each minute thereafter. The caller learned a little about José's life. And Reggie Jackson sold his canceled checks, some for as much as $500.[13]

The business side of sports, both professional and amateur, is well documented. Profits from attendance and television revenues come from winning games. Colleges receive seven-figure incomes because their teams participate in bowl games. This means winning teams—that is, skilled players, demanding coaches, and a whatever-it-takes attitude. One result of this, as everyone who pays the slightest attention to college and sports knows, is that rules are ignored.

The issue is not the player who takes steroids or bets on a game. The issue is the system of sports, both professional and amateur. When the NFL announced that it will accept players who were "ineligible to play for their senior college seasons because they had accepted money from agents," they also announced that their main concern was winning. The regulations that define the game are an inconvenience that can be ignored. This was undoubtedly true in the past, but in the past a pretense of probity was offered to the public. The pretense didn't justify disregarding the rules of the game; it just didn't make that disregard a part of the game.[14]

One way of looking at this is that we are developing a new sort of athlete-hero, an athlete-hero designed very specifically for a cynical society, an athlete-hero who appealed to the avariciousness of the 1980s and who will continue that appeal through the 1990s and into the twenty-first century. This athlete-hero is not quite an anti-hero because he still gives a nod to social responsibility, but he is an athlete-hero who flaunts his wealth. The new athlete-hero is a hero because of national admiration and national recognition—and because he reflects the worst of the nation's values. Perhaps that is what is admired.

It should be considered that in the past, just as the athletes' salaries were rarely discussed publicly, the financial condition of the owners was of limited concern to Americans. Ideally at least, owners in the past were sportsmen before they were businessmen, and perhaps they were although that seems very unlikely. Still, however true it might have been, the 1994–95 baseball players' strike and the 1994–95 lockout of hockey players point out the fallacy of that notion today and demonstrate the current owners' share of the responsibility for the unhappy farce occurring within professional sports.

It has been suggested—by Pat Jordan in the *New York Times Magazine*, among others—that the current owners of the professional baseball teams not only don't like the players (or each other) very much, they don't like the game. One consequence of this is that they ignore the game and deal only with the business; and one consequence of that is the absurd salaries offered to players and the costs of going to a game to the fans. Owners enter into bidding wars for players, making the sport a money game and not an athletic contest. Baseball surely is a business as are all professional sports; that, after all, is the meaning of the term "professional." On that level it is difficult to fault the owners here. Perhaps the problem is that the business-people involved try to sell their business as something more than that.[15]

And that is why all of this comes back to the fans, those people willing to pay $20 for Nolan Ryan's autograph and those who demand a winning team or at least a competitive one. Everyone associated with sports learns early on that winning is what it's about, whatever the cost. They begin to learn it in high school. The lessons continue through college and finally in the pros.

In the movie *Hoop Dreams*, the story of two young men who dream about making it to the pros, a high school coach tells one of them (and the audience) this simple fact: "This is a business, and not a game." Another coach—college level this time—tells another simple fact: "If I don't produce winning teams, I'm out of a job." Can anyone deny that the coaches are right or blame them for doing what they must do to keep their jobs?[16]

This undoubtedly is one of the factors that prompted Tom McMillen and Paul Coggins to protest the abuses that go on in college sports programs, especially in basketball. They note, for example, that all too often television ratings are of major importance to colleges and universities, certainly of greater importance than the scholastic abilities of their athletes. But the students and the fans at the games and the people at home watching the games on television want to see winning teams. And the schools, high school and university alike, as well as the professionals, are satisfying that desire; and so we get dubious ethics and financial excesses in American sports. We can have sports or we can have sports as businesses, but we can't have it both ways. If we choose the latter, we shouldn't be surprised at or complain about the consequences of that choice. [17]

It may be asking a bit much to expect contemporary athletes to behave like the gentlemen of old, as Joseph Bensman and Robert Lilienfeld appear to want them to do. Still, there can be no doubting the accuracy of their assertion that with the professionalization and commercialization of sports, "the byproducts of victory are measured in terms that are far greater than victory, both to the professional athlete or to the owners of the team."[18]

It is not merely that the heroic image of the athlete has changed, nor that the system of professional sports has changed. As suggested above, the system of amateur sports has changed, and not just in academia. The amateur athlete participates in sports because of team spirit or love of sport. At least that was the image presented to the nation in the past. Now the effort is often an investment in the future. The athletes of the 1992 Olympics said just that. They were investing in their future by dedicating themselves to sports, much as one who studies automobile mechanics or dentistry is working for his future. Today, one plans on enjoying a financially rewarding career if one has chosen the right sport and is a successful amateur. Even before the start of the 1992 Olympics, two potential gold medal winners of the Decathlon were advertising athletic gear on television. (Neither won the gold; one failed to qualify and the other was injured during the competition and won the bronze medal.)

The Tonya Harding–Nancy Kerrigan incident, too, reflected the financial benefits of what was once amateur sports. Kerrigan, one may recall, was deliberately injured, supposedly at Harding's instigation, in an attempt to force Kerrigan to withdraw from the competition. This, in turn, would have improved Harding's chances of winning and increased her potential reward. (It didn't work. Kerrigan recovered from her injuries, entered the competition, and won the silver medal in the 1994 Winter Olympics.)

Again, most of us would accept large sums of money for our athletic efforts if offered. But if, as in the past, one criterion for the hero was at least the illusion of some degree of selflessness, that illusion and surely that selflessness, have fallen by the wayside, and the athlete-hero is lessened.[19]

The professional plays for a salary, of course, but also for a team and for a sense of accomplishment. At least this is the way it was publicized, and perhaps even the way it was for a while. Perhaps the Weberian ideal of the charismatic hero did exist and perhaps the money was only a part of the package. This is one of the reasons why some athletes are crowd pleasers. Coupled with their extraordinary skills, they project a reasonable image for a professional athlete: the money is important, but they also care deeply about the game. Magic Johnson in basketball, Jimmy Connors in tennis, and, before his difficulties, Pete Rose in baseball, offered this image. Michael Jordan, too, despite his apparently endless endorsements, always seems first to love the game.

The idealism, that love of the game that is necessary for the existence of an athlete-hero, today seems very hard to find. Of course none of this can be taken to imply that the athletes of the past were at all "pure." When there were problems in the past (and there were), when there were scandals (and there were, especially in the 1920s, the great era of sports heroes), the public tended to ignore them and "the heroes remained heroes."[20]

That's not the way it works today. The system—the culture and the structure, the values and the attitudes we hold, the fans, the owners, the athletes, the media—will not permit it. One consequence of this, as Robert Lipsyte argues, is that "we stopped liking" our athlete-heroes. Perhaps that's why one credit card advertisement tries to get our attention by using this lead: "Next time somebody asks 'Where have all our heroes gone?' point them towards Cooperstown." The implication is clear: athlete-heroes, at least baseball's athlete-heroes, cannot be found on the ball field today. We have to travel back in time to locate them.[21]

Part of the reason for the discrepancy in the public's attitude toward the old professional athletes and the new ones may be the type of negative press each received. When there were headlines about the unhappy behavior of sports heroes of the past, they usually involved details of their sexual exploits, not their petulance because management would not renegotiate their contracts. The former is a lot easier to forgive than the latter. Besides, a sexual scandal is titillating; a contract renegotiation is merely avaricious. Today sex scandals may still be winked at (although not as often as in the past), but current athletes have other problems: drugs and charges of rape and spousal abuse. These do not provide vicarious excitements.

Paul Greenberg wrote in the (Baltimore) *Evening Sun* about Joe DiMaggio's fifty-six-game hitting streak. He saluted that feat and at the same time expressed his dissatisfaction with the changes that have occurred in baseball. He concluded the article by noting that Paul Simon's famous lyric kept coming back to him: Whatever happened to Joe DiMaggio? Where did the Yankee Clipper go? Well, we can answer Simon's question now. Joe left to sell autographs at $30 a pop, and so did all the future Yankee Clippers. In fact, that's one of the reasons why they want to become DiMaggios in the first place. Again, if you were offered $30 for your autograph, wouldn't you sell it? You probably would, but again, such is not the stuff of heroes.[22]

We have athlete-heroes today, of course, and the most skilled of them may be of a quality as good or better than many of those of the past, at least insofar as their abilities on the ball fields and courts are concerned. But their ability to elevate us as people, as a hero should, is waning if it hasn't already disappeared. Money and ego get in the way. Howie Reiser tells of the time when he went to Jackie Robinson's office to meet the Brooklyn Dodger great. This was in 1953 and they (along with Reiser's mother) chatted for well over an hour—a kid and his hero, and they stopped talking only when Reiser's mother made him come home for supper. What are the odds of a star athlete talking to a kid for that length of time today? Our current athlete-heroes won't even look a kid in the eye when his mother is shelling out $10 for an autograph.[23]

And yet . . .

During the summer of 1995, a time when every professional sport appeared to be in turmoil and every professional athlete seemed obsessed with his celebrity, Cal Ripken, Jr. of the Baltimore Orioles broke Lou Gehrig's record for most consecutive games played: 2130. Ripken's 2131st game was played at Camden Yards, the Orioles' home ball field, and they stopped the game (during the middle of the seventh inning when the game became official and went into the record books) so that the fans could cheer and celebrate. Ripken handled the good wishes and attention with grace and charm. He seemed to share his record with the fans who supported him. The point is that even today it is possible for an athlete-hero to have some class, to behave as an athlete-hero should, to be a "good guy." It just isn't done very often.[24]

Chapter 6

Political Heroes

It is hard to disagree with Barbara Kellerman's assessment that the already weakened regard the American public had for the politician-hero was critically injured in the late 1960s and early 1970s. The conflict in Vietnam coupled with the events surrounding the Watergate break-in contributed to the erosion of "our trust in government and in our leaders." Nor was Americans' diminishing admiration for their leaders helped by the economic state of the nation during the next several presidencies.[1]

Amitai Etzioni thinks that the disparagement of our political leaders is as much a reflection of Americans' attitude toward heroes as it is a consequence of our political system. The disparagement, that is, is not merely of the politician-hero, although perhaps it is most apparent when dealing with political leaders, but of heroes generally. We take away all of the illusions of the would-be president before he reaches that office because we dislike all potential heroes. "Long before he becomes President, the halo will be stripped away. In the end, we can't stomach a real hero." We may enjoy heroes but only temporarily. In the end, Etzioni says, we are compelled to destroy them, and rather quickly, especially in politics. Perhaps, then, Carlyle was right: "Democracy means despair of finding any heroes to govern you."[2]

In fact Americans have long been noted for treating politicians with something less than veneration. It is a traditional view that Americans are " 'unreverential' toward politicians," which explains de Tocqueville's observation regarding Americans' "lack of deference to elected officials." Americans generally do not trust centralized government, and that is just one reason why it is difficult to find a living political hero, except perhaps in times of war when the nation tends to rally 'round its leader. (None of this suggests that Americans endorse the political anarchy of the far right, or their use of violence and terrorism.)[3]

A more significant reason that Americans mistrust centralized government is that the nation's political leaders are, virtually by definition, the chosen leaders of only a part of the country. They usually have the support of their party—although there have been exceptions as, for example, Truman in 1948—but the rest of the country may be disinterested in them or may dislike them. A majority of the voters may initially regard them as their political leaders and possibly as their political heroes, but a majority of the American people do not. Those who didn't vote at all are not likely to see them as their heroes or their leaders, and those who voted against them are even less likely to do so.

These are some of the reasons why in the past half century it is so difficult to recall a president who is remembered as a hero save, perhaps, John F. Kennedy, a point that will be discussed momentarily. Truman cannot be regarded as a heroic president, despite the 1992 political testimonies to his memory. He certainly wasn't considered heroic, or even competent, during his tenure—even though he was a war time president—which is one reason he didn't run for reelection. Eisenhower was a military hero, not a political one; Lyndon Baines Johnson was disliked in the extreme while he was in office (and still is)—the reason why he too didn't run for reelection. President Nixon was surely not a presidential hero, and Presidents Ford, Carter, and Bush were clearly not heroic politicians—Nixon was forced to resign the office and the others lost their bids for reelection. Ronald Reagan was not admired by the masses, although the businesspeople of the 1980s may have loved him and although some did indeed regard him as their hero. However, President Reagan's image was tarnished even to his supporters when he "stuff[ed] his pockets with money," that is, when he accepted a $2 million fee from a Japanese company for delivering two brief speeches. As of this writing it seems unlikely that Bill Clinton's tenure in the White House will be remembered as heroic.[4]

The fact is that as a rule American political heroes are political heroes only in memory, as with, for example, Washington, Jefferson, and Lincoln. Fawcett and Thomas are quite correct: "Americans glorify and sentimentalize their Presidents once they are safely dead." The best recent examples here are Franklin Delano Roosevelt and John Fitzgerald Kennedy, who were idolized as were few American politicians, FDR to some degree while he was still alive.[5]

Both men died suddenly, Roosevelt because of illness and Kennedy by an assassin's bullet, and both exuded strength while in office. In both personality and political actions, their years in office seemed examples of imperial presidencies. And in both cases those imperial years took on a mystical aura after a period of time. Arthur Schlesinger, Jr., used the term "imperial presidency" to attack Richard Nixon during his tenure as president. But Nixon's presidency collapsed and he was regarded with disdain by a number of people. In contrast, Roosevelt's and Kennedy's presidencies thrived in memory, and that is critical to the making of a political hero.[6]

Roosevelt is generally accepted as a politician-hero (except by Paul Johnson). FDR saw the United States through its most difficult depression and most horrific international war and even Johnson admits that "Roosevelt appeared to be in tune with the Thirties spirit," although he was a tool of the "Big City Democratic machine bosses."[7]

Other writers usually fail to mention Roosevelt's alliance with, or obligation to, political machines. They do note his inherited wealth and privilege, that he was not especially well trained in economics, and that he was an unlikely candidate to guide the nation through the Great Depression. They also note his political intuition, his ability to communicate with the people, and his deep sense of compassion, based perhaps in part because of his being crippled by polio. Most importantly, they note that he helped people who were looking for work to find work. The CCC, the WPA, and the other "alphabet agencies" that he started gave jobs to those in need of jobs and helped to make him a hero. To a great many Americans, Roosevelt was the man who took them off soup lines and got them paychecks. Roosevelt brought electricity to those who had none; Roosevelt provided the elderly and handicapped with social security checks; Roosevelt supported a minimum wage and labor unions.

Whether or not he should have created so many government agencies and whether or not those agencies should have gotten involved in the lives of so many people is not the issue at the moment. At the time, those creations and that involvement were the stuff of heroes to millions of Americans. Roosevelt was also the war leader, the man who guided the nation through the most devastating war in the world's—not the nation's—history. (Abraham Lincoln, the president who guided the United States through its most horrific war, also died suddenly and was also a political hero—not only in memory, but while he was alive and active.)

That explains why Roosevelt was reelected to the presidency three times. His four presidential terms, which shattered the two-term tradition established by Washington, are an indication of his charisma and of the regard with which he was held by the American people. This is as clear an indication as possible that Franklin Delano Roosevelt was a politician-hero.[8]

Kennedy, too, was charismatic in degree, but it is difficult to separate the memory of the man from the fact of him. The title of Tom Wicker's article about President Kennedy, "From Man to Martyr to Myth," is not an inaccurate representation of America's views of JFK. President Roosevelt died suddenly in April 1945 but not unexpectedly (he had looked quite ill for some time); President Kennedy died prematurely, a young and vigorous man. His death shocked the country, indeed, the world. This feeds the image of hero.[9]

Kennedy brought an unprecedented degree of sophistication to the White House. Roosevelt was as cultured and refined as Kennedy, but he didn't have television to demonstrate that to the public, nor an attractive and urbane young wife (herself a hero). Nor could Roosevelt be seen playing touch football or casually standing at a press conference exchanging quips with reporters. Kennedy managed to reflect the spirit of the times. His youth (he was the youngest man elected to the presidency) was an asset at a time when the young were developing their subculture. Social changes were clearly on the horizon, and Kennedy seemed the man to guide the nation through these changes. There were also the titillating rumors about his affairs, especially with Marilyn Monroe. And there was the assassination. By the end of the weekend following the assassination John Kennedy was a political legend. He received 49 percent of the vote in 1960; after the assassination some 63 percent of those polled reported that they had voted for him. And for a while it seemed as if every street in the country was going to be renamed in Kennedy's honor.

But nothing in American politics is that easy. If Kennedy is deified, and he certainly is, he is also vilified. Ted Sorensen points to the negative views held of JFK by at least some Southern Democrats. ("K.O. the Kennedys" was their political slogan.) Sorensen also notes that Kennedy was regarded as "antilabor" as well as "antibusiness." He was also accused of spending too much on defense by the Left and too much on education by the Right. But all of this was before the assassination; after November 22, 1963, the status of politician-hero fell upon him. His may have been "the death of a prince," but he became a prince only in death. [10]

And Kennedy was an American prince. Godfrey Hodgson points out the extraordinary adoration Kennedy enjoyed, especially by the upper middle class but by no means only by them. Even Paul Johnson, no fan of the Kennedys, says that John Kennedy had "class," and that, "like FDR, he turned Washington into a city of hope," adding that by "city of hope" he means "a place where middle-class intellectuals flocked for employment." Johnson's cynicism aside, hope is one of the things that a hero must be able to give to his followers. That ability is a necessary if not sufficient characteristic of heroes.[11]

Roberts and Olson argue that "Kennedy epitomized America, particularly the rise and triumph of the immigrant," which is stretching things, to say the least. And speaking of stretching things, James MacGregor Burns writes of Kennedy that "he is more than a lion, more than a fox, he's superman." But even this adulation pales beside that of Arthur Schlesinger, who begins an essay on Kennedy with these words: "He glittered when he lived, and the whole world grieved when he died."[12]

But again, the American politician-hero is rarely a politician-hero to everyone. People have questioned Kennedy's abilities as president. Barbara Kellerman notes his failures, especially his ineffective political leadership in areas he himself "designated 'most important.'" Others agree: Roberts and Olson suggest that Kennedy was attacked because of his tepid civil rights program, because he was too closely aligned with business, and because he was "a belligerent 'cold warrior.'" They also note that Kennedy could be quite calculating and that he was extremely concerned with his image as a politician. Kennedy, they argue, was "obsessed with the possibility of his own greatness." Even if this is true it is hardly an unusual presidential characteristic. More to the point, perhaps, if Kennedy the president was not successful, Kennedy the symbolic figure surely was, and that is the sine qua non of the politician-hero.[13]

America's two twentieth-century politician-heroes were different men with different careers and endings. Roosevelt's work was almost finished when he died while Kennedy's had barely started. Roosevelt's heroism lives in the history books and in the memory of those who were enthralled by him and by what he accomplished during an astoundingly difficult decade and a half. Kennedy's heroism is found within his unfulfilled potential and premature death. Roosevelt is a politician-hero for what he did, for the way in which he led the nation. Kennedy is a politician-hero because of what he is thought to have been able to do.

The points here are that Roosevelt and Kennedy were our most recent American political heroes and that their kind is unlikely to appear again.

Barring a true national crisis and a true rescuer of the country from that crisis, the politician-hero is no more. Americans today know that presidential popularity is as much a consequence of theater as of politics. In consequence, people are increasingly cynical about and less likely to be taken in by appearance. Equally important, Kennedy and Roosevelt were able to be regarded by most as being of the people despite being born into the monied class. That has changed. Kellerman writes that politicians today "think it more advantageous to display themselves as being part of a special elite than as one of the people."[14]

But this flies in the face of American political tradition, which has the politician-hero as a man of the people. One of the reasons for the success of both Roosevelt and Kennedy was their ability to use both their wealth and charm to their advantage. They maintained a social distance while creating political empathy. They seemed to set standards for the rest of the nation, yet appeared able to mix with the people and understand their problems.

There is little wrong with being wealthy. Americans may be envious of the wealthy, but that envy is tinged with admiration. The trick seems to be not to appear to be aloof. Two presidents who worked for their wealth, who struggled to achieve their positions of power, Lyndon Johnson and Richard Nixon, never seemed to be of the people. It seemed as if they stood apart from the mass of Americans. Roosevelt and Kennedy, who inherited their wealth, also appear to have inherited a sense of humor and a sense of proportion, two critical qualities for the American politician-hero.

It is of interest that for over one hundred years no Republican president has seemed heroic to the American people during or after his tenure in office. The Republican president who almost attained that status was Teddy Roosevelt, and that was as much for his being an outdoorsman (when killing animals was regarded as manly), an imperialist (when that philosophy was in favor in the West), a trust-buster (which is hardly in keeping with the image of Republicanism), and a Spanish-American War hero (although that was a very unusual war indeed).

John Kenneth White argues that the key to political success—in the terminology being used here, that is, in being a politician-hero—is to possess a common touch, a means of providing a sense of being with and of the people. Perhaps because Democrats often lean toward populist causes they are able to present themselves as sympathetic to the problems of the average American, while the Republicans are associated, justly or not, with the interests of the well-to-do. The Republican image is rarely one of compassion and warmth; rather, the Republican image is that of a rational, hard-headed individualist. That image was fine when a rural nation that was half wilderness needed an abundant number of individualists, but the need for rugged individualists has diminished in an America that is urban and suburban, bureaucratized and well-structured.

The Republican image lies in their association with business executives, making solid, intelligent, impersonal decisions. For example, President Reagan was admired for his administration's foreign policy, but the image, correct or not, of being pro-business, of caring little for the worker—as evinced by his firing the striking air traffic controllers—precluded the public from regarding him as a politician-hero. Firing workers, slashing budgets, cutting programs for the poor, and reducing entitlements may be fiscally responsible, but they don't increase one's popularity among the masses. Similarly, during the 1995–96 battle over the federal budget, polls consistently indicated that most Americans regarded the Republican budget plan as too severe. President Clinton's budget plan was generally considered to be more sensitive to the needs of the poor and the elderly. More importantly, Republicans appeared indifferent to the forced "furloughs" of thousands of federal employees and to the hardships the employees and their families suffered. None of this adds to the image of Republican politicians as warm and caring people.

One other point might be mentioned here. The significance of image is critical to the politician-hero, and image is attained generally through the press. There is some truth to the claim that the media—electronic and print—are liberally biased. This cannot help the Republicans if they seek to be politician-heroes.

In the same vein, one should consider a point just mentioned here and considered in depth in a later chapter: politicians today are subjected to media scrutiny as never before. As noted, Franklin Delano Roosevelt's confinement to a wheelchair was not common knowledge in the 1930s. If it were, his presidential bid might not have gotten off the ground. It is also highly unlikely that President Kennedy's (or President Roosevelt's or President Eisenhower's) affairs would have stayed off the front pages of newspapers or off the television nightly news shows today.

The times, that is, society, allowed for Roosevelt and Kennedy to be politician-heroes. In the ensuing decades the times denied our national leaders that chance, or even the chance to be regarded as just heroic. At the very least, the cynicism of the American electorate today has reached unprecedented levels. That cynicism and broader changing attitudes and social standards, changing technology, increased visibility, and prying

Chapter 7

Entertainment Heroes

INTRODUCTION

Some of the celebrity-heroes that Daniel Boorstin speaks about are athletes, but the overwhelming number of them are in show business. Actors, dancers, "personalities," and especially rock stars are the true celebrity-heroes. Their feats may not be heroic in the traditional sense of that term, and by that account they cannot measure up to past American heroes. Moreover, by the very nature of their activities, entertainment heroes are transitory ones. Nonetheless, according to the American public, stars within the entertainment industry are heroes and likely to remain heroes, even as specific ones fall from prominence. It is important to note here that the "American public" is American youth. The entertainment hero today is the hero of America's young people, adolescents and young adults, and has been for some time.

The higher level of the entertainment hero as celebrity-hero as compared to, say, the athlete-hero may be determined by using the tool by which the status of entertainment heroes is measured: income. If athletes are overpaid, and the consensus seems to be that they are, it should be noted that their incomes are, if not trivial when compared to those of the top movie stars, then certainly a poor second. Nearly ten years ago an observer of the Hollywood scene could write that "the floor for top male stars is now $5 million a picture." That is for a few weeks' work, and that was several years ago. Today a top star would be insulted at a seven-figure offer.[1]

Further proof of the entertainment icon/show business hero, if more is needed, can be found in the August 5, 1991, issue of *Insight*, a conservative weekly news and commentary magazine that takes itself quite seriously. In an article entitled "Kevin Costner Dances with the GOP," the author, Daniel Wattenberg, is enthralled that Costner, a current entertainment hero "is a closet Republican. Maybe even a conservative Republican." What the article didn't discuss is the importance of Costner's political leanings to anyone save Costner, but it wasn't really necessary to do that. Because Kevin Costner is a star and because he is an entertainment hero, the GOP, and especially its conservative wing, wants to claim him as one of its own. This, of course, is only one example of politicians seeking the endorsement of their views by the famous, the entertainment heroes. As a general rule, Republicans and Democrats unabashedly seek celebrity endorsements, especially during election years. [2]

ACTING

In show business as nowhere else, celebrity alone can breed success—and thus more celebrity and thus more success and finally the status of a hero within American popular culture. This is one of the reasons why the children of successful performers have an enormous advantage over their competition and why there are so many people in show business who are related to someone else in show business. Of course nepotism is hardly a new phenomenon, nor one peculiar to the entertainment field. However, the subject here is not jobs, but candidates for the position of American icon. Celebrity literally breeds celebrity and celebrity (entertainment) heroes literally breed celebrity (entertainment) heroes. It is for this reason that successful show people have been termed "America's Royalty."

The notion of entertainment heroes breeding celebrity and celebrity breeding entertainment heroes can be seen in the admiration of past entertainment heroes—often by current entertainment heroes—even if the hero-worshippers cannot possibly have witnessed the greatness of their heroes. Joshua Logan, a man clearly knowledgeable about the theater, and Sir John Gielgud, also a man of some knowledge of the theater, selected, respectively, the ten best stage actors of all time and the six greatest Hamlets of all time. Included in Logan's list were David Garrick and Edwin Booth; included in Gielgud's were Richard Burbage and Thomas Betterton. Garrick died in 1779, Booth died in 1893, Burbage in 1619, and Betterton in 1710. It is unlikely, then, that the selectors of the best stage actors and best Hamlets saw any performances by the people they noted. They were relying upon reputation, and in Burbage's case the fact that he was the first actor to play Hamlet. It is one thing to pick Sir Laurence Olivier's Hamlet over Richard Burton's Hamlet or vice versa. It is quite another to praise the skills of an actor dead for several centuries, but such is the power of name recognition in entertainment.[3]

It was not until the early part of the twentieth century, with the development of the movies, that acting, performing in public, gained national attention and respectability, and actors began to enjoy an increasingly exalted status. One reason for this is that films allowed actors to be known by the masses. The movies were the first popular, that is, relatively inexpensive, entertainment aimed at the urban working class and, most especially, the urban middle class. From their beginnings in cities the movies spread throughout the country, and more and more films were demanded by larger and more varied audiences. Screen actors played to and enjoyed the attention of fans nationwide. The movie star was born and with only rare exception, the loyalty of the fans has remained unabated throughout the century. Larry May notes that actors on the screen developed a unique power over their audiences. People sitting in the movie theater began to "*feel*" the force of actors, and not merely see their images on a screen. This was especially true of stars, those actors with charisma.[4]

To note the obvious, an actor is not the same as a movie star, although they certainly are not mutually exclusive terms as some have suggested. But if the term "actor" is limited here to those working in the "legitimate theater," it is safe to say that the actor cannot qualify as an entertainment hero. Even when the theater was the only form of mass entertainment, actors could attract only a small following relative to actors today. And even today the theater has too limited an audience to produce entertainment heroes. But not so the movies or television. It is a safe bet that more people saw a single motion picture, *Terminator II*, in the first year of its release than saw all of the productions on Broadway in any year, possibly in any decade. And it is probable that more people regularly see reruns of *Cheers* in a single television season than see the entire listing of Broadway plays in any season, possibly in any ten seasons. It is the movie star and, to a lesser degree because the medium is regarded as less glamorous, the television star, who are America's entertainment heroes.[5]

Because today America's entertainment audience is in effect America's youth, the current entertainment heroes of the screen (and of television) do not pretend to be real as they did in the past. A great many of the current Hollywood entertainment heroes, especially the action heroes, are cartoons or fantasy: The Terminator, Rambo, and Dirty Harry. For the kids the most important heroes currently are the Mighty Morphin Power Rangers, also superhuman in essence and skills. Logically following from this, the stars of today aren't the stars of yesterday. Cooper and Gable "have been replaced by Dustin Hoffman and Al Pacino . . . [who] do not inspire images of heroism, or sexual fantasies." Today's movie stars are clearly moneymakers, but they are just as clearly not up to the standards of past movie heroes.[6]

All of this, of course, is contingent upon who is making these judgments. The entertainment hero depends upon an audience for his status. If adults are moviegoers—or, more accurately, if producers think that adults are going to the movies more than adolescents and make movies for adult tastes—the entertainment heroes of the movies will be mature, adult. Such a hero for a while was (again) Kevin Costner as profiled in an article in *Time* magazine. Although at least one letter to the editor in response to that article pointed out that Costner was "just an actor," his movies are often taken to reflect adult fantasies. *Field of Dreams* perhaps best illustrates this point. And this makes him an entertainment hero to an adult audience. Indeed, adult entertainment heroes may become increasingly visible as the baby boom generation ages, unless the movie people insist on pandering to the tastes of adolescents or something happens to keep the baby boomers at home (for example, better quality television shows or excessive pricing at the movies).[7]

Hollywood could, of course, combine the two, make movies for young people and for adults. Vincent Canby argues that "our most popular movies" are enjoyed by people of varying ages "though not necessarily for the same reasons or with the same intensity." But this doesn't happen all that often. In fact, in both absolute numbers and in terms of percentages, adolescents—teens and young adults—make up the bulk of the movie audience (a "real" adult is often defined as someone twenty-five or over). For this reason Hollywood plays to "the eternal adolescent," which is why we've had numerous *Die Hards* and *Terminators*, and why it is impossible to predict when (or if) they and the *Lethal Weapons* will stop coming.[8]

In the 1930s and 1940s, and on occasion in the 1950s, in the years before adults stayed home and watched television, romantic comedy and serious drama played well at the movies. The heroes of these films were adult men and women. Even John Wayne portrayed real human beings on occasion, even in Westerns: Mr. Dunston gets shot in *Red River* and Rooster Cogburn dies in *The Shootist*. And when Gary Cooper was in a fight in *High Noon*, he took a beating that stayed with him for a while. But does anyone expect Rambo to get killed or Dirty Harry to die or the Terminator to be in danger of being terminated? Not as long as there are IIs, IIIs, IVs, and Vs to be made. Does anyone even expect them to show the effects of beatings, stabbings, or shootings?[9]

When Humphrey Bogart as Lew Archer came out of the Fat Man's hotel room after deliberately losing his temper (in *The Maltese Falcon*), he looked at his shaking hand and grinned sardonically. Could Rambo do this? Or Dirty Harry? Or the Terminator? Films for adolescents have dominated the industry for some time now, and the heroes of today as depicted in the movies are the heroes of adolescents. That is one reason why, if you are an adult, watching a movie today "leaves no trace whatsoever."[10]

And so it shall continue, vanishing movies and farcical heroes. Movies, of course, reflect the culture in a variety of ways, as does everything else. Charles R. Morris notes that "a feature film most often must reinforce the cultural values and attitudes of its viewers if it expects to be popular." And they all want to be popular: that's how they make a profit. Thus, if redesigning the entertainment hero into a cartoon is what it takes to make that profit, then redesigned he shall be. If the film was intended for, and the audience consists of, adolescents, then adolescent values will be portrayed on the screen. Today, Costner aside, entertainment heroes designed for an adult audience are rare indeed. Besides, it's quite possible that adults today would be too cynical to believe warmed-over versions of previous entertainment heroes. And that leaves us without any real ones. [11]

MUSIC

Using income once more as a measure of the stature of the entertainment hero, if athletes are a distant second to movie star entertainment heroes, then imagine the status of those whose income trivializes the income of movie stars. Not singers—there are few famous ones left—but rock stars are the entertainment heroes above all entertainment heroes. There is general agreement that "today the rock stars have it all." Mablen Jones's comment that "rock superstars have taken on the role of sacred public magicians" is, if anything, an understatement. [12]

No athlete, no actor, demands or receives the adoration of so many people as today's rock star; no athlete, no actor, can at all be regarded as equal in stature to a rock star as an entertainment hero. Their incomes are measured in the hundreds of millions of dollars, their celebrity is worldwide, the devotion of their fans is apparently without limit. Rock stars defy damaged hearing, morality, and perhaps mortality. They amass fortunes, deceive their fans, and live in insulated vacuums. Their universe is "protected by roadies, managers, public relations writers, lawyers and their record companies." They live in an idyllic world, one in which they are never corrected, never wrong, never challenged.[13]

For all intents and purposes, American popular music began in the late nineteenth/early twentieth centuries. Thus, Howard Husock suggests that, Stephen Foster notwithstanding, "no truly national popular American music emerged until the end of the 19th century." Popular music in the United States continued developing throughout the teens, twenties, thirties, and forties. And in each era the music—ragtime, Dixieland jazz, swing, be-bop, and cool jazz—was regarded as distasteful or vile or dangerous, or any combination of these by older, staid individuals. Dixieland jazz and swing, be-bop, and cool jazz threatened to destroy American youth. But in fact the singers and the songs, the musicians and the music, were different in content only, not in form. Played for and by adults—regardless of the age of the musicians, many of whom were in their teens and early twenties—American music was multigenerational from its inception. Today's classics are by and large made up of those distasteful or vile or dangerous songs of the past.[14]

Welcome to the mid-1950s, to the growth and development of rock and roll, a music designed specifically and exclusively for a particular generation, for teenagers. It may be true that during World War II Frank Sinatra angered parents. He wasn't the tough and battle-hardened GI who was supposed to be the hero of the hour. But Sinatra, the entertainment hero to bobby-soxers, was respectable. Married and with a family, neatly dressed in a suit, shirt, and bow tie (currently enshrined in the Smithsonian Institution), he was a variation from the norm, a diversion; he was not a threat. Rock and roll performers in the 1950s were a threat, at least initially and at least to adults (and perhaps for the very reason that they were heroes to the young).[15]

Rock and roll started as black music, as rhythm and blues (then called "race music")—recall that in the 1950s segregation was usually the fact, and often the law, of the land. As rhythm and blues evolved into rock and roll, it also widened its audience to include white people, but really only white teenagers. One reason for this is that from the first, rock and roll was associated with adolescent rebelliousness, with new and dangerous notions found in *The Wild One, The Blackboard Jungle, Rebel without a Cause*, and *Splendor in the Grass*, films and film heroes intended for adolescents. It was associated with these and other pictures depicting and encouraging teenage contentiousness, teenage rejection of parental authority.

By the late 1950s rock and roll had become a basic part of teenage culture. For a time there was "Guy Mitchell, Frankie Laine, Doris Day, Johnnie Ray . . . and then there was *Rock around the Clock*, Elvis Presley, Chuck Berry, Little Richard, Eddie Cochran, Buddy Holly, the Everly Brothers and all the rest; columns and columns of heroes marching through the charts." But this was only the beginning. Most of the rock and roll stars were comparatively wholesome. Surely these heroes—the Everly Brothers, Frankie Avalon, and Fabian—were no threat to tradition. On occasion even adults could enjoy their music.[16]

Then came Bob Dylan, the entertainment hero to entertainment heroes, and social protest, and the Beatles and the celebrated "British Invasion," and the rest of the 1960s. By the late 1960s and the early 1970s, rock and roll stars (now simply rock stars) were firmly established as the entertainment heroes of the young and only of the young. Bobby-soxers stood in line for hours to see and hear Frankie in the 1940s, but that was trivial compared to the attention, to the unfettered devotion, given to the rock stars of the late 1960s and throughout the 1970s, 1980s, and 1990s by their fans, by the youth of the country. They were entertainment heroes as had never existed before.

It is important here to note that rock music became popular music, young music. The youth generation, the youth culture, took over music to a much greater extent than it did the movies. The movies occasionally play to adults, but this is not the case with pop music. One consequence of this is that talent in the form of singing ability, and of singing ability alone, is only occasionally a requirement for success as a popular singer today. A greater requirement is the ability to put on an event, a provocative extravaganza.

This is not to suggest that today's pop singers (rock stars) are untalented or that they can't sing. It is to suggest that they don't need a lot of talent, that they don't have to be able to sing. Sophisticated equipment that creates amazing sounds has rendered singing an optional extra in the popular music industry, and in any event the popularity of music videos makes good looks more important than singing ability. And this is why there are so many "oldies" stations on the radio and why "country" suddenly became so popular; adults want their own music.

Current success in the field of rock depends upon one of two things, both designed with the adolescent in mind: sex and intensely loud rhythms amid spectacular productions. Adolescent music is concerned with sex as adult music is concerned with romance. Of course, adults also have some regard for sex, but it doesn't overwhelm their music. (Anyone who thinks that this point—the sexual emphasis of adolescent music—is an exaggeration should spend some time watching MTV.)

The second key to success in the music business today is the show and the volume of the music, volume raised to the point of literally shattering eardrums, of endangering hearing. Where once popular music meant a singer and accompanist in, perhaps, a night club (as, say, Bobby Short or Michael Feinstein), rock entertainment consists in the main of elaborate shows with amplified volume—courtesy of enormous speakers and extremely advanced electronic equipment—to accommodate the mass audiences at the shows.

The point to note here is the growth of age-segregated tastes in entertainment in addition to divisions in taste (for example, preference for country or rap). Entertainment (acting and music here), which once was homogeneous, which once had universal appeal in the United States, is now a fragmented, group-specific, heterogeneous entity. This increases the number of entertainment heroes, but diminishes the number of their fans. Each group has its own heroes: Madonna, for example, or Garth Brooks are entertainment heroes to some and unpalatable to others. Paradoxically, they are local heroes on a mass scale.

A GOD AND A GODDESS AND A GOD OF GODS AND GODDESSES

On rare occasions there appears in society a selected few who rise even beyond the status of entertainment hero. They become a god or a goddess to a significant number of people. Adored by fans, these gods and goddesses are deified after they die, especially if they die prematurely. In the movies one such individual was James Dean, who represented the ultimate teenage rebel.

There is no denying the mass appeal of, say, Clark Gable. "Often cast as the ultimate macho male, Gable became one of the screen's greatest sex symbols." And, discounting the cartoon-like roles of Schwarzenegger, Stallone, and Gibson, among others, we've had a lot of other male sex symbols: Grant and Cooper, Redford and Newman, and on and on. But James Dean was different. A publicist put it this way: "I thought Dean was a legend, but I was wrong. . . . He's a religion." A cult of the dead quite literally began when he fatally crashed that car in 1955. "A magazine offering Dean's words 'from the other side' sold 500,000 copies. Dean's death mask was displayed at Princeton University along with Beethoven's."[17]

Forty years after his death, Dean is celebrated, adored, loved. James Dean calendars are still available as are James Dean posters. His pictures are regularly cut out of library books, often by people who weren't born when he was alive; sometimes the books are simply stolen. Decades after his death the studio was still receiving fan mail addressed to him. Dean's premature death and consequently his perennial youth, his symbolization of rebelliousness, ensures him a permanent place in America's pantheon of entertainment heroes. And he did it all with only three pictures.

The disadvantage of death, of course, is that you're dead. The advantage of death, from the perspective of immortality, the studio, the estate, and anyone who receives an income from the hero-worship of fans, is that you forever live in memory as a twenty-four-year-old. Whether or not James Dean would have continued to be an entertainment hero had he lived is unknowable, but it is unlikely. The others who lived longer faded into obscurity as newer stars took their place as the fans' entertainment heroes. In premature death James Dean stayed on, immortal in memory.[18]

And so did the goddess Marilyn Monroe. There have been other Hollywood sex symbols. Each year Hollywood is overflowing with new, extremely attractive, very sexy young women. There seems to be an endless supply of them. And they are needed, for they must replace the extremely attractive, very sexy young women who came to Hollywood only a few years before. The storeroom containing sex symbols appears to be eternally full at the same time that it is eternally being emptied. Among the first of these was Clara Bow, the symbol of the Roaring Twenties. Bow at one time received 40,000 fan letters a week. After Bow there was Jean Harlow, for whom Howard Hughes coined the term "Platinum Blond." Harlow, the sex goddess of the 1930s (who died when she was only twenty-six), played her role to the hilt. In the 1940s Jane Russell caused a minor sensation in *The Outlaw*. And there were others, a great many others; but there was only one Marilyn Monroe. She dominated the 1950s the way no other sex goddess had dominated any other decade. [19]

Part of her notoriety is undoubtedly due to her marriages to celebrated men: Joe DiMaggio and Arthur Miller, as well as her alleged affairs with two of the Kennedy brothers. In addition there was the fact of her premature death and the supposedly mysterious circumstances surrounding it. Was it suicide? An accident? Murder? Was the CIA involved? Were the Kennedys? The Mafia?

But most of the hoopla had to do with Monroe herself. Her sex appeal (although that did not necessarily translate into business success: her pictures were not notable box office hits), combined with her seeming ingenuousness created the female entertainment hero that Americans idolized at the time. And she remains in our collective memory that way. That is why Francine Prose can write that "thirty years after [her] death, her life seems the perfect myth for our times," and why there is endless speculation as to the reason for her life being that perfect myth. That is also why books about her are published year after year and why, thirty years after her death, Monroe has become an industry. She currently earns perhaps $1 million per year for her estate. Marilyn Monroe was loved, admired, idolized, and analyzed—always analyzed. And used, even in death. [20]

Some regard Marilyn Monroe as both heroine and victim, and perhaps she was a victim. But no one can question that she was both a heroine and heroic to a great number of people. And she did this while being only peripherally within the culture. At least insofar as the public was concerned, she was effectively apolitical and uninvolved with current social issues, and she stood apart from feminism and women's liberation. Yet perhaps because of her premature, unexpected, and suspicious death, and perhaps because of the unhappiness and the confusion in her life, she became a symbol for the women's movement, an indication of the use and abuse of women, even as she represented in many other ways all that the women's movement detested. In this way, Marilyn Monroe was an American heroine.[21]

Finally, there is the god of gods and goddesses, Zeus in America's pantheon of heroes, the truck driver from East Tupelo, Mississippi, Elvis Aaron Presley. He died in August 1977, but not really, not to a great number of Americans. Graceland, his home, is a prime tourist attraction, so great an attraction that over half a million people visit it annually. Elvis imitation contests are a regular feature of American popular culture. He is often seen around the country: in Michigan, Hawaii, Texas, and Maryland. People kneel in front of his grave, books have been written about his post-death existence. Pregnant women insist that Elvis is the father of their expected children. A 1991 poll revealed that more than 20 percent of the Americans surveyed either thought that Elvis was still alive or were unsure about his death.[22]

Some have explained the phenomenon of America keeping Elvis alive by arguing that we want to keep our heroes, and that is probably true. But there's more to it than that. A better explanation would include the notion that we keep our old heroes because new ones are not forthcoming (which is also the better explanation for the perpetual celebration of James Dean and Marilyn Monroe). Certainly none are forthcoming to take Elvis's place as an American hero. There can be no doubt that in the history of American entertainment heroes, perhaps in the history of American heroes of any sort, he is at the top of the list.

Which is why Roberts and Olson are right: there really is no reason to mention Elvis's last name except, perhaps, "to give balance to his first." Everyone knows who you're talking about, for unlike so many of the others, "his fame lasted. Even his death has not diminished it. He was one of a kind." Elvis, of course, didn't create rock and roll "but he forged it and focused it, and he was the first great rock superstar." But more than this, he was the singer, the rock star, that all of the other singers and rock stars wanted to be.[23]

Elvis could sing (but so could hundreds—thousands—of others), and he was good-looking (but so were hundreds—thousands—of others). He died prematurely (but again, sadly, so did a great many others). Then why Elvis? Richard Corliss, writing in *Time* magazine, says it's because "he was rock's first superstar . . . [and] the last pop idol who did not control his own career." The result of this was the humiliation of becoming, after the Beatles, "an anachronism" while still young, of making atrocious films—thirty-three of them—of becoming obese and bloated. This was "essential to the creation of a cult religion," as was the poor-boy image, the sense of being at the same time one of us and above us. This is the nature of the hero.[24]

Perhaps Corliss is right, but there's more to the Elvis myth. Elvis Presley displayed a great many of the qualities that Americans seek in their heroes. Even in his drug-induced death, joining Janis Joplin, Jimi Hendrix, and Lenny Bruce, he created the image—this polite young man who evolved into a polite adult—of being the most daring, the most exciting, the most rebellious of the rebels. And some sense of daring, of rebelliousness, is projected from and seen within all heroes. Couple this with his extraordinary ability to touch people emotionally, to charm and to arouse, add to these an unexpected, premature death, and add his talent and looks, and there is formed the quintessential American entertainment hero. Certainly the quintessential American hero of the last half of the twentieth century.

Chapter 8

The Heroes of the American West

THE REASON FOR THE WESTERN HERO

It is probable that there is a direct connection between these two facts: the national hero is gone from the American scene and the traditional Western is generally gone from television and the movies. The western hero is basic to American folklore. As much as anyone else, as much as the Pilgrims on the Mayflower, as much as Washington crossing the Delaware, as much as the soldiers landing on Utah and Omaha beaches during World War II, the western hero is *the* American hero. And he will remain at the apex within the pantheon of American heroes because he can be neither duplicated nor negated. His time is past and irretrievable, he lives in legend, and legends only grow with retelling.

Western myths were plentiful even before the frontier was officially declared closed by the American government in 1891 and by Frederick Jackson Turner in his well-publicized and well-criticized paper of 1893. The closing of the frontier just added more glamor to the myths. One clear reason for these myths is that the western hero has always best manifested what Americans like to think of as their true and typical values. Thus, David M. Potter notes that the ideal of frontier American independence was based upon "an individualism of personal self-reliance and of hardihood and stamina." And that ideal has continued. American stock, that is, is tough and independent and pragmatic. Americans can take whatever is dished out by the elements, by other people, by whatever or whoever comes their way.[1]

Conditions in the West demanded this sort of people. They were, after all, on their own when they settled the territories. There were no law enforcement agencies save the ones they established. Nor were there any religious institutions, medical facilities, or schools for the children on the frontier or in the western towns. Consequently, the times demanded self-reliant individuals, the times called for "a man who could tote his own gun, pray his own prayers, and learn to read, write, and cipher by the light of a pine-knot fire."[2]

Perhaps a more important reason for the myths of the American westerner was the publicity he received, some fairly accurate, some wildly exaggerated. Popular (read cheap) paperback fiction of the late nineteenth century, termed the "penny dreadfuls," contributed mightily to the image of the cowboy, the frontiersman, the tamer of the Wild West, as popular heroes, especially in the East. In consequence, the western hero became the idealized version of the idealized American.

William F. Cody, popularly called Buffalo Bill—actually *the* Buffalo Bill; virtually every buffalo hunter named William was called "Buffalo Bill" at one time or another—was a fine shot, a true outdoorsman, and a skilled and reliable scout. Buffalo Bill worked for General Philip Sheridan, a tough, extremely able cavalry officer, and in 1872 was awarded the Medal of Honor by Congress for his work as a scout. (The medal was taken from Cody in 1917 and restored in 1989). And he may be given much of the credit for institutionalizing the idea of the Old West as a place of heroes. A great deal of the rest of the credit goes to the dime novels of Ned Buntline (Edward Z. C. Judson), a first-rate storyteller. Buntline "borrowed Cody's nickname for a story, *Buffalo Bill, the King of the Border Men,* which began running serially in the *New York Weekly* in December 1869." This story not only started the saga of Buffalo Bill, but prepared the way for Cody's Wild West Show, a basic part of the entertainment world of the time. Buntline had met Cody in July 1869; at the time Cody was already something of an (exaggerated) legend out West, but Buntline contributed significantly to the spreading of the fanciful tales.[3]

But the show was the thing. Buffalo Bill's Wild West Show opened in 1883, and its influence was amazing. In New York City alone (in Madison Square Garden) during a run of a year and a half in the 1880s perhaps a million people saw his show. Six million people saw his 1893 World's Columbia Exposition. Buffalo Bill Cody's show toured for thirty years. Quite literally, tens of millions of people, from poor children to the queen of England, were thrilled by the spectacle and awed by the heroic westerner.

Social change is often traumatic to at least one segment of society, the segment that—often helplessly—watches its traditions and values being altered. It is during these periods of social change that heroes, especially heroes that reflect past values, however romanticized they may be and however little in fact they were admirable people, come to the fore. As the frontier ended and as factories took over the lives of the workers, as bureaucratic regimentation began to be felt throughout the nation and as individuality became a luxury, the idealized westerner, living free, rebelling against authority, became a heroic figure and individual westerners became heroes. By the end of the nineteenth century the glory days of the West were happily recalled and turned into fantasy. One consequence of this is that "normal, if somewhat eccentric, people were being transformed into larger than life heroes as American society tried to maintain its rural, individualistic roots" in the face of industrialization and reconstruction.[4]

The hero by definition must be known to the public; thus one requirement for being an American hero is to have a novelist, historian, or journalist come up with stories of one or more of your exploits. Fame is a necessary condition for the status of American hero. It cannot be surprising, then, that the glories of the western hero were enhanced by increased writing about the Old West—and not only tales serialized in magazines, like Buntline's stories, or those in the "penny dreadfuls." As early as 1871 Edward L. Wheeler had created the fictionalized outlaw-hero Deadwood Dick. *Harper's Weekly* and *Frank Leslie's Illustrated Newspaper* both glorified the West, thereby contributing significantly to the illusion necessary for the western hero. And Frederick Remington's sculptures and especially his sketches and paintings also helped establish the glamor that made up the hero in the American West. More important, in 1902 the western novel was "introduced into American writing" when Owen Wister published *The Virginian*. The popularity of the Western perhaps reached its apex in the works of a former dentist from Zanesville, Ohio, Zane Grey, especially with his *Riders of the Purple Sage* (1912). With help from writers such as Grey, as well as with assistance from movies, especially during the 1930s and 1940s, and television in the 1950s, the western hero became almost synonymous with the American hero.[5]

A great many heroes are heroes only in memory, but thanks in part to the writings of the time, the American West managed to produce living heroes. They were, of course, highly romanticized tales of living men, but the men were living when the tales were told. An idealized Bat Masterson, for example, existed along with the real one. The James boys were written about while they were alive, and Jesse's song was being sung immediately after his death. While they were still alive, the exploits of Wyatt Earp and Doc Holliday, among many others, were often written about back East. And *The Great Train Robbery*, the first feature film, was made a year after Butch and Sundance robbed that train in Montana, the one that precipitated their move to South America. Of course the stories of these daring adventures, the shoot-outs and ambushes and reckless abandon, were embellished as they traveled east. (Easterners were more concerned with their own "preconceptions and expectations [than with] facts.")[6]

It didn't seem to matter that many of the actual heroes of legend were murderers, cutthroats, cowards, fools, or any combination of these. The stories never told that part. Not to be misunderstood, there were some true heroes in the Old West, but the overwhelming majority of these "heroes" were simply petty thieves and cutthroats, and not very good ones at that. It is almost a certainty that, with perhaps one or two exceptions, they'd spend their lives today being sentenced to prison. Many of our more celebrated western heroes rode with former—and notorious—Confederate officers such as William (Bloody Billy) Anderson and William Clarke Quantrill (as did Jesse James, for example). Indeed, the Civil War was one of the main contributors to the creation of the legends of the Old West. The losing side in particular "contributed more to incubating gunfighters than any other influence." A good number of these "incubating gunfighters" probably would have wound up on the wrong side of the law without the benefit of the Civil War. Some, however, were a part of the old southern gentry, well-bred and well-educated.[7]

As suggested, the American West did have genuine heroes, men who were highly regarded for legitimate reasons and not (only) because of dime novel sensationalism. For all his flair, showmanship, and self-promotion, Buffalo Bill Cody was not only an entertainment hero, he was a hero of the Old West in fact as well as in reputation. Cody was a true plainsman, smart and tough, and he had seen it all. Before he turned twenty-five, he had been a Union soldier, a stage driver, a buffalo hunter for the railroad, and a scout in the Indian wars. In the movies and the paperbacks, heroes associate with heroes. This helps explain the friendship and frequent meetings between Wild Bill Hickok and Buffalo Bill Cody. Both were pony express riders—Cody at age eleven—and Hickok was a U. S. marshal. And James Butler Hickok (1837–1876), too, was a genuine western hero.

There is a reason why some have argued that Wild Bill "outshadows such latecomers to legendary fame as Wyatt Earp and Bat Masterson." Hickok had it all. He was good-looking, he fulfilled the image of the western hero with a solid physique, long hair, and a deerskin suit. Wild Bill also had a fine Civil War record, and when called upon he protected Abilene, Kansas, from the ravages of cowboys just ending their cattle drive—no mean feat. Of critical importance, Hickok had publicity. He was the subject of an article in *Harpers Magazine* in February 1867 written by George Ward Nichols, who opted for the Hickok story, in part because of his looks and military record. That story, as much as anything else, made Wild Bill, the former U. S. marshal of Hays and Abilene, Kansas, a national hero. His premature death effectively ensured that he would remain one. Wild Bill was playing poker and supposedly holding two pairs, aces and eights—the celebrated "dead man's hand,"—in the Number 10 Saloon in Deadwood (now South Dakota), when he was shot and killed by twenty-five-year-old "Crooked Nose" Jack McCall.[8]

From the moment of his death, the already substantial number of stories about Hickok increased, and their number never diminished. More than this, as with other stories of western heroes, their drama increased with each retelling. In time these stories became a part of American folklore, their subjects both fascinating and contradictory. Thus, Hickok was seated with his back to McCall (or not), he really was holding aces and eights (or not), he died instantly (or not). In any event, he did have a reputation as a gunman, a well-deserved one (although he only had one *High Noon* type of shoot-out), and was a true American hero. And it always helps the image of the American hero when he dies violently, prematurely, and underhandedly.

All of this, or at least most of it, follows the unstated but obvious American tradition noted above: one becomes a hero because of fame: the public is made aware of the hero because someone writes about one's (real or imagined) heroic deeds. Another American hero, for example, Daniel Boone (1734–1820) became celebrated because his exploits were read around the country. A brief account of his adventures, written by John Filson, was published in 1748, and that "made Boone the representative hero of the trans-Appalachian frontier." In consequence, Boone "helped to define the tradition of the Western hero."[9]

However, save the celebrity-hero, celebrity alone is not sufficient to create an American hero. Having a writer tell the story of a potential hero's exploits doesn't guarantee that the status of hero will follow; it doesn't ensure that people will regard that individual as a hero. Hank Monk surely should be known by more people than only serious students of the American West. His name should be a household word, as familiar as Wild Bill's or Buffalo Bill's. But his feats are generally ignored, and this cannot be because of the quality of his work, the bravery that he displayed, or the literary support he received. All were outstanding.

Stagecoach drivers were among the bravest of men in the Old West, and Monk was a stagecoach driver who "got through on time," no small accomplishment. But this apparently isn't the stuff of heroes, not even when Mark Twain praises your exploits in *Roughing It*. For some reason— lack of charisma, perhaps—Hank Monk never reached the status of American hero in the eyes of the public. Monk may have been heroic, but the public never took him to their hearts, never celebrated him as a hero. It seems that fame alone doesn't make a hero, and apparently a celebrated author is less likely to create a hero than are writers of popular pulp fiction.[10]

Another reason that western heroes became western heroes is that they were protected by their followers. Their foibles and peccadilloes were concealed from public view. The same is true today, of course, or was until recently. However, today it is a lot harder to protect the hero than it was in the past.

Christopher (Kit) Carson, for example, was another true American hero. Carson was an Indian agent and served with the Union as a general during the Civil War, but he first received public recognition as a hero when serving as a guide with John Charles Frémont. In time his reputation grew. He was highly regarded by Buffalo Bill (who named his son Kit Carson Cody), and his name and reputation were well and favorably known throughout the country. Although he deserved both the name recognition and reputation, that recognition was favorable in part because Carson was protected from the bigotry of the times. He twice married Native-American women when this just was not done. Consequently, Carson, in his autobiography (dictated, to be sure—he was illiterate), simply ignored the marriages. And so did the majority of his nineteenth-century biographers.[11]

Wyatt Earp, who is usually classified as an American hero, really was remarkably courageous; on one occasion he single-handedly faced down more than a dozen armed men. He was an assistant city marshal in Tombstone, Arizona, where he lived for two years. He was also a deacon in his church. The OK Corral gunfight—surely the most celebrated gunfight in the West and the high point of Wyatt Earp's career, at least insofar as his fame is concerned—did occur; and Virgil and Morgan, Earp's brothers, along with Doc Holliday, did stand with him. But the gunfight didn't take place on the street where it was supposed to have occurred, nor does anyone really know what happened during the battle. And there are numerous and conflicting stories about how it started.

Earp was only mildly corrupt, no small accomplishment for an assistant city marshal in those days, especially in a rough-and-tumble town like Tombstone. He was something of a compulsive gambler, dealt faro at a number of saloons, and when he wasn't working as a lawman, spent a good deal of time in those saloons either at the gaming tables or in one of the upstairs rooms with the lady of his choice. He died peacefully in 1929, at age eighty-one, in Los Angeles, where he had worked as an adviser on Western films. His peccadilloes—gambling and enjoyment of the company of ladies of the evening—were not known to the general public; today they would be.

Wyatt Earp wasn't the only gunman to die in ways other than a shoot-out. In fact, shoot-outs were rare events despite all of the television and movie nonsense depicting endless gunfights. You'd never know it from the stories detailing their quick draws and pinpoint shooting, but the fact of the matter is that numerous gunmen—lawmen and gunfighters—didn't die "with their boots on." Included here are Clay Allison, Virgil Earp, Frank James, Tom Younger, and Doc Holliday. Bat Masterson, another true American western hero, died in New York City where he worked as a sports reporter.

Western lawmen, outlaws, and gunfighters were an unusual lot, and it is not surprising that American folklore recalls many of them as heroes. Unusual people often attract attention and, with the attention, supporters. In fact, some of the gunmen of the Old West were really heroes by the standards of the time, even if in odd ways. As noted, Bat Masterson—a county sheriff who controlled, among other places, Dodge City (Kansas)— never killed anyone, or at least there is no record of him having killed anyone. Nor did Butch Cassidy ever kill anyone until the now famous shoot-out in South America. This might not be remarkable for most people but Cassidy was, after all, an outlaw, and shooting people is often included in the job description. His gang, as alluded to above, committed one of the last major train robberies in the West (in 1901) before he took off to South America with the Sundance Kid.

Although it is probably best to take these stories with a grain of salt, several reports have it that (unlike most who were so titled) Johnny Ringo deserved to be called "the Robin Hood of the West," and Sam Bass enjoyed a reputation as being gentlemanly. Bass supposedly made sure that his victims at least were left with eating money after he robbed them. Of course if he had left them alone to begin with they wouldn't have had to worry about his being gentlemanly enough to leave them eating money. It's hard to doubt that these stories are largely apocryphal, but that just enhances their contribution to the image of these men as "heroes."

In sum, then, some of the heroes of the Old West were truly heroes and others were, to be as generous as possible, less than heroic in temperament or deed. In stature and in action some were courageous and daring and imaginative. Others, were they alive today, would be robbing convenience stores, if they could figure out how to do it.

The most representative western hero is the cowboy, effectively *the* symbol of the West and therefore of the American hero generally. "What," *Newsweek* asks, "could be more American than the American cowboy?" Few people had a profession with a more romantic image, and few people had a profession that was more unglamorous. It was a dirty and dangerous job. The hours were long, the work was terrible, and the pay was minimal. Among the regular features of cowboys' lives were diseases (hygiene was pretty much nonexistent), accidental shootings (they often unintentionally shot themselves or one another), and accidents of several varieties involving horses (often after the rider had a bit too much to drink). Myths aside, cowboys rarely battled Native Americans (that was the army's job), rarely wore pistols while working (they were dangerous, heavy, and inaccurate), and spent long and dreary hours—perhaps as many as sixty hours per week—in the saddle. And although you'd never know it from the movies, perhaps 30 percent of the cowboys of the Old West were minorities.[12]

The era of the cowboy lasted perhaps twenty years in fact (1867–1887) and forever in legend. These legends grew when the cattle drives stopped; and the cattle drives stopped when barbed wire cut the trails, legislatures banned cattle drives through their states, and business considerations replaced the romantic notions erroneously associated with the work of the cowboy.

The cowboy, the American hero par excellence, is not a hero as an individual. We celebrate cowboys more than the cowboy, except in the movies (as, for example, John Wayne) and in Western fiction when a story is told of a particular man. Individual gunfighters and thieves, scouts and lawmen, are known to historians and to the American public as authentic western heroes. The cowboy is known only as part of a mass of men who roped and branded and moved cattle to the Midwest. He was a fine horseman, but he wasn't a killer. He was young and therefore occasionally a bit wild, but not too wild. His work wasn't very interesting. He did little as an individual to warrant attention, and that is why he is celebrated in a group.

BILLY, JESSE, AND THE COLONEL

It is a part of the lore of the West that the good people there battled with, and often lost to, bad people, to greedy exploiters of decent folk. This is an American version of a tradition carried over from European society where the peasants fought the greedy and evil nobility (but almost never the king); *mutatis mutandis*, the same idea existed in the West. It is basic to the values of this country that violence must be justified. The hero, and in this case the western hero—the gunfighter, for example—must be able to explain his use of violence. That can be done only when he is redressing an injustice. The hero has to be the good guy seeking to right a wrong.

Thus, many of the outlaws of the Old West regarded themselves as rebels against the system, as social bandits, even though their justifications for this claim were generally tenuous at best and often absurd. More often than not their claims did little more than provide excuses for them to do what they wanted to do.

Social bandits, Hobsbawm points out, are people viewed as heroes by the people although they are regarded as criminals by the state. In the eyes of the people, social bandits fight for justice, they help those crushed by the powerful. For this reason, they are admired, even loved. Generally, American western social bandit-heroes claimed a heritage of poverty caused by their family being cheated by some malevolent force such as bankers, Eastern land speculators, and—worst of all—railroad owners. These were the forces that drove the bandits to outlawry. It also caused them to seek vengeance against those who had cheated them. In fact, the bandits' poverty was not a cause of their crime but an excuse for it.[13]

If there is a patron saint of outlaws, of social bandits, he is clearly that celebrated hero-villain of legend, Robin Hood. Although there has never been a positive identification of *the* Robin Hood, there have been identifications of numerous bandit-heroes. Generally, these self-proclaimed Robin Hoods encouraged their image as socially responsible thieves, men who steal from the rich to give to the poor. As we all know, that's the image. And as we all know, the fact is that, with very rare exceptions, they steal from the poor as well as the rich and they keep it all for themselves. But we don't talk about that. The hero is supposed to have a social conscience, even if it exists only in the imagination of the hero-worshiper.

The Robin Hood legend is informed by the idea that "Robin Hood . . . subscribed to the best traditions of Anglo-Saxon fair play and had a social conscience besides." It is this tradition and this social conscience that have fed the imagination of those searching for heroes. In American western folklore two men achieved that status and played that role. One was a killer and the other a killer and thief, and both had a consistent string of stories told, books written, and movies made about their lives or about episodes in their lives. There was a ballet celebrating the life of one and there is a museum dedicated to the life of the other.[14]

The two Robin Hood heroes of the United States lived during the era of the Old West. The first was a New York City-born young man sometimes called Henry Antrim and sometimes called William McCarty, but who is popularly known as William Bonney and who is best known as Billy the Kid (1860?–1881). The second was one of Quantrill's riders, Jesse Woodson James (1847–1882).

To some Billy the Kid was the personification of the outlaw as hero. He was, among other things, the fastest gun in the West, but that cannot be a surprise. Everyone seems to have been the fastest gun in the West. Billy the Kid was also, according to Walter N. Burns, an intelligent young man: he was personable, with a good sense of humor, in addition to being "quiet, unassuming, [and] courteous." And although many have portrayed him as cruel, there is evidence to suggest that he was by no means as vicious and unfeeling as he has been portrayed. On the other hand, according to Dee Brown, Billy was "a sadistic murderer of at least a dozen men," with a face that "appears adenoidal, almost moronic, resembling that of a predatory rodent." A third opinion has him as "not exactly the monster" historians would have us believe. So much for historical consistency.[15]

Despite the questions of Billy's character, there is little doubt regarding his fame. Certainly he achieved a level of notoriety worthy of any celebrated outlaw, and he was the most famous and greatest outlaw the Southwest has ever seen. Whether or not he killed twenty-one men, one for each year he lived, is unclear, and it is unclear whether or not the famous picture of Billy standing with a rifle by his side is really a picture of him. But it is clear that he was in fact a Robin Hood-type hero to many of the people of the Southwest, and especially to the Mexicans living there. He was involved in the Lincoln County (New Mexico) wars. The stories have it that the only reason he was arrested is that he was lied to by Governor

Lew Wallace. In any event he escaped and was arrested again and, somewhat spectacularly, he escaped again, and the legend began.

Billy's death was—is—debated nearly as much as the quality of his character and the tales of his exploits. Was Billy unarmed when he was shot and killed by a friend, Pat Garrett? Was he, in effect, murdered by Garrett? Was he betrayed by him? Or was he just an outlaw who was justifiably shot and killed by a lawman? Although there is a lot of room for debate here, the generally accepted story follows the tradition of the hero: Billy was betrayed and assassinated by Garrett, his friend.

There is no debate that Billy's fame spread almost immediately from his shooting. Less than a year after he was killed, *The True Life of Billy the Kid* was available in New York and then throughout the country. Billy's "legend was on its way." But it didn't last too long. Within a few years Billy seemed to fade from the public's eye. He was rediscovered in the 1920s, now as a full-fledged Robin Hood figure. In 1926, Walter Noble Burns wrote *The Saga of Billy the Kid*, which became a Book of the Month Club selection. He was "depicted as a young man out to avenge an insult to his mother and the death of his employer."[16]

Billy's legend continued to grow, thanks to articles and books and especially movies and television in which handsome and obviously courageous and moral individuals were cast as Billy. He became the hero in all of the portrayals of his life. Even in Pat Garrett's account of his confrontation with Billy, the public sympathized with the Kid, much to Garrett's disappointment.

Doubtless, "Billy the Kid . . . would fare badly under the microscope of psychoanalysis." Virtually all of our western heroes would if they were alive today (and if they somehow could be persuaded to go through psychoanalysis). But they are not alive today, and therefore they are not repressed, or neurotic, or sociopathic. They are heroes, and Henry Antrim or William McCarty or William Bonney or Billy the Kid lives on as one of America's great outlaw heroes.[17]

The second great Robin Hood–type western hero was, as suggested, a killer and thief. Oddly, or perhaps not so oddly, his memory is more closely associated with the outlaw of Sherwood Forest than is the memory of any other western American hero. It may not make much sense, but if America has a Robin Hood of its own in myth (certainly not in fact), that man is Jesse Woodson James. Even presidents have regarded him that way. Harry S Truman commented that "Jesse James was a modern-day Robin Hood."

In a few critical ways Jesse James's life paralleled Billy the Kid's. Like Billy he died young, and like Billy he was betrayed, murdered by a friend. In both cases, these circumstances contributed to their legendary and heroic status. A hero lives in memory as a young man, and how else can one kill a hero but treacherously? Jesse James was less than thirty-five years old when, for $10,000 in reward money, Robert Ford put a single bullet into the back of his head, killing him instantly, and the smaller legend of Jesse James became a grand legend. And Robert Ford became, as the song goes, "the dirty little coward who shot Mr. Howard." ("Howard" was the alias that Jesse James was using at the time.) Ford was killed by Edward O. Kelly in 1892 in a saloon in Colorado.

Their arrogant defiance of authority had already made the James brothers heroes to a number of people. It was well known that Jesse, when accused of a crime, would frequently write letters to newspapers or to the Pinkerton Detective Agency. He either denied the accusation or dared the authorities to catch him. He also was bright—the stories have it that he planned most of the robberies—and according to myth he had a sense of humor, just the sort of qualities that people look for in their heroes. He was also a daring and imaginative outlaw; he is credited with committing the first bank robbery, on February 14, 1866, in Liberty, Missouri. This was a time when banks were almost revered; quite simply, one did not rob them. Jesse and his gang also robbed the railroad, and this helped to make him a hero. To a great many people robbing the railroad was a good thing, like robbing the bad guys.

There are a limitless number of stories of how Jesse helped starving widows and fed orphans, of how he protected the poor and deserving from the unscrupulous bankers and landowners and railroad owners, of how he would feel the hands of passengers on trains and only rob those whose hands were soft, of how he symbolically and in fact represented the individual and the individuality of the Old West. When Jesse was killed, the outrage of the people of Missouri was so great that his brother, Frank, who was tried several times for numerous crimes of which he was clearly guilty, was consistently acquitted. Eventually Frank James retired to his farm, untouched by the law. He sold admissions to the James ranch (at $.50 per visit).

As was the case with Billy the Kid, Jesse's death occasioned an outpouring of writings concerning his daring exploits. The *National Police Gazette* published stories about him, and J. W. Buel and J. A. Dacus published quickie biographies of his life. Dime novelists produced countless stories of the James boys' adventures. In time, and again as was the case with Billy the Kid, movies and television took over. And again as with Billy the Kid, the handsome and the gallant portrayed Jesse James in the movies. Tyrone Power and Henry Fonda, among other leading men, played Jesse and Frank James, respectively. But all of this was unnecessary if the intent was to reaffirm Jesse James as an American hero.

Eric Hobsbawm notes that legend demands that Billy the Kid and Jesse James kill not because they want to but because they have to. They kill, that is, "only in self-defense or for other just causes." He adds that this self-restraint is odd given the environment in which they lived. Nonetheless, tradition has it that Billy killed only armed men and only in fair gunfights. At best this notion stretches one's credulity, but it is possible, and some people do believe that Billy fought fairly. No one ever even said that about the James brothers in general or about Jesse in particular. Jesse James was a stone-cold murderer, and few people of his time would question that statement. He did not kill the vicious or unsavory, the wealthy or powerful; he killed unarmed working people. And that is why a substantial number of people, civilians as well as lawmen, wanted him caught, tried, and hanged. One of the reasons he wasn't captured is that few people knew what he looked like: in those days before mass photography, it was fairly easy to hide out. [18]

Jesse James robbed the railroads and the banks. He fought with Quantrill, and on occasion he "dressed as a girl" in order to trap Union soldiers. It is astonishing to imagine the fierce Jesse in drag, but his mother, a slave owner, taught him to believe passionately in and sacrifice all for the Southern cause. This helps to explain why, despite all of their killing, the James brothers and their gang were so adored by the poor and by those who remained true to the South. Newspapers too helped create Jesse's Robin Hood image. John Newman Edwards, for example, the owner of the *Kansas City Times* and a Southern sympathizer, compared Jesse James and his gang to King Arthur and the Knights of the Roundtable. And the *Liberty Tribune* (of Missouri) published a letter Jesse wrote to the governor in which he claimed that he was falsely accused of various crimes. (Newspapers regularly published the letters Jesse wrote.)[19]

As suggested and as is typical among bandit-heroes, the James brothers had reasons for their outlawry: unjustified poverty and persecution. They were forced into poverty by unscrupulous easterners, by the railroads, and by land speculators. In addition, old wartime hatreds between the North and South continued after the war, and the Jameses were harassed by the Yankees. Proof of this persecution and of the cruelty it produced is suggested by the Pinkerton Detective Agency's bungling an attempt at capturing

Jesse. In the course of the failed attempt the Pinkerton agents managed not only to destroy Jesse's house, but also to kill his half-brother and maim his mother, blowing off her right arm.

Persecution and cruelty are common themes within the Robin Hood tradition. In this case, it goes a long way to explain the anti-Northern actions of the James brothers. The problem with this view is that there weren't any specifically anti-Northern actions by the James brothers, at least in terms of their victims. They mostly robbed southern banks and killed southern clerks, tellers, and coach drivers. The best that can be said here—and it had little to do with refighting the Civil War—is that when Jesse James began to attack the railroads, his stature grew. The railroads had the habit of taking the farmers for all they were worth, and the James boys became symbolic forces of retribution. It seems clear that attacking the railroads helped his reputation substantially more than killing innocent people damaged it.

Within a few years of his death Jesse James had become a true American hero, an icon. His way of death and the reputation that preceded it, the publicity of his exploits, however slight their basis in fact, the willingness on the part of the public to ignore the unpleasant qualities of James's life, the famous hatred of and his attacks on the railroads, all contributed to his becoming a hero, America's own Robin Hood. Like Robin Hood, he supposedly followed his own moral and just code, however preposterous that sounds today. But as Hobsbawm points out, that is a major part of it. Robin Hood must obey an acceptable moral code; he cannot truly be a thief and murderer. There must be a justifiable reason for his desperate acts.[20]

The greatest hero of the Old West was not an outlaw or a lawman or a gunfighter. He was a flamboyant, arrogant, incompetent military officer who was most celebrated because he led his men to slaughter. His story belongs with the Old West and not with the legends of the military, because most people associate him with the Old West.

The books, movies, and television shows about Colonel George Armstrong Custer ("general" was a temporary rank), like those of Billy the Kid and Jesse James, go on forever. Custer's legend was a bit trampled upon in 1934, when a biography depicted him less as a hero and more as an egomaniac, and again in Little Big Man, the 1960s antiwar movie; but the stature—or at least the celebrity—has returned, and rightly or wrongly the memory of his heroism currently outshines the memory of his weaknesses. It is obvious that Americans want—need?—to keep the memory of their past heroes intact; they work very hard at doing just that, especially as regards America's western heroes.[21]

The Indian campaigns during the last half of the nineteenth century were a serious business. It is true that the more intense confrontations between the pioneers and United States Army and the Native Americans occurred before the Civil War, during the days of Boone, Crockett, and Bowie, and that the post-Civil War battles were sometimes little more than slaughters of innocents, of Native-American old men, women, and children. Still and all, even in the final third of the nineteenth century the Indian warrior was a formidable foe. That is why there were 423 Medals of Honor given out in the Indian wars, fought from 1861 to 1898. The wars effectively ended in 1886 when Geronimo surrendered. (It took fully one-fourth of the U. S. Army to force Geronimo and his band of twenty-four Indians into surrendering.)[22]

This is the material that sustained John Ford/John Wayne movies. It is also the material that makes up the legend of Custer. Dee Brown points out that in 1939 a comprehensive bibliography of Custer containing close to 650 items was published. That number has undoubtedly increased substantially in the ensuing half century. All of this, Brown points out, has made Custer America's most celebrated "military hero." The fact that it "is misted with fantasy, giving it a dreamlike quality," is all to the better. Fantasy and dreamlike qualities are what create and sustain heroes. [23]

Custer was intensely ambitious and had long understood the benefits of fame for his career. To say that he was gifted with an extraordinary talent for ensuring that his accomplishments were well publicized is to understate the case. And his gift paid off. During his lifetime he was truly a hero: he was idolized by women and held in reverence by men across the nation. His enemies, and he did have some, could do little more than accept the fact of his status. He taught the meaning of favorable publicity to his wife, who continued to celebrate, advertise, and enhance his reputation after his death on June 25, 1876. Indeed, Libby Custer effectively devoted the rest of her life to preserving the image of Custer as an American hero, as *the* American hero.

Custer was not the only officer to lose a battle to Native-American warriors. A decade before the famous "Last Stand," eighty soldiers led by Captain William J. Fetterman were killed at Fort Phil Kearny. The fort was saved by troops under the command of Colonel Henry B. Carrington. All of this—Fetterman's defeat and Carrington's success—was high drama, marked by courage and daring on the part of the combatants, yet only a few military historians have heard of either man. The killing of Fetterman and his troops received a lot of press at the time and the nation was angry, but eventually this was forgotten by the public.[24]

It was different with Custer. The public response to his death was remarkable: there were newspaper headlines, public speeches, and public prayer services held in his honor—all this for a man who was almost dismissed from the service on several occasions and whose abilities as an officer were at best questionable. Custer was arrogant and notoriously unfeeling toward the men in his command; yet the public always took his side, even during his well-known quarrels with Ulysses S. Grant, president of the United States and hero of the Civil War.

Custer's political ambitions rankled Grant, in part because there was serious talk of Custer running for president. Grant tried to relieve Custer of command. The press published tales of the Grant-Custer feud, and even pro-Grant newspapers attacked him and supported Custer. Eventually Grant relented and Custer stayed in command of the Seventh Cavalry and died at Little Big Horn.

As is usual when it comes to tales of the West, there are a variety of stories and endless speculations surrounding the Battle of Little Big Horn. Perhaps Custer knew that there were 2,000 Sioux and Cheyenne warriors protecting the village. Perhaps he shouldn't have divided up his limited (600-man) force. In any event he did, and Custer, along with 210 men of the Seventh Cavalry, was killed.

The nation went berserk. Anti-Indian sentiment grew, and pro-Custer feelings reached an all-time high. Walt Whitman wrote about the hero's end: "A Death Song for Custer." Custer was officially an American hero, and he still is. In 1990 some 250,000 people visited the national monument at Little Big Horn, which is in effect the Custer monument.

Custer died bravely, or so it is assumed; and he died while still young and full of promise, which is always helpful for becoming a hero. He was fighting courageous Sioux warriors led by Chief Crazy Horse, an opponent who not only possessed considerable valor but who was the better military leader. It may be true, as Dee Brown argues, that had he survived, Custer's incompetence and disregard of orders would have resulted in his being court-martialed. But it is also true, as Dee Brown argues, that at least in myth Custer died courageously and valiantly and that in death he "became a hero."[25]

Custer was a part of one of the most romanticized eras in American history. The United States cavalry truly was a cavalry then, and from a distance, it was glamorous. After all, it's not by accident that those John Wayne films are so popular. The glory of the days of the cavalry, however distorted in memory, produced George Armstrong Custer, the ultimate American hero of the Old West.

POSTSCRIPT

Although the Old West will always be with us in legends and books, on television and in the movies, reality is slowly seeping in, or at least as much reality as we'll allow to seep in. We're slowly deglamorizing the Old West. It has been pointed out that John Wayne, in fact if not in the movies, would have reached for a subpoena, and not a six-gun, in his business dealings out West. The lawyer, not the gunslinger, resolved disputes there. And if the West was tamed, it was tamed more by a windmill than a Winchester. The vaunted rugged individualism—a phrase popularized by Herbert Hoover—was another piece of groundless mythology. The founding of the West was heavily subsidized by the United States government. (In fact, the West is still sustained by government subsidies, for example, water rights.)[26]

The settlers' destruction of the buffalo (depicted to a degree in the film *Dances with Wolves*) is well publicized (although the Native American custom of running buffalo off of cliffs is hardly mentioned). And Frederick Jackson Turner's celebrated seminal 1893 address to the American Historical Society, "The Significance of the Frontier in American History," in which he pronounced the frontier closed and detailed its importance for American culture and America's citizens, is repudiated now as a matter of course.

To a large degree the reinterpretation of the history of the West and the attendant demystification of our western heroes has come about because of a new ethnic awareness—for example, the recent and long overdue acknowledgment of the Buffalo Soldiers, the all-black Ninth and Tenth Cavalry and the Twenty-Fourth and Twenty-Fifth Infantry; and recognition that the cultures of Native Americans were destroyed in the process of the settlement of the West—as well as concerns for the environment, among other reasons. To some degree, then, reality is becoming a part of western folklore.

Of course fantasy still plays a part in our tales of the Old West. In many cases all that has happened is that the heroes have simply become more contemporary, as in, for example, movies and television shows portraying women as fictional western heroes and, simultaneously, showing traditional western heroes as politically correct. Instead of the traditional western tales we now have "Lonesome Dove" (Parts I and II); *Ned Blessing; Dr. Quinn,*

Medicine Woman; *Geronimo*; and an extremely sensitive Clint Eastwood in *Unforgiven*.

Nonetheless, as Bryon Price, executive director of the National Cowboy Hall of Fame in Oklahoma City says, "people don't want to be told that what they believe in is a bunch of hogwash." Others agree: there is a limit to how much and to what extent revision of national lore will be tolerated. For this reason, among others, it is probable that Colonel Custer, Jesse James, Billy the Kid, and Butch Cassidy will remain national heroes. But they are a part of America's past only; they cannot be duplicated—or even recreated—today.[27]

Chapter 9

Intermediate American Heroes

BUSINESS HEROES

Given that few people have denied the accuracy of de Tocqueville's assertion about America noted earlier—"I know of no country . . . where the love of money has taken a stronger hold on the affections of men"—it cannot be surprising that businesspeople exist among the nation's pantheon of heroes. But only successful businesspeople. An imaginative and daring innovator who does not succeed is ignored. For example, few Americans know of John Fitch, one of the several inventors of the steamboat, who died in poverty and obscurity. Fitch was a poor businessman and for this reason was denied credit for his invention. Instead, the credit went to Robert Fulton, who was successful in marketing this mode of transportation. Consequently, it was Fulton who received enormous publicity and is remembered by schoolchildren as the inventor of the steamboat.

Success in business in America, following the logic of de Tocqueville, breeds respect and admiration, a degree of hero-worship. But that was then. Today, we do not, as a rule, regard our business leaders with anything approaching esteem, even though we still maintain our respect for both capitalism and its representatives.

One way to understand the lack of business heroes today, to understand why the men and women in business whose wealth, power, and often self-serving publicity attract our attention are not especially revered, is to consider William Goldman's comments about George Steinbrenner, the owner of the New York Yankees. Steinbrenner must wonder, says Goldman, "wonder fiercely, would he have made it had he not been born so rich and so privileged? And what rips at him, of course, is this: He'll never know.

"I know, though. Not a chance."[1]

In fact, many of America's current business giants are business giants because they capitalized on the wealth and power and influence of their families. This doesn't mean that they are not talented and hard working. Nor does it mean that they aren't bright and creative. It does mean that they generally enjoyed the advantages of the finest possible education, the most sophisticated associates and acquaintances, and the certainty that a part of the roadway—often a substantial part of the roadway—had already been paved for them.

Most of the business giants of the past faced a different situation. Andrew Carnegie, for example, arrived in the United States from Scotland with only pennies in his pocket and wound up owning United States Steel. John D. Rockefeller was not born to wealth, nor were many of those who became America's industrial giants. These men, the industrial giants of the past, were rarely formally educated. Tough and shrewd, often single-minded and pragmatic, they made it on their own, or at least the contemporary image of those business giants has it that way, and that image is at least half true. They were at times mean and crude, hardheaded not to say hard-hearted, even cruel; they were relentlessly avaricious and totally insensitive to the cries of the poor, the families of the workers and the workers themselves, upon whose backs they stood and through whose labors they amassed their fortunes.

The methods they used to achieve their goals reflected their complete lack of social concern. They stole and they cheated, they sold rancid food and faulty weapons to the military. Their workers were paid starvation wages, labored under deplorable conditions, and were forced to live in company towns where the costs were high and the quality of life exceedingly low. When the workers protested their minimal salaries and horrific working conditions, they (along with their wives and children) were beaten by hired thugs. The industrialists justified the working conditions, the squalid living conditions and starvation wages, the brutalities used against the workers who protested, by sounding the alarm about socialism and by boosting capitalism. They used and abused government handouts at every turn, taking government lands for virtually nothing, seeking and receiving government subsidies and support whenever they wanted it, which was often.[2]

But they did establish the nation's industries, and they did make something: they could point to the tangible consequences of their efforts. And they were admired. The October 12, 1903 issue of *The Saturday Evening Post* noted that "we know that the men of trade and commerce and finance are the real builders of freedom, science, and art—and we watch them and study them accordingly." The frontier had produced a particular type of American hero, one whose image was necessary for the long and difficult trek across the country. But when the frontier closed and that type of hero was no longer immediately appropriate except, perhaps, for the purpose of nostalgia, America developed "another type of hero." Americans had found a new individual and individualist to admire. Almost immediately the corporate leader became a hero. The reason for this was individual accomplishment, the ability to rise up through one's own efforts.[3]

Roderick Nash notes that the self-made man is the only rival that the frontiersman "and his athletic surrogate" have as American folk heroes. Indeed, Americans have traditionally admired the self-made individual and turned him into a hero. Especially in early twentieth-century America, this individual was the businessman. Thus in speaking of American entrepreneurs, Fawcett and Thomas note that it is the self-made man who ranks among American heroes. They also note that this view stands in marked contrast to European ideology. In Europe it is not merely acceptable, it is preferable, to inherit one's wealth; in the United States, people admire the individual who succeeds on his own, especially when he has had to fight the odds to do so. And the longer the odds, the better. That is why the self-made entrepreneurs are still the heroes of American folklore. The problem today is the steadily diminishing number of self-made entrepreneurial types, of successful and well-known wealthy businessmen and businesswomen who made it on their own.[4]

The admiration and respect offered the successful, self-made individual is one reason why the newly wealthy industrialists of the early twentieth century not only did not hide their wealth, they went out of their way to flaunt it. And the public respected them for it; the public saw in the displays of the wealthy not the pain of the workers but their own potential success stories. Andrew Carnegie and John D. Rockefeller were important because they "symbolized the possibility of rising from rags to riches." In doing so they forced others to pay attention to them. One way they did this was to show the world generally, but most especially the older, established families, that they had arrived. And they did this by demonstrating—flaunting—their wealth.[5]

It is no accident that Thorstein Veblen, an American sociologist, was the one to coin the term for the ostentatious display of wealth and leisure.

"Conspicuous consumption" and "conspicuous leisure" were a part of the life-style of America's new upper class. They were also signals to the middle class, and perhaps to some members of the lower class, that America allowed anyone to achieve "wealth beyond the dreams of avarice." If in Europe the nobility displayed their social position by titles, in the United States the rich did it with an ostentatious display of buying power.

Henry Ford is perhaps the best example of an American business hero, of an American self-made success. He was regarded as an American hero in a way that his children and grandchildren never will be. The old man created the company while they just ran it, and the status of American business hero is given to one who creates industry and money. Hard work, struggling against the odds, imagination, and creativity are required for the existence of an American business hero. And it is often the case that the further down on the social scale one began, the more admired is one's success. [6]

But as suggested earlier, all of this depends upon the times. It is true, as Paul Johnson notes, that "the heroes of the 1920s had been businessmen," but it is also true that the Great Depression brought about a changed attitude toward the successful old-style entrepreneur and also a changed attitude regarding his treatment of the workers. "Rather than idolizing Henry Ford's efficiency, any Mr. Jones who was hurt in any way by the hard times, probably identified with poverty." Not materialism but tenacity, the ability to take it and outlast the suffering, was the important human quality then, and in some circles tenant farmers became "heroic symbols of . . . popular culture" because of their endurance.[7]

This overstates it a bit. It is safe to say that for most Americans, the majority of whom no longer lived in rural or farming communities, the tenant farmer was not a national hero. Recall that the Okies—migrants from the 1930s "Dust Bowl" of Oklahoma—were often prohibited from entering California. Still, it is true that throughout the 1930s industrial giants and large-scale entrepreneurs, respected figures in the past, were no longer heroes to most Americans. Greed and inequitable labor laws were regarded by many as causes of the Depression, and unskilled workers were organizing to combat the more noxious forces of industry. (The Congress of Industrial Organizations was established in the 1930s.) Just as the crushing recession of the late 1980s and early 1990s negated the symbol of the Yuppie-as-hero of the Reagan years, and as revelations of the scandals and incompetencies involving bankers and Wall Street brokers destroyed the myth of the intelligence of the quick wealth planners, the failure of the industrialists and the entrepreneurs of the 1930s to cope with the Depression damaged their position in America's heroic pantheon.

Time and circumstances again changed, however, and World War II made the capitalist a hero in America once again. The nation needed innovation, enthusiastic leadership in industry, and sound business and engineering practices. American industry, and the people responsible for the functioning of American industry, were invaluable in the Allied victory over the Axis. Credit should have and did go to the workers, but credit also should have and did go to the industrial leaders who made the system work. [8]

After the war the situation changed once more. The businessman was gone, or at least he was on his way out. The individual entrepreneur was disappearing and the giant and all-powerful corporation—necessarily bureaucratic and impersonal—was coming into its own, as were investors and traders. Companies that created products gradually faded from view and money movers and information handlers began to take their place. Corporations and the politics of corporations had replaced the entrepreneur, and permanently.[9]

There was a new game in town, and the game had new rules and new players. Neither the game nor the rules permitted the players to become business heroes, at least not of the sort traditionally regarded as such. The bureaucracy had arrived, and bureaucrats cannot be heroes because bureaucracies do not allow for individualism. Nor do they allow for public attention.

Bureaucracy has dominated business in the last half of the twentieth century, and with that domination has come a change in business personnel. Businessmen have been transformed into bureaucratic men. Perhaps the most powerful statement on this subject comes from David Riesman. Riesman's central argument is that unlike the industrialists of the past, postwar industrialists were concerned—obsessed—by the views of other people. In Riesman's well-known phrase, they are "other-directed." Other-directed people are not guided by their own sense of what should and should not be done, but by the attitudes and opinions of others. Their own convictions mean less than the judgments other people make about those convictions. The American business hero of the past relied on his own judgments. He was, again in Riesman's well-known term, "inner-directed." The inner-directed man is an individualist; the other-directed man is a conformist. That is, the entrepreneur does what he thinks best while the bureaucratic man does what he thinks others will think best. Reisman's methodologies have been reexamined, but his central thesis, that other-directed people now control American industry (and science, education, and other segments of society) is as valid today as when he first proposed his argument. These types are not heroes.[10]

William White, Jr., in *The Organization Man*, explains the effects of industries dominated by other-directed individuals. People start out by accepting the system, they don't argue with it, they don't fight it. This is a wise course if one seeks success—defined by either financial reward or job security—for battling the system is a sure way not to attain that success. But again, this is not the way of the hero. Thus, the "fall from individual man to mass man" was deeply felt in the United States: we lost our business leaders, our entrepreneurial heroes. [11]

The entrepreneur, the individual with courage and imagination and a sense of risk, has traditionally been a hero to Americans. But it is impossible to admire bureaucratic organizations and difficult to admire their leaders. The business hero has passed the endangered status and is on his way toward extinction.

Prior to the 1920s, when industry was becoming dominant in the United States and thrift was an American virtue, the savings bank was king and the hero of the day was everyman. Everyman here was the saver, the one who regularly and without hesitation deposited a portion of his income into his savings account. When America evolved into a consumer-oriented society, the saver was no longer a hero. During the 1920s, there was "a transformed America . . . a new era of the consumer-oriented mass society." This view has continued to today, albeit with a ten-year hiatus during the Depression of the 1930s. The consumer is all important and, reasonably enough, the individual who satisfies the consumer is man of the hour. The "salesman as hero replaced . . . [William Graham] Sumner's savings bank depositor as hero." [12]

But not really. People may admire the successful salesman, but he cannot be a hero. Only the individual who imagines, creates, and leads can be a true business hero to Americans, and that is why there are no true business heroes here anymore. Current business giants, able to match those of the past in glamor, excitement, and respect are extremely rare (if there are any left at all). Perhaps Lee Iacocca, the former head of the Chrysler Corporation, was the last of them, although there is still some question as to whether or not he truly was a business hero.[13]

Even Bill Gates, the giant of the computer industry and an old-style entrepreneur (and currently the wealthiest man in America), is not regarded with the awe his predecessors enjoyed. Perhaps it's because he is involved in the esoteric area of computer technology, or perhaps it's because he is a part of a massive bureaucracy, the one that he helped to create. The reason may even be that computer geniuses are unjustly regarded as "nerds," a far cry from the dirty fingernails type of innovator. In any event, no one favorably compares the technically oriented, highly skilled, successful computer whiz of today with the sleeves-rolled-up, uneducated business-man of the past.

We no longer have any business heroes, and it is unlikely that we ever will again. America's business structure is dominated by bureaucracies, and bureaucracies instill a concern with one's security at the expense of inno-vation and risk-taking. In a word, the company mind-set has finally won, the individual has finally lost, and the business hero is gone.

ADVENTURER-HEROES

The American celebration of adventurers as heroes precedes the exist-ence of the United States. Our admiration for the entry into the "new world" by Columbus and various Spanish, Portuguese, Dutch, and English sailors and explorers, reflects Americans' vision of the adventurer as hero. We join John Keats in praise of "stout Balboa" gazing upon the Pacific Ocean for the first time (although Hernando Cortés actually was the first European to gaze at the Pacific Ocean from its Eastern shores). Our celebration of the voyage of the Mayflower, of the first of the colonial settlements, and of Thanksgiving Day, reflect an admiration for the adven-turer. Similarly, the early European inhabitants of the eastern United States, the settlers and the pioneers, are considered American icons, as indeed should be the case.

Even before the days of Meriwether Lewis and William Clark, then, the adventurer was seen as a hero in the United States. There has always been a spirit of excitement associated with those who first traveled unknown lands. This spirit was part of the appeal of the stories about Daniel Boone, Davy Crockett, James Bowie, and William Travis as well as the appeal of other scouts, trailblazers, and frontiersmen. A desire for wealth may have motivated some of them, as was certainly the case with those other adventurers, the forty-niners, but not for all. In the case of Lewis and Clark, for example, a government order was the motivation. But whatever the motive, there was nonetheless a strong degree of romanticism, an excite-ment, a sense of danger in their actions, at least in the often extravagant versions that are enjoyed today.[14]

When western expansion was completed in 1891, when the European immigrants and their progeny inhabited the continental United States from the Atlantic to the Pacific and from the Canadian border to the Rio Grande, American adventurers began to look for new worlds to conquer. Some, like Robert Peary, looked north. He was the first westerner to reach the North Pole (although there is some controversy here) and the first to offer conclusive evidence that Greenland was an island. Others, like Richard Byrd, looked south, to Antarctica.

But it's difficult to be this sort of adventurer now. There's not much left to explore today except perhaps the oceans, and Frenchman Jacques Cousteau has long established dominance there.

The land has been explored and the sea is being charted. That leaves the air, and America's twentieth-century adventurers have indeed looked up. From Amelia Earhart to undoubtedly the most celebrated American aviator-hero, Charles A. Lindbergh, who, along with Babe Ruth, was *the* American hero of the 1920s, adventurers in the United States have taken to the skies. With Lindbergh there was drama to it all, yet drama with a reason—Anglo-Saxon drama, as Dixon Wecter has it. There would have been drama surrounding Chuck Yeager's sound barrier–breaking flight, too, but almost no one witnessed it and few people knew about it until *The Right Stuff* was published. It was only after the publication of the book and, still more, after the release of the movie, that Yeager became an American adventurer-hero.[15]

At first glance it is reasonable to argue that the space program has produced heroes comparable to Earhart, Lindbergh, and Yeager—Alan Shepard, John Glenn, Gus Grissom, and the rest. After all, the accomplishments of our astronauts were astounding and perhaps as courageous as crossing the ocean by schooner or crossing the Great Plains in a covered wagon. That may be why Stan Steiner argues that the astronauts followed the traditions of the old cowboy-heroes.[16]

But that isn't really true. The astronauts didn't follow in the footsteps of the old cowboy-heroes and they didn't follow in the footsteps of Lindbergh either. The whole point of the Lindbergh flight, the reason for the celebration, was that he flew across the Atlantic Ocean alone. His was not the first flight across the Atlantic, it was the first solo flight across the Atlantic. It took thirty-three hours for him to fly *The Spirit of St. Louis* from Long Island, New York, to Paris, France. It was, as Kenneth C. Davis says, "an act of enormous daring, skill, and flying ability." With all due respect to the courage of the astronauts, no one can claim that they accomplished their extraordinary deeds as individuals.[17]

The space program was a massive effort. The labor, expertise, and dedication of thousands of skilled individuals all went into the preparation, execution, and completion of the flights. While the astronauts have received and clearly deserve praise for their work, they worked collectively, they were each a part of an aerospace team, a wonderfully successful one. The 1995 film *Apollo 13* demonstrated this point: The space program was successful because of the coordinated efforts of a great number of bright and talented people.

If an American adventurer-hero exists in the sense of a lone and courageous individual acting in a traditionally heroic manner, that is, as an individual flying against the odds, then perhaps the last American adventurer-hero was Chuck Yeager. Yeager went it alone, without celebration, publicity, or anticipated glory. And without extra payment. These are the qualities that make up the tradition if not the fact of the hero-adventurer. And he has disappeared.

One other point warrants brief attention here: there are a multitude of American daredevils that claim attention. But while they are brave and entertaining, they are in the main stuntmen, caricatures of a hero-adventurer, not the genuine article.

CRIME, CRIMINALS, AND HEROES

While the gangs of the West—Butch Cassidy's Wild Bunch, the James, Dalton, and Younger brothers—captured headlines, the public's imagination and, in varying degrees, public adulation, the gangs of the eastern cities simply evoked a sense of loathing and intimidation. The western outlaws often saw themselves as social bandits, as Robin Hoods in various forms, and dime novels and the press encouraged others to see them the same way. The urban gangs of the latter part of the nineteenth and the early part of the twentieth century, however, couldn't communicate even a hint of benevolence to anyone.

This is because the western gangs were stealing from people out West, robbing trains and banks out West, and killing people out West. The writers of the dime novels (who lived in the East) and the journalists (the major newspapers were published in the East) could afford to glamorize their exploits. The James brothers, after all, were not much of a threat to people strolling on Fifth Avenue. But New York's local street gangs—the Whyo's and Dead Rabbits, for example—were something else again. They were a threat to the people on Fifth Avenue, including writers and journalists. Consequently, the local gang members were not glamorized at all, but castigated. In the 1930s, this scenario would be repeated; distant (midwestern) gangs and criminals would be celebrated by the eastern press while local gangs and gangsters would be condemned.

There were a large number of gangs in American cities around the turn of the century, but their members did not achieve national recognition and were not at all regarded as heroes. They weren't even regarded as local heroes until the immigrants began to arrive in large numbers and were forced to deal with the prejudice, discrimination, and poverty foisted upon them by the established elite. The established power group here, the old-line White Anglo-Saxon Protestants, did not view with favor the Irish, the southern and eastern European, the free blacks who invaded their cities, and they responded accordingly.[18]

In time the ethnic gangs that formed in the big cities took on an aura of local—that is, ethnic—respectability, even gallantry, not unlike the mythical Robin Hoods of the Old West, the alleged defenders of the weak and the helpless. Mark Haller notes that gang leaders were not always liked by the "respectable" people in the ethnic community. Nonetheless, these same gang leaders had influence in the local communities and, perhaps more important, in city government as well. And because of their influence outside of the local area they occasionally became heroes within the community. This same sort of mythology is propagated today in, for example, the first two *Godfather* movies. Vito Corleone, the Godfather, is depicted as a beneficent protector of his people.[19]

But make no mistake. Like the gangs of the West, the gangs of the East consisted of thieves and killers whose concern for their ethnic brethren was limited to the amount of money they could get from them. In fact, they had relatively little trouble extorting money from their own people, who often didn't trust the politicians or the police until some of their own were represented within the political system and police departments. At the time ethnic peoples were often helpless victims of the street gangs, and most nonethnics were unconcerned about problems within the ethnic communities. Generally, the ethnic gangs attracted little attention outside of their own communities except when politicians used them to scare their constituents.

It took Prohibition and the Volstead Act to provide the circumstances that would call national attention to the leaders of the city gangs, and it took the freewheeling culture of the 1920s to elevate them in the eyes of many Americans to the stature of the western gangs, that is, to the status of bandit-hero. In the exciting post–World War I era, the 1920s, Americans became fascinated by gangsters, especially those who provided them with the liquor they wanted. That fascination has continued off and on until today. To some, in fact, the gangster still enjoys the status of bandit-hero; at least he does within the American popular culture. That explains the success of the television shows, movies, and books about organized crime in the United States. Robert Lacey is right: "Americans cherish their gangsters."[20]

Bootlegging, a consequence of Prohibition and the Volstead Act, provided gangs with a socially justifiable motive for crime; and when flash, wealth, and publicity were added to the equation, it all combined to allow them to achieve the status of social bandit, of hero, first regionally and then nationally. Besides, as with many bandit-heroes, gangsters pointed to the hypocrisy of respectable society. Al Capone allegedly commented: "When I sell liquor it's bootlegging. When my patrons serve it on a silver tray on Lake Shore Drive, it's hospitality." Capone was correct, of course, but not exactly. The difference was that selling liquor was against the law while drinking it wasn't. A legal nicety perhaps, but the difference between committing a felony and not committing a felony.

Still and all, Capone's argument made sense to a great number of people. One consequence of this was that criminals attained a degree of respectability previously unheard of in American society. Because of their newly found respectability, as well as their illegally acquired wealth, they were able to exert considerable authority within legitimate businesses. Then, as today, crime seemed to be—and occasionally was—a pathway out of the slums. But, then, as today, it was not the only pathway out.[21]

Part of the heroic image of the urban gangs was based, on the one hand, on observers not looking too closely at the nastiness inherent in the work the gangs did, and, on the other hand, on a vicarious enjoyment of the flamboyance of some of the gang leaders. Charles Dion O'Bannion, for example, who allegedly killed or ordered the killing of twenty-seven men, was charming, personable, and always in the headlines. Newspaper reporters in Chicago adored him because he made good copy. The exploits of Al Capone, Dutch Schultz, and Legs Diamond, too, made terrific reading. Exciting, interesting, and successful, they were always in the headlines, and they delighted in the publicity. Why not? There was glamor associated with their lives and a great deal of power, political and otherwise, and a great deal of money as well. In time, the publicity the gangsters received, effectively advertising their glamor, power, and money, made them national heroes.

The heroic nature of crime and the gangsters began to diminish as the notorious Roaring Twenties came to an end and the 1930s began. When things are going well, stories about the exciting lives that gangsters allegedly live can be entertaining. In a depression other things attract people's attention, things like finding and keeping a job, buying food, and paying the rent. The illegally gotten wealth of the gangsters looks less glamorous and more exploitive now.

A second reason that the heroic image of crime faded is that the gangs became "organized" in the contemporary sense of the term. When the Mafia, La Cosa Nostra, or the Syndicate—whatever the term—grew out of the ghetto into the mainstream of American life, the heroic ideal evaporated because the men in charge of the organization avoided publicity. And if no one knows who you are, you can't be a hero.

It is, then, a bit unfair to argue that "Frank Costello and Albert Anastasia seemed but sleazy versions of indomitable individualists like . . . Capone." They were different men with different purposes. Capone enjoyed the limelight and the publicity surely helped his business. His notoriety effectively served as advertisement. Costello and Anastasia were part of an organization that neither needed nor wanted publicity; in their case, publicity attracted the wrong sort of attention. In marked contrast to Capone, who thoroughly enjoyed the public's attention and in fact sought it out, Costello and his associates didn't want to be recognized in public. During the famous sessions of the Special Committee to Investigate Organized Crime in Interstate Commerce led by Estes Kefauver in the early 1950s, the television cameras remained on Costello's hands; they couldn't show his face. (In fact, that just heightened the drama and enhanced his image.) [22]

As with the businessman-hero, then, one reason that the heroic nature of gangsterism faded was that the criminals changed. They went from the individualistic, publicity-seeking heroes of the 1920s to the publicity-shy organization mobsters of the 1950s. Bureaucracy began to dictate to criminals as it had dictated to businessmen and to just about everyone else.

One exception here might be John Gotti, a reputed crime boss who is currently in prison. His celebrated battles with various law enforcement agencies has, according to the *New York Times*, turned him into a "folk hero" of sorts. His conviction evoked demonstrations and at least one rap song protesting the methods used by the government to convict him. There is also a comic book about his exploits. Indeed, so well known is Gotti, and for so long, that in 1995 the Arts & Entertainment network devoted an hour to his biography. The story of his rise to a position of prominence within the mob was the feature article in *The New York Times Magazine* as far back as 1989.[23]

As suggested, it was exciting and glamorous in the 1920s, and flappers and gangsters, speakeasies and bootleg hootch were part of that excitement and glamor. But by the 1930s people were suffering under the Great Depression, and that lessened the excitement of the stories of the gangsters. Besides, the repeal of Prohibition ended the glamor associated with boot-legging and speakeasies. Flappers, too, went out of fashion. The murders and arrests of various crime leaders—especially the arrest of Al Capone for income tax evasion—further diminished the excitement and glamor of the gangster in particular and crime generally.

More realistic reporting about the business dealings of mobsters and of the random violence associated with urban crime also helped end the connection between fashionable acceptability and criminality. This con-tinues today. The effectiveness of the Racket Influence and Corrupt Organization (RICO) law, as well as reports from inside criminal organiza-tions, and, most especially, the violence associated with the mob's connec-tions with drugs, have irreparably tarnished any extant romantic imagery of organized crime.

Prohibition was never really accepted by Americans even when the laws were in effect. In this sense it was not difficult to regard the bootleggers as simply providing a tolerable service, especially if one didn't feel connected to or threatened by the violence associated with the gangsters. Drug dealing is a different matter entirely. Drinking has always been more socially acceptable in the United States than using hard drugs. Selling illegal scotch in the 1920s was not regarded as is selling crack cocaine in the 1990s. Moreover, at least in myth, gunfights during Prohibition involved gangsters killing gangsters. Benny ("Bugsy") Siegel is supposed to have said just that: "We only kill each other." Not any more. It is a rare local television news show in the 1990s that doesn't offer graphic pictures and detailed accounts of innocent people, often children, being wounded or killed in gunfights among rival gangs of drug dealers.

Another factor that diminished the glamor of organized crime was the willingness of various members of crime families to inform on their associ-ates. The fact that they did this in exchange for protection lessened the image of their toughness. Perhaps more important, their willingness to talk to the authorities brought into question the idea of a code of sacrifice and honor that members supposedly swore to the organization, a point that will be considered in a later chapter.

The public's fascination with organized crime remains unabated, but the possibility of regarding criminals connected with organized crime as heroes has virtually disappeared. Drive-by shootings, direct consequences of organized crime, are neither glamorous nor heroic.

As city crime was becoming organized and structured and its members were becoming part of a criminal bureaucracy, there was in the 1930s a rise of the individual outlaw reminiscent of the days of old. Just as the glamor surrounding the city gangs of the 1920s was fading, just as the effects of bureaucratization, government pressure, and the repeal of Prohibition began to take their toll on the glamor, if not the revenue, of city crime, the glamorous individualistic criminal was reborn during the Great Depression, the last time that criminals can be said to have been regarded as national heroes in the United States. And these were rural American criminals now, not city criminals; criminals with American names, not foreign ones.

However flawed the heroic notion of the 1930s criminals might be, during the depths of the Depression, when families lost their homes and workers lost their jobs, when businesses failed and banks closed, the more celebrated criminals once again represented rebellion against a system regarded at best as ineffective and at worst as corrupt. The idea of the social bandit had resurfaced in America, however specious the reasoning and however brief the return.

The criminals fought back against poverty and against the Depression, and because most people couldn't or wouldn't do that, and aided by a favorable press, they were able to create and sustain a heroic image. Some in the 1930s saw criminals as brave and daring men. In myth, at least, they were willing to challenge the system, and their status reflected their image of having the courage to do that.[24]

The "social bandits" who became criminal-heroes in the 1930s were not very successful, but they didn't have to be in order to be heroes. Their heroic stature rested upon fiction of their heroic gestures, upon the notion that they, as no one else, had the courage to fight the established (and unjust) order. That is, the outlaw-heroes of the 1930s were heroic only in the press or in the imagination of their fans (generally people who never had any contact with them). Charles Arthur (Pretty Boy) Floyd, for example, received a great deal of attention from the newspapers, most of it negative and some perhaps unfair. Nonetheless, to his Oklahoma neighbors he was a folk hero, albeit "a menace to every bank in the Southwest, and a deadly killer to police everywhere." Woody Guthrie wrote a song about Floyd, portraying him as a folk hero, and a lot of people agreed with Guthrie's view. In the tradition of Jesse James, Floyd was called "The Robin Hood of the Cookson Hills." Floyd died when he was thirty-three.[25]

Some even admire Bonnie Parker and Clyde Barrow, Bonnie and Clyde. Hobsbawm, for example, regards Bonnie and Clyde as "the heirs of Jesse James." It may be the case that they were "historical throwbacks" to the days of the Old West, but if they were indeed a 1930s version of the James Boys, that fact belittles Jesse and Frank. Despite the 1960s movie of their adventures, they were not at all made of the stuff of heroes. They were a pair of sociopaths, dangerous because they were emotionally and intellectually defective. They weren't even successful as thieves; their robberies generally netted them little money. [26]

Other celebrated outlaws of the 1930s weren't much better. Francis ("Two-Gun") Crowley, who died when he was twenty, was tough only by virtue of specious reporting by the press. In fact, he was a violent and petty thief, and George R. ("Machine-Gun") Kelly wasn't much more than that. His image, too, was a product of an imaginative and inaccurate press.

There was, however, one Robin Hood–like bandit-hero of the 1930s, John Herbert Dillinger, that daring bank robber. He was born in 1903 and may have died in 1934, for, as with Butch and Sundance, there are those who say that he is still alive today, or at least that he didn't die outside of the movie theater in Chicago that hot July evening. (If Butch and Sundance are still alive they'd be in their mid-150s and Dillinger would be in his mid-90s.)

Dillinger has been called a member of "the last of the buccaneering school of gangsters," and tales about his exploits are legendary. Movies and television shows have been made about him, and his betrayal by the "Lady in Red" is well known. So are tales of his generosity. He has the classic Robin Hood image: he stole from the rich and he was a friend of the poor. One story has Dillinger robbing a bank, but refusing to take money from an elderly man. "We only want the banks," he is supposed to have said. Of course this is something that all bandit-heroes say.[27]

Still and all, there is no denying his supporters. One wrote that "Dillinger does not rob poor people. He robs those who became rich by robbing poor people. I am for Johnnie." And, if you choose to believe it, he died young. A supporter of the poor and waging constant war against unjust authorities, a victim of betrayal and premature death, Dillinger had all of the qualities needed for the bandit-hero.[28]

If he was one, Dillinger was the last of the criminal-heroes in the United States. Bank robbers just aren't heroes anymore. Everyone these days knows that a daring bank robbery is not really daring; it's just a foolish and desperate act that warrants no admiration. Of course there are some criminals who do attract attention these days—assorted serial killers, for example—but they are rarely regarded as heroes by society. What can one possibly say about Jeffrey Dahmer that could in any way be complimentary?

Today's criminals all too often engage in excessive and unnecessary violence, and they aren't regarded as challenging a corrupt and unfair system. When they receive publicity, it doesn't make them heroes: it just enhances their chance of being arrested. These conditions preclude the existence of a criminal-hero. His days are past. Perhaps it is this that lends credence to the "Dillinger didn't die" tales. Dillinger was the last of the bandit-heroes, and we can't afford to lose any more of our heroes, even criminals.

Chapter 10

Lesser American Heroes

THE BRAINS: SCIENTISTS AND INTELLECTUALS AS HEROES

Scientists

At one time scientists were, if not heroes in the popular sense of the term, heroes in the abstract. When Bruno Bettelheim, the noted psychoanalyst, died in March 1990, The *Los Angeles Times* called him just that, a "genuine hero." Other American scientists, native-born or not, have also been so regarded. For example, Lee De Forest, James D. Watson, John Dewey, Enrico Fermi, Albert Abraham Michaelson, and, most recently, Jonas Salk, are heroes to the nation even if the nature of their work is known to and understood by a limited number of cognoscenti.

The two most celebrated American scientist-heroes are undoubtedly Albert Einstein, a refugee from Nazi Germany, and Ohio-born Thomas Alva Edison. Einstein was the theoretical genius, Edison the brilliant technician.

George Bernard Shaw once proposed a toast at a public gathering at the Savoy Hotel in London: "I drink to the greatest of our contemporaries, Einstein." Shaw was not alone in his assessment. The international scientific community honored Einstein with the Nobel prize for physics in 1921. Edison, who patented over one thousand inventions in his lifetime, was nominated for the Nobel prize only once and unsuccessfully. Instead, he was honored by the government of the United States: the U.S. Congress accurately stated that Edison had "revolutionized civilization" through his inventions.[1]

The point here is that some scientists were once among America's heroes; they were recognized as heroes by the government and by the public.

Science in the United States in its several forms was perhaps at its peak beginning in the late 1940s. In the aftermath of the Second World War new areas of expertise were in demand and various sciences were used to meet those demands. The social sciences, for example, had reached new levels of acceptance in American society by the early 1950s. As the United States became increasingly consumer-oriented, people became increasingly aware of the social and psychological causes of human behavior and of the social and psychological causes of people's spending habits. For this reason business in the post-war era was quick to adopt several of the views and especially the methodologies of the social sciences, for example, survey research and experimentation. Attention was also given to studies concerning a variety of social issues, such as racial prejudice, poverty, and stability within the American family.

The social sciences, however, could not produce heroes of the stature of Einstein or Edison. The closest the social sciences came to producing a hero was Alfred Kinsey, who conducted research in human sexuality. In pre–World War II America, sex and sexuality weren't even discussed in polite company much less clinically analyzed. Because of his work and the recognition it received, Kinsey was regarded as a hero, despite his resistance to such recognition. His enemies—and because of the nature of his work he had many—were forced to view him as "a heroic figure." His scientific integrity and his demand that his efforts be regarded as true scientific inquiry evoked admiration, even if it was given reluctantly.[2]

The rise of the status of both social and natural science in the postwar era reflected America's awareness of the social changes that had ensued since World War II. To some degree it also reflected a realization of the failure of other areas of American expertise and the weakening search for new American heroes. But that was all right. Everything from the Cold War to the baby boom now seemed amenable to scientific analysis—and for many people to scientific analysis alone. Even if businesspeople, politicians, and all of our other heroes had vanished or were in the process of failing as heroes, science and scientists would save us and protect us and provide us with heroes.[3]

Physical scientists, already enjoying a considerable reputation due to the technological advances made during World War II, truly came into their own in the late 1950s. After the United States was frightened by the Soviet Union's launching of Sputnik I in 1957, the space program started in 1958—NASA was funded and Explorer I was launched—and anyone involved with science, engineering, research, or technology became something of a savior of the nation and, therefore, a hero to the American public. Scientists could and would save us from the technologically advanced Soviets. In January 1961, for example, *Time* magazine had not a man of the year but fifteen American scientists as its collective men of the year, pointing out that everyone—priests, statesmen, builders, etc.—is at the service of science. "Science," *Time* said, "is at the apogee of its power."

But it should be noted that *Time* magazine honored scientists, not a scientist. The cover told of the men of the year, not of an Einstein or an Edison or even of a Kinsey, but of fifteen scientifically gifted people, a collective. And that is not unreasonable, for the fact is that since the Second World War science and technology have become too complex. No single scientist can master all that must be mastered. Consequently, today the scientific team, the collective, has replaced the individual scientist as hero. Robert Kargon has remarked that scientists today work on systems that are so complex that they "are made up of little steps." In consequence, one "cannot say that one person invented" the entirety, which is why in science today it is impossible to assign "credit [for an innovation] to a single individual." In science we can no longer have specific heroes; we can only have heroes *en masse*.[4]

Physicians today specialize and specialize again within their area. Physicists are expert only in relatively small portions of the subject. Topics are divided and subdivided and subdivided again. Research is done by teams of scientists. And because no single individual can claim the success as his own, no single scientist can be the lone scientific hero. This means that the work of several groups must be coordinated, which is one reason that science is so influenced by its structure, by bureaucracy. But bureaucracy has its own logic, and that logic has nothing whatever to do with scientific inquiry.

We all enjoy the image of Edison diligently working in his makeshift, cluttered lab. One percent inspiration and ninety-nine percent perspiration, he said. But today the individual scientist toiling in a garage-like laboratory is a myth (it was something of a myth to begin with). Science today demands a modern laboratory, and that is possible only with the financial backing of a major corporation or government agency. Today a scientist can function only within a scientific organization because only an organization can provide him with the necessary equipment for the work he must do. Even those few scientific projects that begin as small operations quickly turn into giant ones that are controlled by the organization. And, Kargon notes, "working in a large laboratory can strip the inventor of his heroic status." Anonymity defeats the possibility of heroism, and being a part of a large organization necessarily means being anonymous. In consequence, by design or not, the organization takes credit for scientific innovations within its structure.[5]

None of this suggests that scientific teams do not succeed; they do and often spectacularly. The growth of scientific knowledge has resulted in the number of diseases and the trauma caused by those diseases being dramatically reduced. Because of science and teams of scientists, our knowledge and understanding of the world has increased exponentially, and the quality (and length) of our lives enormously improved by the efforts of scientific teams—which, ironically, leads to another problem.

Success leads to expectations; American society views fewer things with greater disdain than unfulfilled expectations. Within a few years of its celebration on the cover of *Time* magazine, American science found that it was failing all too often, at least in the public mind. The threat of a nuclear holocaust was on the minds of many Americans during the Cold War, and especially in the 1960s as portrayed, for example, in *Dr. Strangelove*. In addition, during the conflict in Vietnam a number of Americans were somewhat disenchanted when napalm was regularly used in bombing attacks on North Vietnam. These two factors were significant in reversing America's almost universal love affair with science. But there were other factors. Concerns about nuclear accidents and potential nuclear accidents—for example, at Three Mile Island and, farther away, at Chernobyl; problems concerning nuclear storage; rockets that exploded on the launching pad; and the 1986 national tragedy of the space shuttle *Challenger* all contributed to a lessening of scientists in the mind of the general public as had, earlier, the terrible consequences of the drug thalidomide.

Concerns about the environment didn't help the image of science, and various social movements—from the anti-vivisectionists to Greenpeace—raised the specter of science run amok. Oil spills, nuclear waste dumping, and problems with the ozone layer all helped undermine the image of science as a faultless tool of the nation. When science is questioned, so are scientists. Once American society was quite content to write a blank check and give it to scientists, but not any more.

The questioning of the limits of science and scientists has been heightened by recent developments in areas such as genetic research. While few question the importance of genetic research, a number of people have expressed concern regarding its limits and the morality surrounding it. Where once Americans believed that American science could do anything, and where once American scientists enjoyed the absolute confidence of the American people, neither situation obtains today. Neither science nor the scientist has the absolute trust of the American public. For some people, science had been the great destroyer, not the great savior.

Another major cause of this new skepticism directed toward science may be the absorption of science by industry. As suggested earlier, when industry dominates science the individual scientist and his creativity is often lost in or subjected to the whims of the maze that is bureaucracy. More than this, when industry controls science not only does bureaucracy become the dominant structure of science, but business starts to control the direction and the interests of science. Concern for profit becomes the dominant motive of science. Justly or not, drug manufacturing companies especially receive negative attention here.[6]

Traditionally, there was an ideology of science that at least paid attention to the ideal: science for the sake of knowledge. This is not to suggest that scientists never thought of money; it is to suggest that the public perception in the past had it that money was secondary to the scientist, that his attention was directed toward scientific matters. In addition public perception had it that the sciences were and ought to be run by scientists. Edison may or may not have made a great deal of money from his work, but in either case he was his own man. Einstein was associated with Princeton University, an academic setting not a corporate one.

The various corporations that dominate the several fields of science today are collectives, then, not individuals, and they exist for the purpose of profit, not knowledge. None of this is morally wrong, for it produces usable information. What it does not produce is heroes within the sciences.

Yet as business increasingly controls science and as the rewards for scientific achievement grow, the temptation to do things unscientific in order to gain the rewards also grows. Revelations concerning dubious manipulation of data in breast cancer research, AIDS research, and tobacco research cannot help the image of science or of the scientist. Fudging data is not new to science, and it is unquestioningly true that the overwhelming majority of scientists retain their integrity. Yet, increasingly, the scientific community is questioned as to its ethics.

Equally worrisome, there have been occasions when the scientific community seems to have caved in and protected errant scientists and not cared too much about the truth of the matter in question. This behavior, however rare and however limited in scope, from people who are supposedly, if naively, thought of as dedicated only to the truth, is reminiscent of behavior of politicians who protect one another because you never know when you'll be the one relying upon your colleagues for that same protection. There is a lack of integrity in fields other than science, of course. The problem, as Barbara Ehrenreich writes, is that "science is different, and the difference does define a kind of sanctity."[7]

One consequence of all of this is that people increasingly mistrust the motives of those engaged in applied as well as in theoretical science. And it hardly needs to be said that trust is fundamental to the acceptance of a hero.

One final point might be mentioned here. It is partially because American scientists are expected to be as successful as they were in the past that these attacks on science occur and why there aren't any more American scientist-heroes. American science is no longer regarded as the best in the world. Justly or not, Americans often view the scientific communities of other countries as better than our own—more advanced, more efficient, even more ethical. In the minds of many Americans, we place a poor second, or even third, in the world in electronics, innovative communications systems, advanced theories in biology, chemistry, or physics. Consequently, American scientists are no longer looked upon as geniuses, as heroes. As noted, Max Weber included continued success in his definition of charisma, of heroes. The flip side of this is that nothing tarnishes charismatic individuals—heroes—like failure, real or perceived. The perceived failure of American scientists as compared with foreign scientists has diminished their stature and therefore their status as heroes.

With all due respect to Bruno Bettelheim, the last American scientist-hero was probably Jonas Salk, the man credited with creating the first effective polio vaccine. *Time* magazine noted that "for a time" he was "America's greatest hero," while Paul Greenberg argues that with his death the nation has "run out of scientific folk heroes." The image is that he worked alone to create the preventative of that horrible disease. Whether the image is true is not really at issue. At worst, the popular image is incorrect—the popular images of most heroes are incorrect. But at least with Dr. Salk we had a recent (post–World War II) hero and standards by which to measure future heroes, however implausible those standards might be today.[8]

Intellectuals

In the United States intellectuals are less recognized as heroes than are scientists. Indeed, one might argue that today there cannot be an American intellectual-hero, just as today there cannot be an American artist-hero, a point that will be considered momentarily. However, the significance of the intellectual is recognized in the United States, even if in limited ways, as for example, by the MacArthur Grants, popularly known as the "Genius Grants." Since 1981 the MacArthur Fellows Program has given various sums of money to "creative" people "to be used however they please." [9]

This is a far cry from the past. At one time the United States was capable of both producing and recognizing scholars, men and women whose ideas, insights, and ways of perceiving the world helped to change our understanding of ourselves and of other people. Our perception of the world was, in part, shaped by the efforts of American thinkers, and in time their ideas became a part of American culture. In earlier years William James and John Dewey, Thorstein Veblen and George Herbert Mead, Charles Sanders Peirce and William Graham Sumner contributed to our understanding and our knowledge of human existence. And they were recognized for doing so, if not by the population at large, then by enough people to cause them and their intellectual abilities to be respected, even celebrated.

Perhaps the best example here is Mark Twain, Samuel Langhorne Clemens, arguably America's most celebrated writer. When he returned from a European trip it "was a national event." Not only was Twain greeted with enthusiasm, he was regarded as a "popular authority on foreign affairs," and his views were published in the *New York World* just prior to his arrival in the United States. This wouldn't—couldn't—happen today. We do not have an intellectual or will not recognize a writer of Twain's stature.[10]

It has been argued by Richard Hofstadter that Americans are anti-intellectual. A kinder way of looking at this might be to say that Americans are a pragmatic people. Yet America has still produced its share of intellectuals, an accomplishment all the greater for the supposed cultural indifference to, or disregard of, ivory-tower views. Further, the intellectual had a role, albeit a limited one, even in the anti-intellectual United States. The intellectual was an iconoclast, a scholarly curmudgeon (although the latter term seems to be reserved for H. L. Mencken). And the intellectual is necessary, for in a society that is forever changing—and especially one changing so rapidly—the intellectual points to the direction of the change, points to the problems and to the issues that may arise, the problems beyond the current ones.

Surely Rachel Carson's *Silent Spring* (1962) said things about the environment that were worth noting. Carson made people aware and got them to do something to alleviate that situation. John F. Kennedy was influenced by the book as well as by Barbara Tuchman's *The Guns of August*, a study of the beginnings of World War I. The point here is that American intellectuals have helped to shape American society and have been recognized for their contributions. An article in a 1956 edition of *Time* magazine had as its cover story "America and the Intellectual: The Reconciliation." Forty years later America's intellectuals seem to have vanished. Paul Fussell argues that "except for [Ada Louise] Huxtable and Tom Wolfe, we have hardly any critics who are not the captives of corporate money or university taste." Tuchman herself wondered; "What has become of American wits?"[11]

William H. Honan points out that people are wondering why American intellectuals "are in hiding." Daniel Bell notes the "sense of exhaustion [that] marks [American] intellectual life." He argues that American writers today, unlike those of past generations, "have retreated into silence." The reason is that "the habitat, manners, and idiom of intellectuals" have changed since the end of the Second World War, and not for the better. All in all, this does not paint a happy picture of America's intelligentsia, and certainly is not the stuff of American intellectual heroes.[12]

Politically neither Left nor Right seem capable of producing the profound and influential thinkers they both had produced in the past. And they seem to recognize this. Those on the Right suggest that intellectuals have burned out on Marxism; those on the Left argue that the intellectuals have been absorbed by the institutions they should be criticizing, or at least monitoring. The former assertion is unprovable; although it is undoubtedly ideologically satisfying to state it, one cannot simply conclude that intellectualism in the United States collapsed with the Berlin Wall. However, there is persuasive support for the latter view, that is, support less bounded by ideology.

Writing in the *New York Times*, literary critic Christopher Lehmann-Haupt suggests that insofar as the public is concerned, intellectuals "are invisible," they are "lost in the universities." Others support this view: intellectuals today do not speak in public or to the public, but generally "only as academics—only to each other, and mainly to get tenure, or to earn a raise." This is the central thesis of Russell Jacoby, who argues that the nation has lost a generation of thinkers and social critics. [13]

Today Left-leaning intellectuals, at least insofar as public awareness is concerned, seem generally to be interested only with being attendants for the "politically correct." Ever vigilant, they watch to ensure that everything that is done in society is done in accordance with their definition of what is and what is not morally acceptable. In the main, however, they seem to do little more than impose their views on a limited number of college campuses.

Right-wing intellectuals today have achieved a greater degree of publicity in the form of articles, books, and panel shows. (The moral wing of the Right, Christian conservatives, rarely get intellectual respectability; they seem content in seeking validation of their ethical position.) However, as stated earlier, the Right wing can rarely muster a hero, even an intellectual one. William F. Buckley, Jr., for example, stands out as spokesman for the Right, but while he is surely admired by the conservatives in the country, it would be stretching the point to claim that he is a national hero.

The intellectual—Right-wing, Left-wing, or middle-of-the-road—is today generally concerned with social position and economic security and has therefore entered into the teaching profession. This is a blow to the political Left (traditionally the intellectual was Left-leaning), although it gives an academic imprimatur to the Right. More important, it leaves a vacancy in an area that was once filled in America. The provoker, the troublemaker, the one who looked at the nation and poked fun at its foibles seems to have vanished. The members of the Algonquin Round Table have disappeared, but we have substitutes: radio talk show hosts. Rush Limbaugh and Howard Stern and G. Gordon Liddy and dozens of others are happy to tell us what's wrong with the nation and why. They have their followers and may be heroes to those followers. But they are a long way from Mencken, Carson, and Tuchman.

THE ARTIST AS HERO

If American intellectual heroes are only on very rare occasions acknowledged as such, American artistic heroes are noted on even rarer occasions, and then only by a select group of people. The nation at large sort of takes the word of that select group and accepts the artistic hero as artistic hero because those in the group say he is.

This is the main reason that recognition of the artistic hero is generally reserved for practitioners of specific "high" or "fine" arts: dance and classical music, as for example, the accolades given George Balanchine or Isaac Stern. The designators of American artistic heroes offer an occasional nod to some popular composers, George Gershwin perhaps or Edward "Duke" Ellington or Irving Berlin; and to a few exceptional playwrights such as Arthur Miller or Tennessee Williams. American practitioners of other arts, of painting and sculpting, literature and poetry, photography and architecture, rarely receive the praise in the United States that they do in other countries, that is, national recognition as artists of extraordinary ability. American movie, rock, pop, and television performers are, as a rule, classified as celebrities rather than artists as that term has traditionally been used.

There are only a limited number of followers of the arts in the United States, and that itself precludes there being a national artistic hero. Americans tend not to celebrate artists on a national scale. We've heard of Jackson Pollock, perhaps, but Ivan LeLorraine Albright is not a household name; Frank Lloyd Wright may be, but it is unlikely that many people could name other contemporary architects. Similarly, even though Walt Whitman is universally regarded as a national treasure, how many Americans know that in 1995 Robert Hass was named the nation's poet laureate? (He replaced Mona Van Duyn, who was named poet laureate of the United States in 1992 and who was the first woman to hold this title.) And why is it necessary to hope that a 1991 biography of Carl Sandburg will "lift the poet and biographer of Abe Lincoln from his present obscurity?" Why should a talent such as his be in obscurity to begin with?[14]

There are, of course, exhibits of some of the country's greater artistic talents. The National Gallery, for example, will exhibit Georgia O'Keeffe's work and that of Willem de Kooning and Andrew Wyeth. And most Americans know the paintings of Norman Rockwell, if for no other reason than there are postage stamps acknowledging his enormous gifts. The photographs of Man Ray may be widely known, and even if most people do not recognize Joe Rosenthal's name, they'll recognize his photograph of marines raising the flag on Iwo Jima, just as they know Alfred Eisenstaedt's "V-J Day, Times Square, 1945" photograph, the one of the sailor kissing the nurse. But it is questionable whether or not most Americans know Eisenstaedt's name. Generally, the American artist-hero is an elusive figure.

Yet in some ways the arts are becoming popularized in the United States. Andy Warhol saw to this, as did Peter Max and the generation that grew up in the 1960s. These days newspapers and news magazines run features on artists as a matter of course. The Kennedy Center in Washington, D.C., honors various American practitioners of the performing arts, and its awards presentation is nationally televised. Thus, Marshall Fishwick can argue that in the United States today we can indeed have the artist-as-hero. That is possible, of course, but not very probable, especially if it is, as Fishwick suggests, "on the people's terms" and not on terms specified by "the elites." The arts of the masses, of the people, come from television, the movies, and popular music; and as enjoyable as they may be, the talents here are unlikely to gain prominence within the cultural realm of the United States.[15]

The arts and artists can gain broad fame in the United States, but usually that happens only when there is more notoriety than celebration as in, for example, the photographic exhibits of Robert Mapplethorpe. Whether or not those photographs were indeed art and whether or not the government should have helped subsidize the work via National Endowment for the Arts (NEA) grants is not at issue here. What is at issue is that it seems to be only through such notoriety that the artist and the art seem to be able to gain widespread recognition in America.

It wasn't always this way. As recently as the 1950s Lawrence Ferlinghetti, Gregory Corso, Allen Ginsberg, Jack Kerouac, and the other "beats" received national recognition even if they wrote for a small group and even though, like Norman Mailer, they occasionally wrote self-advertisements. They were known and they were highly regarded as American artists—if not by everyone, then at least by a greater number of people than is usually the case with artistically talented Americans today. And the 1950s also gave us perhaps the last two American classical artists famed throughout the country, Van Cliburn and Leonard Bernstein.

But the times do not seem to allow for a Whitman or even for a Kerouac, and Van Cliburn plays for that select group of people mentioned earlier. Classical American artists have been replaced by popular artists, and for some time now. *Time* magazine noted the "neo-Dada embrace of pop by artists and independent intellectuals of the 1950s and early 1960s," and suggested that "their approach was off-center, cool in every sense."[16]

But the artist-hero cannot be a fad, nor can his work be tongue-in-cheek. The media—films, radio, and (especially) television—could have enhanced the position of American artists, but they did not choose to do this. Instead, with the aid of the public, they have transformed whatever American artist-heroes they could find into the celebrities that so worry

Daniel Boorstin. It was, after all, a popular artist, Andy Warhol, who allotted everyone fifteen minutes of fame, artists included.

MORALISTS AS AMERICAN HEROES

America has traditionally had a complex relationship with its moralists. Americans' attitudes toward their spiritual leaders have varied from love to hate, from trust to skepticism. Cotton Mather, Joseph Smith, and Brigham Young; Henry Ward Beecher, Mary Baker Eddy, and John Humphrey Noyes; Carry Nation, Billy Sunday, Daddy Grace, and Aimee Semple MacPherson; Martin Luther King, Jr., Jerry Falwell, Billy Graham, and Pat Robertson have been admired, loved, and on occasion regarded as heroes to the faithful. In the United States the faithful often count for a substantial number of people.[17]

Yet Sinclair Lewis depicted the hypocrisy of the moralist in *Elmer Gantry*, and scandal surrounded a number of evangelists in the not too distant past. Ralph Abernathy writes of Martin Luther King, Jr.'s affairs; Jimmy Swaggart was involved with prostitutes; Oral Roberts told his followers that if he didn't get immediate donations totalling $8 million he would die (he got the donations); Jim Bakker was imprisoned for bilking his followers. Pat Robertson has come under criticism for his business dealings. A recent survey had nearly two-thirds of the American public holding an unfavorable view of television evangelists.[18]

Americans, perhaps more than other people, admire men of faith, spiritual leaders. And Americans, perhaps more than other people, enjoy seeing moralists fall from grace. Americans may on occasion raise a moralist to the level of hero, but few things elate them as much as a holier-than-thou individual tripping and winding up in the mire of what he himself preached against.

The reason may be that, unlike the ancient Greek hero who often suffered doubt about his convictions, the modern moralist is unshakably secure in his vision of the universe. He sets himself up for a fall, and the nation is there to witness it—and gleefully. Thus headlines regarding men of the cloth who are involved in sexual scandal and financial impropriety are among the juiciest news items available. We expect our politicians to be immoral; it seems that we are relieved to find that our moral leaders are as well.

Being a moralist and being a hero is almost an impossible task in the United States today. How is it possible to find a position that almost everyone can support? How to find one that a substantial number of people will not oppose on ethical grounds? America is increasingly a society where diverse views are accepted. This necessarily encourages moral relativism, and that necessarily flies in the face of those who take themselves to hold absolute truths. Even when there is agreement on, say, the importance of family values, there is disagreement as to the exact meaning of "family." (An easy way to start a heated debate at a party is to raise the question of whether or not same sex couples constitute a family.)

In the past there were few questions to discuss. Abortion was immoral, as were divorce, virtually all forms of non-traditional sex, and on and on. But partially due to the acceptance of the explanations of the social sciences regarding variations in human behavior, partially because technology has made what was once a necessity an option, and partially because an understanding of other cultures has contributed to a tolerance of once questionable patterns of behavior, greater choice now exists within American culture.

Sociological and psychological understandings of human behavior, the development of the birth control pill, the willingness of people to seek divorce where they once would have remained unhappily married, has meant that fewer and fewer people will not question at least some of the moral rules that were once basic to society. More and more people now demand the right to analyze and examine issues that, at one time, were beyond discussion. In consequence, many people today disregard traditional moral views.

All of this may or may not be fine, depending upon one's personal views of morality. From a social point of view, however, it reduces the possibility of the existence of the moral hero, and thus the hero generally. Among his other qualities, the hero must be able to sustain social probity. Sustaining social probity necessarily means that there is a generally agreed upon standard of probity and a generally agreed upon standard of social norms. That no longer is the case; nor has it been for some time now.

This point will be considered in some depth in the following chapter. For the moment it can be said that, for better or worse, the values that represent America are changing. Consequently, any opinion based upon a moral position—except perhaps for an extreme one: molestation of children, for example—will lead to intense debate and possibly to conflict. No one can speak for the nation at large anymore on a moral level; at one time we had people who could at least come close to representing all of the

Addendum: Why Few Heroic American Women Are Recognized as Heroes

The purpose of this section is to explain why half of the population of the United States is generally excluded from the category of American hero, to explain why, although women have often done heroic deeds, they are rarely accepted in the United States as American heroes.

As discussed earlier, there is a difference between one who is a hero and one who does a heroic deed. The difference is, in a word, recognition. Society creates and sustains its heroes. Conversely, society dismisses out of hand those it will not perceive, or those it will not permit to be perceived, as heroes. American women have only rarely been heroes because in the United States the heroic deeds that women have done have been at best infrequently acknowledged as such, and the women who accomplished those deeds have been infrequently recognized for having done them.

The argument here is perhaps best summed up by Christina Hoff Sommers. She acknowledges that there are a limited number of women mentioned in history books, but argues against the notion that reason is "due . . . to the bias of male historians." Instead, the reason lies in the social system, in the fact that "women have not been allowed to make history in the way that men—and relatively few men at that—have been allowed to make it." *Mutatis mutandis*, this is why few women have been regarded as heroes in the United States: they have not been allowed to become heroes.[1]

Complicating matters, today many of the women who are celebrated as heroes are celebrated—and especially by women—for various "firsts," as, for example, Gerty Cori, the first woman to win a Nobel prize (in 1947 for medicine or physiology). But women "firsts" are effectively local heroes.

They are often heroes only within the women's movement, celebrated by women as evidence that women can make significant contributions in whatever field. This was clearly the purpose of the "Congratulations to 125 of America's top achievers. (What?! You were surprised they're all women?)" full-page ad in the *New York Times*. In fact, no one should have been surprised; the purpose of the ad was to demonstrate the contributions by women to the nation.[2]

That is also the reason for the establishment of the National Women's Hall of Fame, founded in Seneca Falls, New York, in 1969, site of the first Women's Rights Convention (held in 1848). None of this, of course, diminishes the efforts or accomplishments of the women noted. It does, however, reduce the number of their admirers and, consequently, their fame and their status as American heroes. And it explains why Lucy B. Hobbes's accomplishment of being "the first female dentist" should qualify her as an "authentic American heroine." There can be little question as to the prejudices and discrimination that Dr. Hobbes faced and overcame or of her courage in doing so, but there can also be little doubt that an "authentic American heroine" requires a higher standard than that.[3]

In the headlines of the 1920s and the 1930s, according to Grace Lichtenstein, two athletic stars, Helen Wills and Suzanne Lenglen, were bigger names than Babe Ruth and Jack Dempsey. That claim may be a bit exaggerated, but there can be no doubting two points here: the abilities of these two tennis greats and the fact that they have been forgotten.[4]

This is the fate of a great many female athletes and the fate of a great many possible female heroes—heroines, if you prefer. Partly for structural reasons, partly for physical (biological) reasons, and partly for cultural reasons, the accomplishments of America's female heroes are sporadically recognized at best and ignored at worst. Thus, Barbara Holland can argue that it's been some two hundred years between American female heroes. To Holland, Jacqueline Kennedy Onassis is "our first national heroine since Betsy Ross."[5]

Holland does not say what Jacqueline Kennedy Onassis did to be regarded as a national heroine, although most Americans would allow that her grace, elegance, and stature permit her that status. More to the point, Holland doesn't say why the accomplishments of so many other women within that two-hundred-year span, often heroic and significant accomplishments done by heroic and significant women, are ignored. Yet Holland's views are not atypical, her reluctance to acknowledge other American women of consequence is not unusual. For those reasons she is correct in her assessment: we've had only two women heroes within those two hundred years. Virginia Apgar and Frances Kelsey (scientists), Jessie Benton Frémont (a writer), Belle Moskowitz (a behind-the-scenes politician), Mary ("Mother") Jones (a union leader and organizer), Julia Morgan (an architect), Clara Barton (a nurse and founder of the American Red Cross), and Grace Murray Hooper (an admiral and computer innovator), among numerous other women, are generally ignored by the American public. And because heroism requires recognition, these women, regardless of their abilities and despite the significance of their work, cannot be regarded as American heroes.[6]

As a rule, on those occasions when America's heroic women and their accomplishments are acknowledged, they are acknowledged for a brief period of time and then quietly forgotten. Barring some exceptions, American folklore tends to exclude women from those who are admired as heroes, whatever their accomplishments. This is part of an unjust but well established tradition; and although feminists and others have worked to reverse this tradition, generally they have not succeeded.

To Joseph Campbell, for example, the hero is "a prince, warrior, saint, or god," but the hero is not a woman. For Campbell the hero is always a man. But Campbell doesn't totally ignore heroines. In *The Power of Myth*, he denies that heroes are necessarily male, which implies that he is aware of the possibility of female heroes. And indeed, he includes mothers as heroes: to Campbell giving birth is a heroic act. He cites the Aztec notion that "the heaven for warriors killed in battle was the same for mothers who died in childbirth." But the heroism of battle and the heroism of giving birth are two different things. If one expands this notion and considers women in the military, women who were in immediate danger because of their proximity to battles—those who served in Vietnam or the Gulf War are the most obvious examples—Campbell's notion equates every woman who has been pregnant with every woman who has risked her life in the service of her country.[7]

Campbell's seeming disregard for women who truly were heroes is, like Holland's, not unusual. Still, not everyone ignores the contributions of women in society. Sidney Hook is among the few scholars who cite female heroes in history, women who, to Hook, have affected the lives of numerous people. The United States government, too, has honored and recognized the contributions of women in several fields, but only sporadically. For example, as of 1991, that is, before the new tradition of putting celebrity-heroes on postage stamps, only about 13 percent of the people pictured on U. S. postage stamps were women. Included were Rachel Carson, Helen

Keller, Anne Sullivan, and Sojourner Truth. Similarly, Lynn Sherr and Jurate Kazickas point out that there are some statues in public parks dedicated to (and, one might add, streets named for) American women who were true heroes, but not very many. The fact is that American women who are heroes are rarely given the national recognition that is given to their male counterparts.[8]

That is unlikely to change. As our present culture and structure prohibits the creation of new heroes save the celebrity-hero, the possibility of women currently being regarded as heroes is slender at best (as it is for men).

Part of the reason for the lack of recognition of women heroes is structural, that is, a consequence of social organization. Specific positions lend themselves to producing heroes while other positions almost guarantee that they will not produce heroes. Those positions that have in the past produced the most American heroes were rarely open to women. There were, for example, few female military heroes who were recognized as such. One woman has been awarded the Medal of Honor: Civil War surgeon Mary Walker.

In recent years women have entered the military in record numbers. The all-volunteer armed forces, new technologies that reduce the demand for physical power, and changing attitudes within the nation, among other factors, have all worked to give women new opportunities within the military. And women in the military are increasingly placed in harm's way. Today women fly combat missions and serve aboard combat-ready ships. Of course, women in the military have always been placed in dangerous situations whether or not this fact was acknowledged by the nation at large. The work that military nurses did in the past was heroic beyond any possible question.

In the main, however, America gets its military heroes from those involved in ground combat, and women are currently excluded from serving in the U.S. infantry. This may change, but it is well to recall that in the past three wars—Korea, Vietnam, and the Gulf—we've had no military heroes in the traditional sense of the term, male or female. For reasons discussed earlier, the likelihood of a future American military hero in the traditional sense of that term, male or female, is minimal at best.

At least women's contributions to the military are being recognized, if collectively rather than individually. A memorial is being erected to honor the nearly two million women who served in America's armed forces from the American Revolution through the Gulf War. The memorial will be placed over the entrance to Arlington National Cemetery. The recognition may be late in coming, but it is coming.

Until recently women were rarely admitted into politics, especially on a national level, which means that their potential as heroes here was limited (as noted politician-heroes are a rare commodity to begin with). The famous—or infamous—"glass ceiling" restricts movement on the part of women up the corporate ladder. Thus, even if there could be business heroes today, opportunities for women remain limited here.

The classic heroes of the Old West were male; the women were hangers-on. They were often alcoholics and prostitutes and led lives that were not only completely lacking in glamor, but were generally filled with misery. Belle Starr (Myra Belle Shirley), for example, was a petty thief. Calamity Jane, "a mean, ugly, tobacco-chewing sometimes whore," has been portrayed by Doris Day, Jane Russell, and Betty Hutton although "the frame and profile of Robert Mitchum would have done [her] justice."[9]

Only through Hollywood distortion could their lives be made to seem appealing, and Hollywood has rarely chosen to do even that. There were women who deserved the accolades generally reserved for Belle Starr and Calamity Jane, for example, Ann Bassett. But, like Hank Monk, Bassett is relegated to arcane histories of the West. However, belated recognition is coming to the women of the West as it has to women in the military, and their contributions to the settling of the plains may eventually receive its due.[10]

The gangsters of the 1920s and 1930s—the Robin Hoods manqué—were generally male. Bonnie Parker of Bonnie and Clyde fame is perhaps the most famous of the few women outlaws of the era and she, like Clyde, was no hero. Most of the other women who lived outside of the law, as they would say in the 1920s and 1930s—Ma Barker, for example—were well known because of their children's notorious exploits rather than their own.

America's women adventurers, too, are rarely noticed. Amelia Earhart was correctly regarded as a courageous adventurer, but her continuing fame is more a result of her untimely (and possibly deliberate) death than a result of her daring. This is why her name is well known while few people today have heard of Blanche Scott, another adventurer and pilot ("aviatrix" was the term then), whose courage and abilities matched those of Earhart. Contrast this with the celebrity of Robert E. Peary, whose courage and daring were no greater than Scott's but whose recognition certainly is.

Female athletes of prestige were all too often disregarded and their accomplishments dismissed or forgotten, which is the point of Grace Lichtenstein's remarks noted earlier. Mildred "Babe" Didrikson Zaharias was a heroic figure; however, her fame is due as much to her tragic and untimely death as to her remarkable athletic skills. Helen Wills, as noted, has unjustly suffered obscurity as have other outstanding female athletes, for example, Helene Madison (an outstanding swimmer in the 1932 Olympics) and Hazel Wrightman (a tennis star several decades ago). It is only with the release of A League of Their Own, a movie that told the story of the All-American Girls Professional Baseball League, that women as hero-baseball players received notice.[11]

The point to all of the above is that social structure hampered, not to say destroyed, the chances of female heroes receiving the recognition required to be regarded as heroes. Generally, women were not allowed in the areas that created American heroes or, if they were—as in sports—their accomplishments quickly faded from the nation's memory.

Physical (biological) factors also limited recognition of potential female heroes in the United States. The advent of televised sports and the popularity of sports celebrities generally, along with the rise of feminism and its demand that female athletes and male athletes receive equal recognition, have contributed to the increased recognition of female sports stars. The increased participation of girls and young women in high school and college athletics, respectively, furthered the nation's acknowledgment of women as athlete-heroes. Today women are recognized for their athletic abilities in tennis, swimming, and a number of other sports.

Yet they do not have the clout of male athletes. With the exception of Chris Evert, Mary Lou Retton, and a few other sports stars, few female athletes are hired to do television commercials. It may be that while young men consistently identify with male athletes, young women do not identify with female athletes, or at least that is what advertisers seem to think. The reason may be that in virtually all popular American sports men are the better athletes, and a part of the reason for this is that most male athletes are bigger (taller and bulkier), stronger, faster, quicker, than most female athletes—although there are some exceptions to this rule—and Americans tend to prefer the power play in whatever sport. To many Americans physical contact is synonymous with athletic events, and bigger and stronger are better than smaller and weaker. Football, hockey, and basketball—physical, not to say violent sports—to all intents and purposes represent sports to a considerable number of Americans. The exception is baseball; but even here power and speed are generally the major crowd pleasers, although other factors—for example, "hustle"—also count.

In sports where there would seem to be little need for size and strength, in golf, for example, there is a sexual division; no one wants to eliminate the Ladies Professional Golf Association (LPGA) and have women golfers compete with the men; nor is anyone asking that men and women compete with each other in bowling, also a sport that relies as much on skill and finesse as power. Certainly in tennis, the sport in which women athletes have earned the greatest following, the women cannot compete one-on-one with the men, although the top professional women here are superb athletes. Men and women professional tennis players often do not even play the same number of sets; men sometimes play the best three of five sets while women almost always play the best two of three sets (the WTA TOUR, formerly the Virginia Slims Championships, is the exception). When Renée Richards, a transsexual, was admitted to the women's tennis tournaments, several of the women tennis players protested. Richards may be a woman in any number of ways, but she retains the musculature of a man.

Besides tennis, the sports in which women have gained the most fame and respect are ice-skating and gymnastics, where diminutiveness—but certainly not physical weakness or lack of courage—is a distinct advantage, and diving and swimming. It is no accident that all of these sports, like the more successful of all of the sports in which women participate, are noncontact sports.[12]

For both structural reasons and physical ones, then, women have effectively been limited in many of those areas that have historically produced America's heroes. Limitations in other areas, in entertainment and the arts and sciences, are more of a cultural than a structural issue. Similarly, restrictions placed against women's participation in areas from which occasional American heroes arise (generally the intermediate or lesser heroes)—literature, intellectual activities, and science—are cultural; surely they are not based on the women's physical strictures.

The cultural limitations on women as heroes take two forms: the way children are socialized into viewing heroes and the biases that prohibit women from achieving the status of hero. Children see that television heroes and movie heroes are overwhelmingly male, especially when they represent real people (however distorted the representation). This, of course, connects with what was said earlier: the qualities that make heroes in the United States, especially to children, are physical size and strength and the use of force. As a rule, these are taken to be masculine qualities. If children regularly see males as heroes and only sporadically see females as heroes, it can hardly be surprising that the image of the hero is the man and not the woman.[13]

Some people have suggested that there is another point to consider regarding culture and the status of heroes in the United States: the masculine and feminine quest for that status. To some, men are taught to seek fame, to strive for greatness, if that is the appropriate term, to a greater degree than women. This is the opinion of Leo Brady, author of *The Frenzy of Renown*, who argues that seeking fame is "historically a masculine pursuit." Esther S. Person agrees: women's "passionate quest" is usually "interpersonal, and has generally involved romantic love [while] for men it has more often been heroic, the pursuit of achievement or power." She argues that men need to find their masculinity before falling in love: in literature, the man faces heroic external challenges: in "real life," he faces "his own consciousness."[14]

This is possible, but in the end the issue is one more of social acceptance than of psychological inclination. Currently, however unjust it might be, American society willingly endorses the male hero and is reluctant to endorse the female hero. For structural, physical, and cultural reasons—that is, because of social organization, physical differences, and perhaps because of variations in socialization—the number of female heroes celebrated in the United States is limited, unrecognized by the nation at large. So are the arenas in which women can become heroes.

Perhaps the future will see the number of these areas expanded. That is the hope; the reality is that American heroines, no less than American heroes, are likely to be found only in the world of the celebrity. That is, they will be transitory heroines-manqué. It is somewhat ironic that as women are entering in record numbers into fields that once produced heroes in the United States—science, for example, or politics or business—those fields are no longer as highly regarded as they once were. And in any case, they don't produce heroes anymore.

Conclusion

There are virtually no heroes left in American society save, as noted, the celebrity-hero/entertainment hero, the local hero, and the transitory hero. The heroes of America's past, the ones that reflected and defined the nation's purpose and character, no longer are allowed to exist. Geography and time and, more important, structural and cultural forces in society have combined to eradicate the American hero—and permanently.

The Western hero vanished with the closing of the frontier, and his image has been tarnished in any event as new interpretations of the history of the American West emerge. Military heroes have diminished due to technology, among other factors, and American skepticism has damaged if not eliminated the political hero within the United States. Bureaucracy has reduced the business hero to a cog in a mighty machine and has done the same thing to America's outlaw-heroes. A bit of reality therapy, too, has taken its toll on the criminal-hero. There are few places left for the adventurer-hero to be an adventurer-hero, so unless one regards daredevil pranks to be on a par with the exploration of new lands, the adventurer-hero, too, is gone from American life. Moral heroes have become suspect, science is too big and organized to produce an individual hero, and artists are too scarce and infrequently recognized as heroes. We are left, then, with celebrity-heroes—in entertainment and in sports—and with local and temporary heroes. We have traveled a considerable distance from the people who once represented the nation. It has been a difficult journey.

The elimination of the American hero is not a phase that the nation is going through, a brief period in history that causes the people to regard heroes critically, wherein people seek out failings that would force a hero into the shadows. The characteristics of American society that deny the hero his place, including here a substantial degree of cynicism, are fixed and more than likely irrevocable. This does not change the American people's desire for a hero nor ease their unhappiness that none is forthcoming. It just makes their frustration greater and, in consequence, their standards lower in their search for one who may be regarded as a celebrity-hero. Increasingly and necessarily, as the people's frustration mounts and the search for heroes intensifies, the qualities required for the status of hero in the United States will diminish.

Because neither America's social structure nor culture allows the existence of the American hero today and because they both did prior to World War II, it is reasonable to consider the social changes in the years after the war that caused the hero to disappear from American society. To that end, the next chapters will examine several specific aspects of America's changed social structure and culture. These include changes in the population and organization of the country, changes in the power and the effects of the media, changes in the general attitudes of the people, and changes in American values. All of these and more caused the traditional hero to vanish.

Part III

Why America's Heroes Have Disappeared

Introduction

Given the number and the diversity of America's heroes of the past, why is it that there are, by consensus, no American heroes today? Some answers to this question were suggested in the previous chapters: in several instances where heroes existed, external—that is, nonsocial—circumstances caused them to vanish save in memory. Adventurers vanished as more and more of the earth was explored and there were no longer exciting places to discover. In several areas, and especially in science, increased knowledge and technology as well as the burden of equipping a modern laboratory demanded group efforts. These required the creation of a bureaucratic structure within science and, consequently, the disappearance of the individual as innovator.

In other cases, social and historical circumstances caused the disappearance of the traditional American hero. The heroes of the Old West, for example, disappeared when the frontier closed, when civilization moved from the East to the West, and when law and order effectively eliminated the old way of life. And while it is true that modern technology reduced the contributions of the individual soldier and thus his recognition as a hero, it is also true that in the aftermath of the Korean conflict and especially in the aftermath of the war in Vietnam, America's conception of the military changed.

In the late 1930s Americans, concerned with events in Europe and Asia, started to rally round the flag. People in the United States began to view the Axis powers, totalitarianism, as a force to be defeated. Most important here, that view directed the United States socially, politically, and militarily until the Vietnam era. Many Americans volunteered to do military service in World War II, and to a lesser degree, in Korea. There was a sense of pride, of self-sacrifice, in serving one's country.

But by the time of the war in Vietnam things had changed. For the draft-eligible the situation was different. A substantial number of Americans did what they could to avoid military service. The pride that had once been a part of a uniform had all too often evolved into a "misfortune." Among other things, the growth of a youth culture, the ambiguity of the cause, the diminished trust in government had taken their toll on Americans' willingness to respond unquestioningly to a call to arms. That is one reason why World War II produced military heroes and Vietnam didn't, and why, discounting the excessive adulation for the collective members of our armed forces during the conflict in the Persian Gulf, American military heroes pretty much disappeared throughout the 1960s and 1970s.

Similarly, political heroes also seem to have vanished, and especially after Watergate. The trust that once existed, or at least the lip service that was paid to the trust that Americans offered their politicians, started to disappear during the Kennedy/Johnson era. Godfrey Hodgson is correct in noting the significance of the changes that occurred in the United States during the Vietnam-Watergate era: "What happened in the age of Kennedy and Nixon was something more than a mere acceleration in the pace of change. There was a real break in the continuity of the American experience." [1]

Some suggest that one reason for the disappearance of the American political hero is that the politicians themselves have failed. Others argue that the system is at fault, that, for example, the press stopped granting presidents a lengthy "honeymoon." All of this is well and good and undoubtedly contains some truth, but the fact of it is that above all else cynicism has eliminated the possibility of an American political hero today.[2]

Cynicism has become a part of American political life. Consider Pauline Kael's comment: "You remember the pictures of Winston Churchill? On the cover of *Life*? That bulldog face and that big fat cigar. The idea was that there were men in charge who knew something. You couldn't pose leaders in that style anymore. People would laugh at it." She is right; people would laugh at it. They don't believe that there are leaders like that anymore. And they're right; there aren't.[3]

However, the process that led to this political cynicism specifically and to the "break in the continuity of the American experience" started well before the Kennedy-Nixon era. It started in the years following World War II and has accelerated consistently since then. The conformity of the 1950s led in time to a questioning of the political hero; the chaos and mistrust of the 1960s led in time to doubting him; the disillusionment of the succeeding decades completed the job.

Throughout these years other changes occurred in specific areas of society that contributed to the disappearance of the American hero. Among the most important of these, subjects to be considered in some detail below, are America's changing values and attitudes; changing American demographics and an attendant ethnic awareness; the completion of the bureaucratization of various systems in American society; America's love affair with and the consequent domination of American popular culture by the nation's youth; the relentlessness, ubiquity, and power of the mass media.

These changes, in addition to several lesser social factors that will be noted throughout this section, are the primary reasons that Americans search in vain today for a hero.

Shortly after the end of World War II attaining the good life became the key motivator in the United States. In general and compared with previous generations, the post–World War II generation was not raised to know hardship, or even minor deprivation. Indeed, a substantial number of the baby boom generation could not even think of hardship and deprivation as possibilities. In the late 1940s, throughout the 1950s, and well into the 1960s, the United States became enormously wealthy compared with other nations. More important, because this is the criterion by which people measure their current situation, the standard of living of a great many Americans reached a level that was almost unimaginable in the prewar years. John Kenneth Galbraith's *The Affluent Society*, written in the 1950s, was a true reflection of that era.

Increasing numbers of people in the United States were earning a greater income than ever before, and the security and pleasures this wealth provided were especially sweet when compared with economic conditions throughout the rest of the world and with their own memories of the Depression. A 1959 survey showed that "Americans were the most confident people in the world" and that "few of them doubted the essential goodness and strength of American society." Critically, Americans drew a connection between these views and their newfound wealth; they believed that their affluence was a right. It reflected the "essential goodness and strength" of the nation.[4]

America had, after all, stopped the Axis powers and won the war, had rescued Europe from economic collapse and Berlin from starvation, had stopped communist aggression in Greece and Turkey using its economic power, and in Korea by its military power. Americans were, and deserved to be, the leaders of the free world and America's wealth and power were justly earned. It surprised no one when, in his 1961 Inaugural Address, President Kennedy asserted that "God's work must truly be our own." Everyone in the nation believed that the United States would and should lead the free world. America's rightful claim to universal leadership existed because of America's military, financial, political, and moral superiority. Indeed, that superiority existed in every possible arena.

Attitudes like this both reflect and effect cultural values, both reflect and effect the structure of the society, both reflect and effect peoples' expectations. They also evoke disappointment and anger if those expectations aren't satisfied.

Of course, throughout these years things were never quite as idyllic as they were supposed to be; and all along some people began questioning America's hegemony in numerous arenas. Among other issues, racial disharmony and inequitable political representation, poverty and the challenges directed at established conventions, provoked dissatisfaction among several groups within society. As questions within these various areas persisted, disillusion, cynicism, and self-absorption became significant themes in American society. Alvin Toffler argues that beginning in the 1950s with the "beats" and continuing through to the 1960s and the "hippies," the "pervasive cultural theme" in the United States became "pessimism about the human condition, not optimism." Both movements, Toffler says, "did much to replace knee-jerk optimism with knee-jerk despair."[5]

By the time of Vietnam and continuing after Watergate, "America had lost its postwar illusion of omnipotence." Recall President Ford speaking about Watergate, "our national nightmare," and hoping that we would put it behind us—we didn't—and his failed battles against an increasingly weak economy. Recall President Carter speaking about America's national malaise, the continuing economic turmoil of the 1970s, and the embarrassment of the United States at the hands of Iran. Was it possible to have ideals, to have a hero in these circumstances? By the time of the Reagan era all pretense at ideals, and certainly all dreams of having an American hero, had vanished.[6]

A great deal was made of the "me generation" of the 1980s, people who represented perhaps the culmination of an attitude of working only to assure one's self-satisfaction. Indeed, there is little doubt but that Tom

Wolfe's tag was an accurate description of many of the notable people of that decade. But the "me generation" did not burst upon the scene from nowhere. The thing that stands out about the Yuppies, the representatives of the "me generation," was not their self-interest but their reluctance to hide it, their obviousness about their desire for wealth, their greed, and their selfishness. The system had changed, perhaps, but what is more important is that attitudes had changed.

De Tocqueville early on observed that Americans valued money a great deal. But Americans also valued subtlety, or at least a pretense to it, in their desire for wealth. The Yuppies of the 1980s who, incidentally, evolved from the hippies of the 1960s, made no pretense to subtlety. Recall the poster picturing a man, expensively dressed and with one foot on the bumper sticker of his Rolls-Royce. The caption under the photograph said "Poverty Sucks." Recall Gordon Gekko, perhaps Hollywood's quintessential Yuppie of the 1980s, unequivocally asserting in the movie *Wall Street* that "Greed, for want of another word, is good." Clearly understatement was out and unabashed avarice was in.

Viewing post–World War II Americans broadly, then, the initial salient feature was pleasant conformity. Then came the short-lived idealism of the early 1960s as reflected in, for example, the "Freedom Riders" and those who joined the Peace Corps. This idealism yielded to the chaotic youth culture of the mid-and late-1960s, whose attitudes reflected self-absorption, skepticism, and mistrust. It cannot be surprising that these attitudes prompted people to question America's moral values, sense of justice, and purposes. Nor can it be surprising that, effectively by the end of the 1960s and almost completely by the early 1970s, through the disillusionment of Vietnam and Watergate, the American hero, along with American idealism, had disappeared. The members of the "me generation" of the 1980s were too self-absorbed to worry about heroes, except perhaps those who successfully matched their views of money and self-interestedness. Who better to do that, to become American heroes in the 1980s, than celebrities: sports and entertainment stars, "Material Girls," and people featured on "Lifestyles of the Rich and Famous?" Who better than the flamboyantly wealthy?

Other social changes also affected American society and contributed to the disappearance of the American hero. One such change was the growing influence and respectability of the social sciences. As suggested earlier, both sociology and psychology achieved new attention and occasionally intense consideration beginning in the postwar era. That attention and consideration permitted, among other things, an "understanding" of the actions of people that did not exist earlier. Science generally—including here the social sciences—attempts, among other things, to explain the mystical. But mystery is a part of heroic existence; explaining the hero can only destroy him.

In today's psychological world the heroic are often regarded as merely foolhardy, neurotic, or confused. One should have a passion if one is to be a hero, but in psychological terms, an intense belief may simply reflect an unfulfilled need, or be some type of sublimation, or indicate that the hero falls under the general, all-purpose term and label "maladjusted." The hero it seems is someone who needs a few hours of intense counseling. Certainly Daniel Boorstin is correct: When looked at sociologically and psychologically, qualities once regarded as heroic disappear within "a blur of environmental influences and internal maladjustments."[7]

Finally, it might be mentioned that along with the other factors noted here, revisionist history (often in conjunction with ethnic consciousness) has harmed the American hero. Revisionism may be justified, but, as will be considered below, it has diminished the status of past American heroes, of traditional American heroes. And it has helped to limit the creation of new heroes.

Chapter 11

Values

INTRODUCTION

Among the most explicit statements of American values is that given by Robin Williams, Jr., who cites fifteen that most significantly reflect Americans' goals and motives. These values include various moral judgments, physical comforts, and political philosophies, and are basic to American culture. That is, they apply by and large to the nation as a whole and have been consistent over the years, even if some have in theory and in practice occasionally contradicted others. In a sense, Williams explains the values that Americans use to define themselves. The concern here is considerably more modest: to note a limited and vanishing number of values that people in the United States have traditionally recognized as part of an American hero's makeup. That is, the concern here is to identify several specific values that Americans have traditionally regarded as reflected within their heroes and to explain why those values no longer seem to mean very much to Americans.[1]

American heroes are embodiments of specific values because a nation's values represent a nation's ideals. American heroes "personify traits which Americans have always admired." These include "courage, self-reliance, and physical prowess," among others. Of course, values change as society does. As one obvious example, physical prowess is less valued today than in the past, although it is still admired. Nonetheless, some of the values manifested in American heroes have remained a part of the American ideal. In addition to courage and self-reliance, they include trust rather than cynicism, a sense of fairness, sacrifice for a noble cause, loyalty to an ideal and a sense of integrity, and an acceptance of responsibility. At the present time, and for a while now, these are rarely found in American society. Some have vanished completely from the culture.[2]

ON TRUST AND CYNICISM

Most of these social values began to lose their effectiveness within the United States at the end of the Second World War, although the most dramatic reductions in their influence occurred from the mid-1960s through the mid-1970s. Most obviously, critical changes in the attitudes and actions of Americans during the Vietnam/Watergate era permanently altered the character of American values. This point is especially clear when these attitudes and actions are compared with similar attitudes and actions Americans manifested during World War II.

In the Second World War, for example, there was a relatively equitable distribution of people in the services in terms of class. "In World War II everybody who was fit went." Even if they didn't go happily—and most didn't—they went willingly. Politicians and movie stars, professional athletes and celebrities all served in the military.[3]

This was not the case in Vietnam. A disproportionate number of American casualties there were sons of America's poor families. College students were exempt from the draft until 1972, and by the time they finished school they had learned enough about the draft to be able to beat it. Attitudes and actions had changed. Students adhered to "a cops and robbers view of national obligation." But it wasn't only college students who felt this way. For this generation, "avoiding Vietnam became a . . . preoccupation." Baskir and Strauss point to a survey indicating that perhaps 60 percent of those men eligible for the draft who weren't in combat "took . . . steps" to that end, that is, to ensure that they wouldn't be in combat. Another survey found that a majority of Americans regarded those who went to Vietnam "as suckers."[4]

As Vietnam altered our view of contributing to and sacrificing for the nation, Watergate completed the picture. Watergate verified that trust placed in the government was trust that was misplaced. Revelations of the inner workings of the Nixon administration proved the impossible: at the highest levels of government there was bribery and deception, lying and willful—even malicious—abuse of power. The president and vice president, the attorney general, and assorted subordinates with power and influence had violated the laws of the land. A key legacy of the Watergate relevations is that in the ensuing decades and very likely for many decades to come, the trust necessary for politicians to do their job was not and will not be forthcoming from the American people, a point considered earlier. Numerous polls indicate that twenty years after the Watergate scandal public confidence in the integrity of politicians remains low.

It is unfair, however, to regard the conflict in Vietnam and the Watergate affair as the only causes of Americans' lost sense of heroic values. Robert K. Merton, for example, traces that loss back to the immediate post–World War II era. Richard S. Tedlow notes that as early as 1946 Merton had argued "that cynicism about public statements from any source, political or commercial, was pervasive." That cynicism was helped by doubts about Harry S Truman's abilities as president, McCarthyism, and the Korean "Police Action." Things did not change during the Eisenhower years; the country then appeared almost tranquil and Americans seemed determined to maintain the status quo.[5]

With John and Jacqueline Kennedy in the White House, with the world enjoying Pax Americana (except for a minor conflict in little-known and distant Vietnam), with the nation apparently prosperous, all seemed fine in the early 1960s. Idealism managed briefly to replace both cynicism and tranquility among many of the nation's young, and that idealism was accompanied by an optimism that saw every problem as soluble. Charles R. Morris points out that in 1962 Kennedy said "that there were no great ideological issues left." The only problems that remained were "technical [and] . . . administrative," and it was inconceivable that America could not solve them.[6]

Kennedy's assassination helped put an end to both the idealism and the optimism. Cynicism returned to the United States and continued throughout the later Johnson years and into the Watergate era, by which time it was pretty much a fact of American life. Through the tenure of Presidents Ford and Carter, and the "me generation" of the 1980s and beyond, it has remained intact. Ronald Reagan and George Bush were, perhaps, calming influences through the 1980s, much as President Eisenhower had been a calming influence in the 1950s. But calm doesn't mean trust, and every once in a while a new scandal comes along—"Irangate," the "S & L Scandal," and the "Whitewater Controversy"—to assure that our cynicism does not fade away. As of this writing, President Clinton cannot claim to have diminished America's sense of cynicism.

Leo Gurko has noted that "the deflation of the hero has marched with the deflationary times." As the trust and the optimism of the nation faded from the time of the post–World War II years, so did the nation's ability to produce heroes. Trust and optimism are necessary for the existence of a hero if for no other reasons than mistrust and cynicism cannot be conjoined with admiration for a hero. We live in a cynical time, in a deflationary time, and consequently we live in a time without heroes.[7]

One consequence of this cynicism was the acceptance of moral relativism. Beginning ironically enough during the 1950s, the age of conformity, Americans began to feel that they should not impose their views on others. Richard S. Tedlow notes that "pollsters at the end of the 1950s were finding the belief widespread that the individual did not feel it was his place to condemn. Moral relativism, it seemed, rather than adherence to . . . moral absolutism, was the rule." And moral relativism has remained a significant value within American society for the past several decades.[8]

In James Grady's *Six Days of the Condor*, a novel published in the 1970s, two men who work for the CIA are chatting. The younger of the two asks the older man, who began his career with the forerunner of the CIA, the Office of Strategic Services (the OSS of World War II), if he misses the old days. The older man replies that he misses the clarity of the old days. There once was a certainty as to who were the good guys and who were the bad guys. Moral relativism works to eradicate that distinction. Neal Gabler argues that "moral relativism challenges the predicates of our moral system. It says any behavior is all right, as long as there is some culture or subculture that permits it." [9]

That is why moral relativism demeans the hero. Heroes serve causes, and one cannot be a hero, one cannot serve a cause, if the cause of each is morally equal to the causes of everyone else. If moral relativism is the social norm, if all causes are equally regarded, the hero is superfluous at best and an ideologue at worst. He is transformed from a man of purpose and integrity to a myopically driven egoist who unjustly regards his views as superior to all others.

Moral relativism, when carried to an extreme, allows that all views are equal. In consequence, sacrifice for an ideal, a hero's work, is transformed into fool's work. This is not a perspective conducive to producing heroes.

ON WINNING AND FAIRNESS

Vince Lombardi created a slogan that in a relatively short period of time came to represent all things to all people in America: Winning isn't everything, it's the only thing. America adopted that slogan, took that idea to heart.

Of course the idea of winning being crucial to Americans is not new. Fawcett and Thomas point out that "self-confidence is meant to run in the American blood. However daunting the obstacle, Americans would roll up their sleeves to shove it out of the way. Where else, the historian Eric Goldman has asked, would people joke: 'The difficult we do immediately. The impossible takes a little longer.'" Fawcett and Thomas also suggest that there is a competitive edge here, that "doing well means doing better— either than others or than one's own past. Winning is an American passion."[10]

The American attitude toward winning has traditionally meant that the hero had the courage, the intelligence, the imagination to win. It meant that the hero was willing to endure the sacrifices necessary to win. It also meant that the hero won fairly, that there were rules to be followed, and that the hero did in fact follow the rules.

But the rules no longer seem to mean very much. When the idea that winning is the only thing takes hold, the means used to win becomes a secondary matter. Any action that provides success is ipso facto a success and socially acceptable, even if not necessarily ethical or even legal. In business "the man to be admired was the smart operator and dealer who handled himself well," an attitude that is hardly surprising in a highly competitive world espousing a view that winning is the only thing. Nor could it be surprising that with very little effort this view has been extended beyond the world of business. In time "there was no clear boundary between the social world of the smart operator and the wider society." Given all of this, the excesses and abuses of the 1980s and beyond were almost to be expected. The criterion that was established—and it was established well before the 1980s—was that the victory, not the means to the victory, was what counted. Sports commentators are forever reminding their audiences, who really don't need reminding, that the record books don't say how, they just say how much.[11]

It is easy to blame an ideology of "victory by any means" on the excessive financial rewards that are routinely a part of victory today, and of course the financial rewards do play a part in the importance of achieving one's goals regardless of the means. If a single victory in whatever contest one enters ensures the victor considerable wealth, a life of luxury, it cannot be surprising that the goal becomes all.

But this view extends beyond the financial rewards accompanying victory. The victory itself has become so important that people are prepared to sacrifice all for it, often without concern for the accompanying rewards of that victory or for the accompanying penalties. James M. Jarvis, a sports psychologist offers an example. He notes the result of a survey reported in *Sports Illustrated*: More than half of the Olympic try-outs would be willing to take a drug that ensured a gold medal even if taking the drug would kill them. Jarvis points out that "winning has become so overvalued in our society that some athletes and coaches will do anything to capture victory."[12]

This desire—obsession—with winning is not at all limited to the field of amateur or professional sports. Alfie Kohn is correct in noting that "the preoccupation with being No. 1 suffuses our classrooms . . . our work places, playing fields and families." Reasonably enough, given this attitude toward winning, the rules regarding the methods of achieving the goal have dimmed in importance where they haven't vanished completely. Studies show that a considerable number of high school and college students have few qualms about stealing, lying to get a job, cheating on examinations, and taking financial aid with little thought of paying it back.[13]

The idealistic notion of winning fairly (because to win any other way is not really winning) has been a traditional characteristic of the hero. But this sense of idealism, this form of integrity, seems to have disappeared in the United States. Stephen Toulmin puts it this way: "In America these days, idealism is out of fashion, even in bad taste."[14] In consequence, rules of fairness no longer seem to be considerations in the struggle for victory. Consider three areas of American culture that currently provide us with our celebrity-heroes: movies, sports, and television.

Movies: Butch Cassidy is up against Harvey Logan, who was a man truly to be feared. After refusing to engage in a gun fight with Logan, Butch is forced to face him in a knife fight. But first he wants to talk about the rules of the fight. The idea is absurd to Logan; there aren't any rules in a knife fight and he says so. Just as Logan ends his comments, Butch "delivers the most aesthetically exquisite kick in the balls in the history of the Modern American Cinema." Logan crumbles and Butch knocks him out and is safe. The hero has won. [15]

Like Butch, Indiana Jones is in some difficulty. He is facing a huge and brutal-looking Arab who is armed with a large scimitar. Things don't look good at all. Jones is stuck for a moment and then he casually reaches to his holster, pulls out his revolver, and kills the Arab with one shot. Indiana is safe. The hero has won again.

Audiences responded to the scenes described above in pretty much the same way: a bit of shock and perhaps relief and then laughter. The hero had outwitted the bad guy even if he couldn't outfight him. But he didn't win fairly.

Again, Americans are a pragmatic people, but pragmatic or not, fairness used to count. There used to be rules of behavior, even in fights, even if the odds were against you, even if it meant sacrifice. In fact, the odds were supposed to be against the hero; he was supposed to make sacrifices in order to win fairly.

Would John Wayne have kicked a bigger opponent in the balls? Not the Duke, not on your life. Would the Lone Ranger have shot an unarmed man, or a man without a firearm? Would Shane or Matt Dillon? It would never happen. There was a time in America when at least the fictional hero fought fairly, even if he lost. Today that would be at best a sign of ingenuousness and at worst a sign of stupidity. There was a time when kicking was called fighting dirty. Now it's called karate. Even for fictional-ized heroes, when idealism went "out of fashion" so did obeying the rules when it was not convenient to do so. If this is so for fictional heroes, it is reasonable to expect the same from living ones.

Sports: On October 6, 1990, the University of Colorado was playing Missouri in a difficult football game. In the last quarter Colorado managed to get the ball over the goal; they won the game 33 to 31. But they didn't win, not really, because the referee had made a mistake and allowed them an extra down. Colorado had scored the winning touchdown on a fifth-down play. The civil thing to do, the sportsman-like thing to do, the right thing to do would have been for the Colorado team to discount the score. They didn't; the score stood and they won. The Colorado coach flatly refused to take the points off the scoreboard. Perhaps most bizarre of all, the National Collegiate Athletic Association refused to alter the score and give the game to Missouri. Winning fairly used to count, but not anymore. Fairness is one of the qualities of the hero.

Television: Thanks to the movie *Quiz Show*, many people today are generally familiar with the story: In 1959, Charles Van Doren was some-thing of an American hero—and an intellectual hero at that. He was a successful contestant on the immensely popular television quiz show "Twenty-One." Bright and articulate, handsome and personable, the young Columbia University instructor became "the new all-American boy," accord-ing to several magazines, "and to millions [of people] he was that indeed."[16]

The show was also a winner. It managed to maintain audience suspense by such devices as turning off the air conditioner in the booths in which the contestants were placed so that they were sure to perspire. After selecting an area of expertise and after correctly answering some relatively simple questions, the contestant would return each week to answer increasingly difficult ones. The home audience that regularly watched the show didn't like to see contestants lose, especially likable contestants. And Van Doren was likable. Hence, a dilemma. If a personable contestant lost, the public's reaction might be negative, clearly not a good thing for either the show's popularity or its effectiveness as a mechanism for selling the sponsor's products. But as the questions got harder and harder, the probability of a contestant answering a question incorrectly increased. There is, after all, only so much knowledge that an individual can retain.

The solution to the dilemma was to offer kindly assistance to appropriate contestants, Van Doren among them. The contestants were given books to study to help in preparation for the following week's questions, all reasonable and above board. Less reasonable and less above board was the innovation of letting the contestants know that some pages in these books were considerably more important than other pages, of pointing out the important pages, and of simply giving the contestants the answers.

In August 1958, a defeated and disgruntled contestant, Herbert Stempel, revealed the subterfuge. Initially Van Doren, who had won $129,000 on the show, adamantly denied that he had done anything wrong. Eventually, of course, it all came out. There were vociferous and possibly heart-felt apologies from the show's producers and a lot of commentary about American values and morals.[17]

The movie *Quiz Show* took several liberties with the truth in telling the story of the scandal. Perhaps the biggest liberty—and surely the most interesting point here—was in showing the public response to the scandal in general and to Van Doren in particular. The movie portrayed the public as disillusioned and Van Doren as tormented because of his transgressions. In fact both the show and the "all-American boy" were quickly forgiven by the public. Indeed, most people sympathized with Van Doren. Moreover, a great many of the people who were questioned said that they'd have done the same thing. Newspaper editorials "treated [Van Doren] extraordinarily gently." Clearly a new attitude toward winning had become a part of America's values.[18]

It hardly has to be noted that heroes win fairly or not at all; they don't cheat. Or at least they never did. (Or if they did cheat they were smart enough not to get caught.) As foolish as it sounds today, heroes used to have something called integrity; if any still exists it is diminishing rapidly. The lack of integrity so apparent in the United States these past decades, Americans' reluctance to follow rules they deem inconvenient, may be a natural consequence of the excessive rewards offered to victors these days, but that's not the whole story. More to the point is the flip side of Vince Lombardi's commentary: if winning is the only thing, then the method we use to win isn't anything.

CAUSES, LOYALTY, AND INTEGRITY

Heroes fight for causes, noble ones that they and the people who cheer them on care for deeply. Heroes sacrifice, do battle, and take risks for reasons beyond just winning, for reasons beyond their own personal gain. At least they used to. Today avarice, vindictiveness, and weakness are valid reasons for sacrifice, battle, and risks. Consider one of the most intriguing of pursuits, spying, and the reasons for doing so. Consider, too, those who spied against the United States and for the Soviet Union.

It has been suggested that "a generation or so ago, the spies who served the Soviet Union were uniformly sympathizers with the Russian Revolution." People in the past, that is, spied because of the belief that they were working to make the world a better place. Those beliefs were misplaced and the people naive, but the spies intended that the end result of their actions was a general good. They worked not for self-interest but for a higher purpose.[19]

Presumably, a generation ago spies who served the United States worked for the same reason, a belief in a cause, noble and higher in purpose than personal gain or satisfaction. Things changed in the later years of the post–World-War II era. Francis Gary Powers was the first of the well-publicized entrepreneur/spies of the Cold War era. Powers didn't fly for the United States, he was merely employed by the United States. Powers flew for money, and he made a lot of it—$30,000 a year, a considerable wage in the late 1950s. (Before flying for the CIA his and his wife's combined income was some $8,400 a year.) But even if he spied for profit, at least Powers worked for his government and not against it.[20]

Spying has never been a particularly noble profession. Nathan Hale, who remains America's most famous spy and who was hanged by the British during the Revolution, was celebrated less for his activities than for his patriotism and his courage in the face of death. But suppose it turned out that Hale had been paid to spy, that he hadn't acted for the good of the nation but for the good of his bank account. It is safe to say that this would have changed our view of him. The cause for an action is significant. An action motivated by patriotism is not the same as an action motivated by personal gain even if the actions are identical.

With some few exceptions, spies in the early years of the Cold War were concerned with causes. When, for example, Kim Philby, Guy Burgess, and Donald MacClean gave secrets to the Soviet Union, no matter how ill-advised their actions, they were undertaken with the intention of bettering the world; that purpose was the driving force of their actions. Similarly, assuming for the sake of argument that Julius and Ethel Rosenberg were spies for the USSR, they acted not for profit but because they believed that the world would be a better place for their action.[21]

There surely are spies working today who act for selfless motives, for country and honor. But at least those spies of recent decades who were caught did not spy for idealistic purposes or for noble causes, but for profit or out of personal anger at the system or because of pique or for kicks. J. Anthony Lukas refers to them as "a banal new generation of traitors." Surely he is correct; they are banal. And some are wealthy. John Walker, a former Birchite, spied for the Soviet Union for seventeen years. "By the time the FBI caught up with him . . . [Walker] had earned something like $750,000, a $44,000 annual average." At the same time, "Jerry Whitworth, Walker's most serviceable recruit, made $332,000 in ten years." It is reasonable to suspect, then, that when John Walker and his associates spied for the Soviet Union and against the United States, it was not for ideological reasons.[22]

There have been numerous others, people who committed treason for money. Perhaps the most infamous is Aldrich Hazen Ames, an American employed by the Central Intelligence Agency (CIA). Ames was a spy for the Soviet Union, a terribly effective one, who betrayed at least a dozen of America's "best secret agents working . . . within the Soviet Union and the Soviet bloc during the 1980's." The consequences of Ames's actions were the deaths of at least some of those agents. And there can be no doubt as to why Ames did what he did: in his own words, "money—money was . . . the motivation." Others spied for personal, petty reasons. Edward Lee Howard, for example, who spied for the Soviet Union, had a problem with liquor and petty theft and was angry because he was fired from the CIA. He did not spy for noble reasons but because of pique. And if the accusations are true, Felix Bloch, a former CIA agent, spied for the Soviet Union because he was angered at being passed over for promotion. If he did spy—he was dismissed from the CIA but no formal charges were brought against him—it was not because of ideology.[23]

If a requirement for being considered a hero is to serve a cause, preferably a noble cause as Nathan Hale had, then the point here is not just that contemporary spies cannot qualify as heroes. The point here is that they can serve as metaphors explaining why the American hero does not exist. Spies today, at least the ones noted above, are businessmen who sell out their country for money and a flashier life-style or because of petty slights, real or imagined. They risk the security of their nation as well as their lives, careers, families, homes, and integrity for so very little.

Implicit in the discussions of spies is the issue of loyalty to one's country. But loyalty takes a variety of forms and is directed toward a variety of people, ideas, and things. Loyalty—to a nation, a cause, an individual, or a group—is fundamental to the makeup of the hero. That is why a willingness to sacrifice oneself for a cause is part of the heroic makeup. But that sort of loyalty seems nonexistent today. Recall that the Watergate scandal that destroyed Richard M. Nixon's presidency might never have reached the level it did had not James McCord, initially, and John Dean III, subsequently, revealed what they knew about the affair.

It may have been naive of Richard Nixon to expect his subordinates to accept full responsibility for the Watergate affair and sacrifice themselves for him, but then again it may not have been naive of him. Nixon may simply have been old-fashioned; there was a time in American history when one did sacrifice one's own interests for those of one's superior.

Finally, consider what is perhaps an odd illustration: loyalty within organized crime. For years the federal authorities had a nearly impossible time limiting the activities of organized crime. The reason was the tradition of *omerta*, the code of silence, but that code no longer seems to be in effect. In 1962 Joseph Valachi became the first member of organized crime to testify about organized crime. Valachi spoke before a Senate investigating committee, revealing the inner workings of what became known—due to Valachi's testimony—as La Cosa Nostra.

Valachi may have been the first member of La Cosa Nostra to betray the code of *omerta*, but he surely wasn't the last. A key figure in organized crime, John Gotti, the "Teflon Don," was convicted of thirteen charges, including murder and racketeering. He was convicted in large part because of the testimony of a trusted associate, Salvatore Gravano. Nor was Gravano the only recent member of organized crime to reveal what he knew to the government and thereby to see several of his former associates arrested and himself to get a more palatable arrangement from the government in exchange for his testimony. The loyalty of members of organized crime families to those families, once beyond question, has dissipated.[24]

Of course to some people both McCord and Dean—and perhaps Gravano, although not at all Ames—may be considered to be heroic in their actions if not heroes themselves, and perhaps they are. This is not the place to examine the ethics of McCord or Dean, Valachi or Gravano. It is the place to point out that loyalty, once a prerequisite for the hero, is at best in limited evidence these days, and that as the value of loyalty has dimmed in recent years, so has the aura surrounding the hero.

RESPONSIBILITY

One more change in American values and its effect on the American hero should be considered here: the virtual disappearance of individual responsibility and the growth of what some have called "The New Culture of Victimization." It seems today as if no one is to blame for anything, that nothing today is anyone's fault. So pervasive is this "New Culture" that a recent television show was devoted to a single question: "Are We a Country of Victims?" The answer, to some, is yes. More than that, we celebrate victims; indeed, "only the victim shall be the hero."[25]

Everything from excessive shopping and drug use and even murder are the responsibility of someone else or something else. They are never the responsibility of the shopper, drug user, or murderer. Illness in one form or another appears everywhere and some take exotic forms. People who spend too much money are victims of "compulsive buying." Drug users—just about all of them but especially the famous ones, celebrity-heroes manqué—are victims of compulsions or, failing that excuse, victims of pressures of their position and deserve sympathy. If you kill someone it's because you were abused or misunderstood or perhaps because you ate a cream-filled dessert. Lack of self-esteem is a current reason for claiming that one is a victim, that one is helpless, that one cannot accomplish anything. One could, of course, consider the logic of Harold W. Stevenson: "Meaningful self-evaluation and positive self-esteem are usually the result, not antecedents, of accomplishment." But that would diminish the concept of victimization, and we can't have that. [26]

If you brutally beat someone, if you sexually harass someone, if you drink too much, eat too much, smoke too much, or do anything that you're unhappy about, it's always someone else's fault. If you can't find an individual to fault you are still not to blame. Perhaps you are the victim of a psychological problem, a mental illness, and none of us is responsible for being sick.

The notorious Kim Philby was a spy because of a mental disorder, schizophrenia, although as Ron Rosenbaum points out, "schizophrenia doesn't really explain Philby so much as excuse him." And that of course is the point. No matter the action, there is an excuse, not responsibility. Even an inability to write well is not one's responsibility but a mental disorder. Stuart A. Kirk and Herb Kutchins point out that Code 315.2 of the *Diagnostic and Statistic Manual of Mental Disorders* cites a "Disorder of Written Expression."

Of course if you don't suffer from victimization because of an emotional disorder (not of your own making), then perhaps society is to blame. Wendy Kaminer's *I'm Dysfunctional, You're Dysfunctional*, Alan Dershowitz's *The Abuse Excuse*, and Charles J. Sykes's *A Nation of Victims*, document this current trend, one that has been noted by George F. Will, Mike Royko, and almost everyone else who observes the American scene. Their point is we've all learned that we're really innocent of the consequences of our actions, their point is that we've all discovered that we're just victims of previous or current injustices or of illnesses or of society or of anything else that subverts our own responsibilities for our actions. Their point is that we no longer take responsibility for what we do. Their point is that we should. [27]

Quite obviously, the current attention to victimization is beneficial and significant to those who are truly victims. There is now a long overdue appreciation of the extent and consequences of child abuse, spouse abuse, and abuse of the elderly. These had been either ignored or hidden or considered merely "domestic squabbles" in the past. No one would argue that these issues should be ignored; no one can argue that there aren't real victims. But when everybody becomes a victim, when people are no longer responsible for their actions, the plight of the true victim is reduced to a cliché, a triviality. True victims may be seen as people just looking for sympathy or seeking excuses for their troubles. True victims may be regarded with contempt and not offered the help they deserve.

Because victimization has become an ideology, one that protects people from taking responsibility for their actions, it has demeaned the hero. Any assertion of heroic activity includes an assertion of responsibility for that action. If the hero fails he does not seek to blame others nor seek to discover excuses for his failures. For example, General Eisenhower had two messages in his pocket during D-Day, the invasion of Normandy. The outcome of the invasion would determine which message he transmitted to the world. The first proclaimed that the operation was a success; fortunately that was the one that was sent. The second acknowledged the failure of the mission. What is of consequence here is that in the second message Eisenhower accepted full responsibility for the failure. The "fault," Eisenhower said, was "mine and mine alone." He did not fault inept soldiers, weapons, or field commanders; he did not blame the weather, the tides, or the equipment. He took responsibility for his decisions. He acted heroically; it is known that he acted heroically, and those are two reasons he was regarded as a hero.

CONCLUSION

The lack of reverence for once admired institutions, the intensive cynicism that is directed toward officials, the reluctance on the part of Americans to trust those in power have all harmed the American hero. These are a part of the changed values of the nation, most especially, perhaps, the acceptance of a winning-is-all view. That view dispels the notion that adherence to the rules that permit social life to function and that make heroes possible is required. This attitude resulted from and contributed to extreme rewards, which in turn contributed to diminished fairness in contests, weakened loyalties, and failure of individual responsibility. Fairness, loyalty, and responsibility, however, are inherent in the makeup of the American hero. Or at least they were in the past.

Chapter 12

Bureaucracy, Rationality, and the American Hero

Some of the effects of bureaucracies on the existence of the American hero have already been considered. The titans of business, individualists such as Ford and Rockefeller and Carnegie, have vanished in a world of "other-directed" people. So, too, has the fact, and to a large extent even the concept, of the self-made man disappeared in a society dominated by organization men.

Europeans have often been confused by Americans boasting about having achieved wealth and status despite—because of?—an impoverished childhood. Americans took pride in the fact that without a formal education, economic advantages, or "connections," they were able to succeed. Americans adored the "self-made man." Europeans, on the other hand, regarded as absurd the idea that an individual entrepreneur was admirable, that he might be considered a hero. But it wasn't an absurd idea in the United States of the past, and it still isn't today, not really. It's just an impossible idea, a fantasy and generally recognized as such. The reason is the bureaucratization of America.

Bureaucracies develop a life and a power of their own, which is not in and of itself a bad thing. However, bureaucracies can and often do develop to the point where individuality becomes their victims. Thus, Ronald Gross and Paul Osterman point out that bureaucracies limit behavior, and while "limiting behavior is not in itself bad . . . the limitations can be carried to such an extreme that individuality is suppressed. This is exactly the effect of life in a large bureaucracy." And this is exactly the effect of the bureaucratization of America.[1]

One consequence of bureaucratized American society is the destruction not merely of the individual American entrepreneur, but of American individuality generally. Another consequence is the passing of the self-made man and the romantic (if fanciful) idealization of what and who he is. Because the individuality of those who work in bureaucracies "is suppressed," and because more and more Americans are "employed by bureaucracies, both public and private," the potential of the self-made individual has effectively vanished.[2]

Traditionally both American politics and America's economic system celebrated the individual; the "heroic archetype" was "the self-interested go-getter." But today that archetype is disparaged. Although we still "cling to [our] belief in the primacy of the individual" and to the values manifested by individuality, such as deferred gratification and hard work, these beliefs and values really don't mean too much in contemporary society. Further, no values parallel to those manifested in individualism have "arisen to fill the gap" created when individualism no longer was admired in America. The individual has been replaced by the group, and in that process romanticism has been replaced by rationality. None of this is in itself bad, for clearly rationalism and group efforts have produced marvelous benefits for society. Yet both have also diminished the existence of the American hero, the quintessential individual.[3]

David M. Potter notes that "individualism" is among our "sacred terms," and that Americans have often "placed an immense premium on the individualistic values." These values have taken several forms here. As suggested, one of these is the self-made man, the financial success who starts with nothing and achieves great wealth, the person who works hard and patiently awaits the fruits of that work. A second form is the individualism in which one is able to take care of oneself. This doesn't imply financial achievement; it suggests the rugged individualist, the free spirit embodied in the mountain man. These people did not acquire wealth, but they demonstrated self-reliance, defiance, and perhaps eccentricity. We have also honored, on occasion and if the circumstances and the fields of endeavor were correct, nonconformists. To a large degree the anti-hero can be understood in this light. Another possible interpretation of "individualism" is offered up by de Tocqueville, who coined the term in the 1830s. By individualism he meant a form of "self-withdrawal," a way in which people close in upon themselves. That is not, however, the standard American view of the term.[4]

Yet individualism, as David Riesman has noted, "depends on historical setting." Warren I. Susman agrees that "individualism can exist only if the culture permits it," if it has "necessary function within the structure of the culture itself." As the setting—the society—changes, then so does the definition of what we mean by "individualism" and so does the need for individualism. Today in the United States "individualism" means fitting in. Ironically, individualism now and for some time in the past, has come to mean conformity; individualism now means being a team player; individualism means not being an individual. Potter puts it this way: "individualism is not justified if it serves only individuals." [5]

The reason for this is that individualism is no longer necessary or even wanted in the American today. Stuart Samuels is clearly correct in arguing that due to structural changes throughout the society, "the . . . rugged individualist" is no longer the accepted American model, the man to emulate; the new American model is the man who works in the "world of the group—[in] big universities, big suburbs, big business, and big media." If one is to succeed in a big organization, in a university or business, one has to be able to fit in. And since the growth of the suburbs, one even has to fit into the area in which one lives. Some communities limit the color one may choose to paint one's house; some prohibit parking one's car in one's own driveway; others prohibit keeping the garage door open unnecessarily. It is an odd paradox that, in contrast to the moral relativism so prevalent today wherein we tolerate a wide range of individual opinions on ethical matters, in organizations and in our communities we are often reluctant to tolerate any individuality at all.[6]

Starting in the 1950s and continuing to the present, "conformism . . . replaced individuality as the principle ingredient for success." One had to be a part of a team and be accepted by the team. To succeed, that is, one knew that acceptance was the goal to be sought, and to reach that goal one "played the game." Playing the game meant adjusting to a new culture. While the old culture, the "Puritan-republican, producer-capitalist—demanded something called 'character' . . . the new culture insisted on 'personality.'" The difference is that " 'character' . . . stressed moral qualities" while " 'personality' . . . emphasized being liked and admired." The former implies probity and integrity, individual characteristics; the latter implies personality and charm, group characteristics.[7]

The logical consequence of this was a conflict between a need for individual recognition and the importance of conforming to the group. In the end, conformity won. People increasingly "submerged themselves into some larger mass." And because "group work and group think were the ideals," a new attitude developed: "Individual acts of heroism were suspect." Consequently, the nonconformist who spurns "normal" society and the gutsy entrepreneur who gambles all to make his fortune are looked upon with some skepticism and barely tolerated. The individual is now to be sacrificed to the social good.[8]

The idea of the hero being sacrificed for the good of the group is not new. For example, with the development of the polis in ancient Greece, the Homeric hero "whose primary needs were for courage and skill in battle" was altered. M. I. Finley points out that "it was necessary to tame the hero in order that the community might grow." But that is not the same thing as eliminating the individualism of the hero in the name of bureaucratic conformity. In the first instance the hero is controlled for the good of the community; in the second he is not allowed to exist.[9]

The reason that there is a difference between controlling the hero for the good of the community and destroying the individuality of the hero in the name of conformity is that the essence of the hero is individual responsibility. When bureaucratic conformity prevents the existence of the individual, it isn't just the individual who disappears. Individual responsibility disappears as well, a point considered earlier.

To some historians individual responsibility vanished years ago. Paul Johnson argues that "the nineteenth century saw the climax of the philosophy of personal responsibility—the notion that each of us is individually accountable for our actions—which was the joint heritage of Judeo-Christianity and the classical world." But Johnson exaggerates a bit, for surely there was a willingness to accept individual responsibility in this century, even in the last half of this century.[10]

When Edward R. Murrow devoted his television show to an attack on McCarthyism he knew what he was doing, and he took responsibility for his actions: "I don't know whether we'll get away with this one or not. . . . things will never be the same around here after tonight." Surely Martin Luther King, Jr., knew what he was doing when he went to jail. "The laws [he] violated were either unjust laws—they applied only to a minority or they were undemocratically passed—or proper laws being applied unjustly . . . and King was willing to accept whatever penalty was imposed."[11]

Murrow's willingness to accept the consequences of his actions and King's willingness to sacrifice himself for a valued cause exemplify the critical difference between the hero and the nonhero, the noble deed and the publicity stunt. Today we lack the hero and the noble deed, but we have in excess the nonhero and the publicity stunt.

This was seen during the riots of the 1960s as well as in more recent demonstrations of civil unrest. The first thing the leaders of the protestors during the 1960s asked for was amnesty, a full and unconditional pardon for their actions. Whether the causes and methods of those various protests were just may be subject to debate. What is not subject to debate is that, unlike, say, the actions of Martin Luther King, Jr., their protests and sacrifices seemed to be contingent upon self-preservation. This condition, the concern first with assurances of escape of liability rather than the purpose of the action taken, reflected the new bureaucratic tradition in America: a tradition of the nonheroic, of a lack of individual responsibility for one's actions, of the conformist culture of American society.

It should be noted that the idea of conformity is not entirely a consequence of the post–World War II era. In 1936 Dale Carnegie published a book stressing that "success is measured by how well one fits in, how well one is liked by others, how well others respond to the roles one is playing." The book was more prescient than one might then have imagined; this was, after all, a time in the United States when the individualist was still admired. Among other things, Carnegie seemed to be pointing out that the future would include "a strange kind of individualism for individualistic America."[12]

The point of it all, of course, is that "our ideal is increasingly smooth absorption into the group rather than self-realization in the old-fashioned, strong-minded, don't-give-a-damn-sense." The logical question is: "Where does the great man fit into our homogenized society?" The logical answer to the question is that he doesn't fit in, not anymore.[13]

Dixon Wecter has argued that "hero-worship . . . tends to the heart rather than the head," which is a variation on Ralph Waldo Emerson's comment that heroism is always right because it "feels and never reasons." If Wecter and Emerson are correct, the loss of individual heroism in the West was predictable. A century ago Max Weber pointed out that western society was becoming increasingly rational. Whether for good or ill—Weber thought the latter—people's relationships within western societies had become the sort that sociologists call secondary; they are based in the main upon rational calculation, not feelings. But it is unlikely that even Weber, prescient though he certainly was, could have understood the degree to which rationality would eventually dominate western industrial society.[14]

One consequence of the rationality of modern society is the diminishing romanticism of modern society, for rationality and romanticism are, at best, antithetical concepts. The romantic has diminished at a rapid rate precisely because the rational has ascended at a rapid rate. As the reasoned forces of analyses increase, the romantic notions of idealism vanish along with the hero. This is only logical; after all, romance is one of the requirements for the hero.

Heroes traditionally "were superior to the ordinary man and isolated in lonely grandeur by their extraordinary powers." This superiority and grandeur were among the elements that made up the hero. The hero vanished when his romanticized image disappeared into explanations of actions by science, especially by the social sciences of psychology and sociology, as has been discussed, and into the ever probing eye of the mass media, which will be discussed. But sociology and psychology—science generally—are by-products of rationality. The point to emphasize, then, is that rationality, not scientific explanation nor probings by television cameras, is one of the main contributers to the demise of the American hero.[15]

When Max Weber argued that western society was becoming increasingly rational—and no society is more western or rational than the United States—he meant, *inner alia*, that we seek a logical explanation for everything. We examine everything. We want to know how and why things work. This is all fine, of course; it is the basis of modern science. It is the reason we have the technology of heart transplants and why we can send messages around the world in seconds. This tendency toward rationality—to question, examine, and test everything—and results of this tendency have immeasurably improved our lives.

But a hero cannot bear close examination. A hero needs to have at least a portion of his being shrouded in mystery; there has to be a certain aura of romanticism surrounding the hero. A hero is only a man; today he is a man whose "lonely grandeur" would be examined until it was neither lonely nor grand, neither mysterious nor romantic.

There has always been a battle between romantic idealism and scientific inquiry. The first wants to keep the magic of the unknown, the excitement of the mysterious; the second seeks to explain all that is explicable, to understand each and every aspect of the universe. In the past we could maintain a sense of mystery. Today rationality and its consequences—advanced technology, a desire for understanding and reluctance to accept the idea of the inexplicable—have mitigated against the romantic era necessary for the existence of the hero.

Bureaucracy has helped to destroy the hero in two ways: by demeaning the individual (and attendant individual responsibility) and by substituting analysis for romanticism. Sean O'Faolain has pointed out that for Ernest Hemingway "the only possible hero of our time is the lone wolf." Hemingway was right, of course: the hero is necessarily an individual. But there cannot be a lone wolf when the bureaucracies within the structure, when a rational and nonromantic culture, prevent his existence. How could we have had a hero in the campaign in Somalia when hundreds of photographers were on the beaches there waiting to take pictures of the American invasion? That not only diminished the import of the landing, it demeaned the actions of the men who took part in that invasion. They went from being soldiers to being photo opportunities.[16]

Chapter 13

The Effects of Homogeneity, Heterogeneity, and Population on the American Hero

INTRODUCTION

The more homogeneous a society the more likely the existence of a national hero or, more to the point here, the more heterogeneous a society, the less likely the existence of a national hero. The reason is fairly obvious: in a homogeneous society there is greater possibility of agreement on values and agreement that a single hero represents those values.

America's constantly changing ethnic population helps create conflicting interest groups, and this precludes the universal admiration of a single individual. In a society as heterogeneous as the United States, one group's values may be—indeed, are likely to be—different from those of another group. Consequently, the representative of a group's values, their hero, may be something less than a hero to a second group, and may be considered an enemy by a third group. When groups of people disagree on values and goals, on the purposes the hero is supposed to represent, they necessarily disagree on who is and who is not a hero. The result here is the existence of the local hero and his supplanting of the national hero.

More than this, American society is structured so that a great many contentious, zero-sum arenas exist: that is, one group's gain means that a second group suffers a loss. Consequently, any individual who can ensure gains for a group will be a hero to the members of that group, and a villain to the group that has lost any advantage that it had as a result of his actions. When, as has happened on occasion, there are common goals among all of the groups in the society, the existence of a national hero is facilitated. But that is rarely the case in America today. Today the United States is awash with conflicting and competing groups, and overtly.

HOMOGENEITY AND HETEROGENEITY

It may be true that Americans never "looked the same, spoke the same language, worshipped the same gods and believed the same things." But it is also true that for much of American history the people here behaved as if the United States was a single, unified society with a single (although multifaceted and occasionally contradictory) ideology. That ideology, designed by and created for the white, Anglo-Saxon Protestant Europeans who first settled the land, was accepted throughout the United States as *the* American creed.[1]

There can be little doubt that this ideology existed at the expense of other peoples, of ethnic immigrants who did not fit into the mold already established when they arrived on these shores or, in the case of Native Americans and African Americans, before and while they arrived on these shores, respectively. The groups that immigrated here—the various ethnic groups that made up the United States—struggled to become assimilated within the nation. That meant adopting the values, behavior patterns, and attitudes of the WASP establishment. It also meant adopting the established view of who were and who were not American heroes, and why they were or were not American heroes.

As the sons and grandsons, daughters and granddaughters of those immigrants worked here and raised their families here and fought the nation's battles, they came to feel a part of the fabric of American society. They were not, after all, immigrants struggling to learn the language and the customs of a new nation. They were born here and helped to define and sustain the changing meaning of the nation. The need to accept the older ideology and to be accepted by the older establishment began to fade. So too did the acceptance of the established criteria of the older American hero. One consequence of this is that the "national memory" of American heroes, if that term is acceptable, became fragmented.

If it is true, as Robert Hughes argues, that the American creed was "born of immigration, of the jostling of scores of tribes that become American" and that it exists "to the extent to which [the tribes] can negotiate accommodations with one another," then the American hero exists to the extent that those tribes can agree on a hero. All of this presupposes an agreed-upon culture, but, as Susman notes, a culture itself "presupposes some common ground." For some time now Americans have publicly turned their attention to their differences, to their specific ethnic cultures. In consequence, that common ground is diminishing.[2]

All of this means that one of the causes for the lack of national heroes in the United States today is the increasing fragmentation of American society, the increasing awareness of the heterogeneity that exists within the nation. Because of the continuing ethnic diversity within the United States, it is impossible to find a national hero. We may have a greater number and variety of heroes, but they are necessarily more particularized, that is, more group specific and local. A national hero cannot be found.

From one point of view, American heterogeneity makes the country exciting and different, an interesting mixture of unique groups. "America is a land of fascinating cultural diversity. The *Harvard Encyclopedia* contains accounts of some 125 American ethnic groups, and the list is by no means exhaustive. The *Encyclopedia of American Religions* includes information on nearly 1,200 groups—an unbelievable number. Indeed, it is this *tremendous range of associational groups* that sets America apart from so many other cultures."[3]

America was once by definition white, Protestant, Anglo-Saxon, and its attitudes reflected that definition: middle-class, Republican, middle-aged, New Testament moral. America was by definition patriarchal, monogamous, drug-free, divorce-free, heterosexual, and abstemious, at least overtly. Each of these characteristics has been weakened in recent decades, and the leaders of those who represent members of the groups that support changes in these characteristics are often regarded as heroes to the members of those groups. But they may not be heroes to the members of older, well-established groups or to members of other groups who are competing for a part of the traditional American dream.

Partially this is because the group hero was often among the first of the members of the subgroup to confront the larger society. A clear example here is Malcolm X, who challenged the white establishment and was (and is) a hero to a great many African Americans although not necessarily to white Americans. Similarly, Margaret Sanger, who fought tirelessly for the right of women to elect to use birth control, was a hero to women and a villain to conservative moralists. Can anyone seriously entertain the idea that George Armstrong Custer, who is regarded as a hero to Americans generally, is a hero to Native Americans? Similarly, most Americans celebrate Columbus Day, but some celebrate "Indigenous Peoples' Day." There are now black comic book heroes as well as comic book heroes representing other groups. The point, then, is this: different groups often have different heroes, this trend is increasing, and the chances of America celebrating a national hero is thereby diminished.[4]

Further, while any number of local heroes existed within these various groups and ethnic enclaves, they have produced few, if any, national heroes. America's political leaders were still white, Anglo-Saxon, and Protestant. Thus, Warren I. Susman notes that from the mid-1930s through the mid-1940s "there was one phrase, one sentiment, one special call on the emotions that appeared everywhere in America's popular language: the people." And there was no question as to who the people were, they were the American people and they shared a specific and agreed-upon set of values, values inherited from the country's founders.[5]

But beginning in the 1960s—perhaps due in part to the election of the first, and as yet only, non-Protestant president—there was a question as to whom, exactly, "the people" referred. "The People, Yes!," a slogan used in New York City during the 1960s would now prompt the question, "which people?" This is not the place to discuss the merits of multiculturalism. It is the place to point out one clear consequence of multiculturalism: it makes establishing a national hero virtually impossible. [6]

Still and all, acknowledging that there are ethnic differences in the United States, one can reasonably ask how great these differences are. Regina Markell Morantz points out that "education, mass media, and the increase in leisure time among all social strata have tended to homogenize popular culture and narrow behavioral differences between social groups." In *Cheers*, for example, no one has a Boston accent, and in *Designing Women* there is a limited stress on a Southern accent; in *Dallas* there was no Texas drawl that was noticeable, and the Huxtables on the *Cosby Show* spoke "white" English as opposed to what some linguists have termed "Black English."[7]

There aren't any realistic nationalist movements in the United States. The United States has nothing like the Quebecois in Canada. America may have "Basques in Idaho and Nevada, but no militant separatists campaigning for ETA, 'Land of the Basques and Freedom.'" Except for fringe groups—the Marcus Garvey "Back to Africa" movement of a few generations ago or the white separatists/militia today—no real attempt exists to split the nation on national, ethnic, or any other grounds.[8]

Inter-ethnic disputes and separatist/militia actions ought not to be discounted or minimized. The contrasting reactions of (most) blacks and (most) whites after the jury announced its verdict at the conclusion of the O. J. Simpson trial and the tragic 1995 bombing of the Federal Building in Oklahoma City that took the lives of 169 Americans demonstrate this point, if the point needs demonstrating. However, most separatist movements and interethnic clashes are as yet local and controllable, and they are likely to stay that way. They do not threaten the integrity of the nation. The Civil War was concluded well over a hundred years ago. Significant interethnic differences and the militia movements do, however, indicate the improbability of the United States producing a single hero.[9]

There is an addendum to the contributions of ethnic diversity in the United States towards the disappearance of the contemporary American hero. A "reality therapy" of sorts exists if one supports the idea of ethnic recognitions in America, and a demeaning and divisive revisionist history of sorts exists if one doesn't. Especially, but not exclusively, among Native Americans and African Americans, there have been serious complaints regarding the celebration of various heroes of America's past. For Native Americans perhaps the most villainous of the group of past American heroes is, as suggested earlier, Christopher Columbus. African Americans argue that slave traders and slave owners are celebrated as a matter of course in American history but that black soldiers who helped settle the West are ignored. Mexican Americans, too, have reason to question the celebration of some traditional American heroes, most especially those who defended the Alamo against Antonio López de Santa Anna.[10]

Beyond the question of Columbus, slave traders and owners, the Alamo defenders, and other American heroes who are not heroes to members of specific groups, the questioning of past American heroes by some has led to the questioning of past American heroes by a great number of others, as noted. With some consistency, books, magazine articles, and newspaper articles now critically examine the basis of the celebrations of past heroes, most especially the heroes of the Old West.

And beyond these examinations, revisionism is becoming increasingly nasty. What was once perhaps a demand for recognition of one's ethnic group's contributions to the nation has evolved to the point where the efforts today seem to be only partly directed toward a celebration of one's ethnic heritage and heroes. An equal (or greater) effort seems to be directed toward discrediting as many of America's traditional heroes and myths as possible. This may be good history and important for the recognition of the contributions of various ethnic people to America's development as a nation, but it does not help the nation as a whole. People with political views as diverse as Arthur Schlesinger, Jr., and George F. Will have argued that multiculturalism has at the least a dangerous potential insofar as national unity is concerned. And it should be clear that multiculturalism virtually destroys the possibility of a single American hero. It allows Americans to have heroes in the only two areas in which there is some, but usually limited, ethnic contention: sports and entertainment.[11]

POPULATION

One final comment regarding the effect of the population of the United States on American heroes is warranted: the way the sheer number of Americans has helped diminish our regard for heroes.

The population of the United States increased dramatically after the Second World War. Between 1946 and 1964 more than four million babies were born every year. These people, of course, make up the baby boom generation. Although the baby boomers did not have children in proportion to their size, the "echo effect" of the baby boom (as demographers call it) was, by sheer weight of numbers, sufficient to cause a continued and unprecedented population growth. Add to this improved medical technology, new medicines, and increased health consciousness on the part of the people, among other things, and it is easy to understand why, even though most Americans use birth control, the population of the United States today exceeds a quarter of a billion people.

The issue here is that the very size of the population has affected the number of heroes and Americans' views of them. Consider the issue of awards, the purpose of which is explained by William J. Goode: "Formal awards, prizes, and other honors are mostly given to individuals, but they are simultaneously *public announcements*, typically made by an organization, and meant to convey information to as many people as possible in as many different social networks as possible."[12]

But Goode also notes how the number of awards has increased. He points to "the continued increase in the number of organizations that give awards and prizes," which logically leads to an increased number of awards. Awards, prizes, medals, and other forms of recognition of heroes—almost always local heroes, but they occasionally get national attention—have increased in proportion to the increase in population. Daniel Boorstin agrees: we consistently add to the number of prizes, awards, and titles that are presented each year, and we create and support numerous halls of fame to enshrine more and more people. This occurs even in the supposedly hallowed arena of scientific achievement. In the 1970s, for example, perhaps several hundred scientific prizes of major significance were awarded in the United States. The number today is several thousand.[13]

We have Ellis Island Awards to celebrate our ethnic diversity and Horatio Alger Awards for those who overcame adversity. We have awards for everything and everyone and we give them out freely. There are well over two thousand plaques in the Hollywood Walk of Fame. The Walk once celebrated extraordinarily gifted actors. If everyone gets a plaque, can the actor who is being recognized truly be gifted?[14]

A similar form of generosity has affected education in the United States. In high schools and colleges grade inflation has reached a point where it is almost more difficult to get a "C" grade, the traditional standard for average work, than to get an "A" or "B" grade. Teachers seem reluctant to give average grades to students anymore. Today students everywhere are above average, and no one seems to notice the inanity of this academic standard. Thus, Peter Jay, writing in the *Baltimore Sun*, points out that today we do not recognize excellence, that we live in "dreary egalitarian times." The consequence in high schools and colleges is that "most academic honors have been made meaningless because everyone gets them."[15]

Until recently it was virtually impossible to get an "F" grade at Stanford University (in 1994 the faculty voted to change the system). Indeed, throughout the university system, grade averages have consistently moved up, though efforts are now being made to halt or even reverse this trend. In the same spirit the College Board changed the scoring system for the Scholastic Assessment Tests (SATs), increasing the mean so that, by definition, those who take the test now will get a higher score than they would have before the change.[16]

Similarly, and as a preview of the hoopla that was to accompany returning American forces after the Gulf War, consider the invasion of Grenada by United States combat forces in 1983. The invasion was a success and there are two measures of the extent of that success. First, there was a Clint Eastwood movie about it. Second and more to the point here, although American forces involved in the operation totaled 7,000 troops some 8,612 medals were awarded to those troops.[17]

Now it is clear that some, perhaps most, of those medals were deservedly awarded, were earned by the recipients. But it is unlikely that all were, and it demeans those whose bravery and sacrifices were justly acknowledged if a similar acknowledgment is offered to those who were less brave and who sacrificed less.

Awards, recognition of significant contributions, should be given because the recipient is or has done something special. If all are honored for something, if all get good grades, medals, and awards, who is there to celebrate as a hero? How do we tell the hero from the mass of recipients?

Addendum: Adolescents Take Over

If one is old enough, one might recall when popular culture, the major source of American heroes today, was adult-centered. That was when the young were anxious to grow up, to become adults, and before adults wished to revert to adolescence. It is strange today to read that in pre–World War II America, "youth wanted what age had achieved: dignity and respectability" and that as late as the 1950s "young Americans accepted the values of the older generations." This is one reason why, until the 1960s, American popular culture was an adult culture, and the culture heroes of American society were adult culture heroes.[1]

This doesn't mean that American heroes weren't young or that some weren't frivolous. It means that young people wanted to be regarded as adults and that their heroes were the same as adults' heroes. It means that at least insofar as age was concerned, Americans shared a common culture.

This was one of the selling points for cigarettes during these years, for example. Smoking was a sign of maturity, of sophistication, of being grown up. Adult heroes smoked cigarettes. But cigarettes were just the most obvious product that indicated that one had achieved adulthood. Advertisers sold virtually all products intended for the youth market that way: use this and you'll be regarded as an adult. Today, of course, it is just the opposite. Advertisers now sell youth to adults instead of selling maturity to the young. Fawcett and Thomas note the "norm of youth" in contemporary America, while Morris comments that "adults wore their childrens' ideas like their clothes." Morris was speaking here of the 1960s. The process continued through the 1970s, 1980s, and 1990s.[2]

Despite arguments to the contrary, the 1960s did not initiate the youth movement in the United States, nor, in fact, did the baby boomers, although they were the beneficiaries of that movement and rode it to fruition in the 1970s. The leaders of the initial phase of the youth movement—the rock and roll stars, the speakers at the rallies in the 1960s, the leaders of the various antiwar movements—weren't teens, but young adults who were born before or during the Second World War.

But the baby boom generation responded to them. Beginning in the mid-1950s, and increasingly throughout the 1960s and 1970s, American youth attacked the power of adults, established their own areas within American popular culture, and gradually took control of and in time thoroughly dominated it: "Youth culture virtually took over the country." As noted, the mid-1950s saw the beginning of distinctly teen music—an easing over of the rhythm and blues music played on black radio stations to white stations; in time this music evolved into rock and roll. Television and movies began increasingly to be directed toward the tastes of the baby boomers. *Life* magazine noted that "as everyone once wanted to be rich, now everybody wanted to be, or seemed to be young." By December 12, 1966, when *Time* magazine's Man of the Year award went to "The Younger Generation," and continuing through today, popular culture in America was defined as American youth culture. As the power of popular culture in the United States today is a reflection of the power of the younger generation in the United States, so are today's American heroes a reflection of that power.[3]

To put this into some sort of sociohistorical perspective, one must consider the phenomenon of the baby boom and the effect it had on American culture. The key reason for the domination of American popular culture by American youth was, of course, the sheer number of baby boomers. By the mid-1960s the population of the United States exceeded by perhaps 30 million people the number that demographers had anticipated. Those 30 million people were the baby boomers, now becoming teenagers.[4]

Babies are good for business. So are toddlers, school-age children, and teenagers. It cannot be surprising, then, that with these numbers came the money generated by their existence. Reasonably enough, businesses directed their attention to that market and advertisers played to them. The baby boomers were the first group specifically targeted by Madison Avenue, and the advertising industry had discovered new and sophisticated methods of persuasion. Records and movies, cameras and toiletries, were all redesigned with America's young in mind. The reason is that baby boomers not only were a massive group, they were a massive group with a substantial disposable income. Business encouraged them to take advantage of that fact. As a result, the baby boomers enjoyed considerable economic and social power. This situation continued throughout the ensuing decades and continues today. An article in the *New York Times* points out that there is currently a "growing market of teen-agers with oodles of disposable money, much of it from their Baby Boomer parents."[5]

The wealth enjoyed by the young influenced their sense of self-worth. Speaking specifically about the 1950s, Charles R. Morris notes that members of the baby-boomer generation were consistently reminded of their significance. Life in the suburbs revolved around them and they knew it. That is, the youth of America recognized and understood the significance of their economic and social power.[6]

America's youth weren't (and aren't) stupid; they took advantage of their economic power and the attention they received and began to forge their own culture, new and distinct, loud and celebrated by everyone. By "the middle 1960s there was a subliminal, but almost tangible, moment when power shifted away from adults to young people." The shift continued throughout the 1970s and was completed by the 1980s. Popular culture since then has remained solidly in the hands of the young; each succeeding generation assumes control over American popular culture.[7]

America's youth in the 1990s did not steal or usurp American popular culture. It was given to them by the aging baby boomers who not only idolized youth but kept trying to be a part of the increasingly younger generations. They perpetuated the idea that youth should be forever celebrated. *Newsweek* quotes one baby boomer: "People my age can't let go of their youth." He adds, quite correctly, "we don't have to." And the baby boomers passed this idea on to their own children. In consequence, America's young people today are to a large degree free of the idea of adult America and not especially receptive to it.[8]

Morris is incorrect when he suggests that the "tyranny" of America's youth "over taste and culture" will in time pass. It is here to stay. The individuals have changed, but the "tyranny" has not lost any of its force. If anything, youth culture has gained in power, respectability, and economic clout. Not only movies and music and television shows, but magazines and electronic gadgets and just about anything else one can imagine are specifically designed for the youth market.[9]

Because American adults gave popular culture to the young, the heroes of popular culture have been the heroes of the young; and necessarily the heroes of popular culture are transitory if for no other reason than the young, by definition, are transitory. Every generation grows up—every baby boomer remembers when thirty-five was terribly old—and each new generation wants and chooses its own heroes. That is why there are always new heroes ready to take the place of current entertainment heroes and celebrity-heroes. Moreover, because each new generation is by default in charge of the new version of popular culture, they decree who the next entertainment heroes, the next stars, will be. In the past stars lasted; the lengths of their careers were measured in decades. It doesn't work like that anymore. The celebrity—the star—vanishes as quickly as he appeared. Because the control of popular culture perpetually awaits the next generation, the United States is assured that its current popular culture heroes are temporary. The continuance of a specific popular culture hero within American society for any length of time is highly improbable (although there are some exceptions: the Rolling Stones seem eternal).

Youth will always need heroes, which suggests that they are receptive to new leaders, new idols. Adolescence, as virtually everyone who has studied it asserts, is a time of uncertainty, of instability, of identity seeking. Heroes provide youth with stability and identity, qualities needed more and more today.

Uncertainty and a weakened identity are often a consequence of a rapidly changing society. Beginning in the 1950s, but especially in the ensuing decades, the United States underwent dramatic and rapid change, much of it directly involving the nation's youth. In the 1950s the nation's young lived in a crack-free, AIDS-free, relatively crime-free, and fairly stable world. Such is not the case today. Most especially, changes that have occurred within the American family over the past few decades have been nothing short of revolutionary. Family life in the 1950s was not nearly as idyllic as it is often portrayed. But family life since then has been devastating to a great number of people, the young especially.[10]

Because of these changes in their lives, there is an intense and immediate need on the part of adolescents for a hero, for someone who offers stability, who serves as a model upon which the young can base their behavior, and who suggests something to which they can aspire. The paradox is that this very demand, the speed with which a hero is required, prevents the existence of a true hero. A hero must be a hero for an extended period of time, for more than a moment in the nation's history. But youth is in a hurry. That is why the celebrity-hero satisfies the needs of the young. The celebrity-hero is an instantaneous hero, the perfect answer to the demands of youth. And the rapid turnover of celebrity-heroes explains why they necessarily fail as traditional, time-honored American heroes. All of this also helps explain why, as noted in the earlier discussion about James Dean, celebrity-heroes who die young and unexpectedly evolve into cult heroes of newer generations. They have remained young and therefore acceptable as heroes to succeeding generations.

There is a danger in youth not having heroes, so it may be to society's advantage that they seek out rock stars, movie stars, and other celebrity-heroes. As vacuous as these celebrity-heroes are, they do serve the function of being there when they are needed, however briefly they are adored and however superficial their true worth.

When the hero is a hero to a particular generation of Americans, two things can happen as the next generation comes along. The old hero can either fade into history along with the older generation or he can be maintained by the new generation and still regarded as a hero. As suggested, a national hero must exist beyond his own lifetime or else he is of consequence for his generation alone and not for the nation. In the past this happened: heroes existed beyond their own generation. That is why we still celebrate George Washington, Jesse James, and Babe Ruth. But more and more we produce generations with their own cultures, with their own specific attitudes and values, and this necessarily reduces the chances of a transgenerational hero.

Each generation wants its own representatives, people who will speak for them alone and not for earlier generations. But this doesn't mean that heroes of the recent past should be forgotten; there should be room within the current pantheon of American heroes for the heroes of previous generations. At the moment there doesn't seem to be.

Chapter 14

The Media and Heroes

Barbara Kellerman is speaking about politics when she suggests that one of the characteristics of television is that it "demystifies." But demystification is not limited to either television or to the political arena. Indeed, Kellerman, in citing the work of Erving Goffman, seems to agree that demystification can be put in a broader context.[1]

Goffman, in his classic sociological study *The Presentation of Self in Everyday Life*, makes a distinction between the "front region" and the "back region," areas that are public and areas that are private. A restaurant dining room where people are served their meals, for example, and the floor of a department store where salespeople greet potential customers, are front regions. In these regions the workers maintain public faces; they are civil and perhaps flattering. The kitchen and the employees' lounge are back regions where the workers discuss their customers in less than flattering terms.

In front regions one is always aware of and concerned with appearances because one is always before an audience. In back regions one may do and say things one wouldn't do or say in public. Today, due in large measure to the media generally and television in particular, the dividing line between these two areas has vanished, especially in the case of celebrities or potential celebrities.

This is one reason why Howard Stringer, president of the CBS Broadcast Group, argues that the mass media effectively destroy the potential hero: he cannot "survive the age of information and mass media." And indeed that is how it works today. There used to be boundaries respected by the mass media, albeit with some exceptions. In the past it was the case that one's private life was of no one's concern except by invitation; one's public image was one that the individual chose to project. More significantly, the media helped maintain the individual's privacy and his chosen public image. Due to changed attitudes within the media, the private life of anyone in the public eye is now to all intents and purposes that individual's public image.[2]

Equally important, the American public seems to revel in learning all of the details of this newly-discovered public image. Again, it wasn't always like this. In the past the public seemed to want glamor, to keep the more unpleasant aspects of their idols hidden from view. Today the public seems to eschew glamor in favor of revelation of those unpleasant aspects of their idols' lives. But the hero needs parts of his life to remain unexamined, and since privacy has disappeared, so has the hero. No one can withstand an intense examination of every detail of his life except perhaps someone who is excruciatingly dull, and that too is a fault. One's private life is rarely what one would like one's public image to be—or to have it shape the attitudes of the public.

As suggested above, more than any single factor, the workings of the media today, the new way those responsible for getting the stories to the public view their job, is critical for the changes that have occurred in the way the lives of heroes and potential heroes are exposed to public scrutiny. As one example, consider that in 1848, during his presidential campaign, Grover Cleveland was charged with fathering an illegitimate child. Throughout the campaign the mother of the child, Martha Halpin, was effectively invisible, which is astonishing. There can be little doubt that had Halpin lived today, not only would her story be a standard feature in the tabloids, she would be a regular on the talk show circuit.[3]

As another example, consider a story going around concerning Babe Ruth. The story may be apocryphal, but it is not improbable, given the Babe's life-style, and it too illustrates the point. Two journalists were in the dining car of the train on which the Yankees were traveling. Ruth, naked, came running through the dining car and into the next one; a few seconds later a young woman, similarly dressed and carrying a large knife, followed after him. One journalist turned to the other and said: "It's a good thing I wasn't here when that happened or else I'd have to send in a story about it." The reason the story is not improbable is that the press tended to ignore Ruth's "excesses and . . . crudities." Ruth's "boorish personal habits were nicely overlooked by talented sportswriters," who were happy to give the people the hero that they wanted. And indeed they did.[4]

Today the press would not only report the "excesses" and "crudities," they would interview the young woman and have her on national television within twenty-four hours. There once was a time when sportswriters avoided harming the image of our athlete-heroes. More than this, the press generally worked with the people about whom they reported, and not only sports heroes such as Babe Ruth. Rare is the photograph of Jacqueline Kennedy Onassis smoking a cigarette, or perhaps more to the point, of President Franklin D. Roosevelt in a wheelchair. There was an unspoken rule regarding photographs of FDR, the most powerful man on the face of the earth, who had literally to be carried from the presidential car to his wheelchair. Whether or not a wheelchair-bound individual should be president of the United States is not the issue; at the time public knowledge of the effects of his bout with polio would have hurt FDR, and the press did not exploit that.

In his memoirs Richard M. Nixon writes that newsreels "never showed a wheelchair or crutches, nor did newspaper accounts mention [President Roosevelt's] disability. The media actively kept the secret for him." And John Gunther noted that when he lived in Europe in the 1930s he regularly "met men in important positions of state who had no idea that the President was disabled." Part of the reticence concerning Roosevelt's disability, Gunther suggests, was due to "personal affection" on the part of the press for the president. But it is highly unlikely that every single journalist felt "personal affection" towards Roosevelt. There were, after all, a number of bitterly anti-Roosevelt newspapers. It is more likely that respect for the man, the office, and the right to privacy protected the president's secret.[5]

Today we have the paparazzi and a seemingly endless number of talk shows. The tabloid press as well as the traditional press often report on the doings of the famous and the infamous, the hero and the anti-hero. And they do so as sensationally as possible. As suggested earlier, the relationship between just about everyone associated (however remotely) with that 1995 tragicomedy in California, the O. J. Simpson trial, and the press—both print and electronic, both tabloid and traditional—illustrate this as nothing else can.

Celebrity examinations and interviews are not especially recent trends. It is a bit disquieting to note that Edward R. Murrow did a home interview show with the famous and would-be famous in the 1950s. He did not, however, peek into their bedrooms, dredge up old and sorry tales from their past, and sensationalize the interview. He had, in a word, a sense of dignity both for himself and for those with whom he spoke—Senator and Mrs. John F. Kennedy, for example.

Today's journalists have traveled a considerable distance from Murrow. All too often they are unencumbered by anything such as dignity, regard for others, or common sense. The media may have hit an all-time low when they revealed that Arthur Ashe, the late tennis star, had AIDS. Richard Rosenblatt is clearly correct in asserting that "the earth would have continued to spin without anyone knowing that Arthur Ashe had AIDS; that was the press's doing." This is a polite way of saying that the media's intrusion on his privacy was grotesque; that his being ill with the fatal disease was his business, his family's business, and no one else's damn business. [6]

One result of this probing into the personal lives of celebrities is that the fabled Byronic hero is now a relic, a historical curiosity. His dark and mysterious past, the mystery that helps make a Byronic hero a Byronic hero—his intensity, brooding, and pained soul—would today be examined under the glare of the late evening news. This cannot help but destroy the hero.

Branches of the media seem to work, and work assiduously, to contribute to the destruction of the current and potential hero, a point that will be considered below. Here the efforts of various biographers to (negatively) analyze, probe, examine, and reveal all of the unpleasant aspects of the hero seem particularly noteworthy. Daniel Boorstin notes that in the past American biographers tried to flatter their subjects. He also notes that this is no longer the case. Can anyone doubt that he is correct? [7]

FDR is attacked because he allegedly abandoned the Jews during the Holocaust, and there is still a public debate concerning General Eisenhower's alleged affair with his driver, Captain Kay Summersby, during World War II. Thomas C. Reeves's *A Question of Character: A Life of John F. Kennedy* and Nigel Hamilton's *JFK: Reckless Youth* question Kennedy's integrity. Robert A. Caro seems to have worked tirelessly to demolish the memory of President Lyndon Johnson in *The Years of Lyndon Johnson*, vols. I and II. David Stockman and Michael Deaver paint unflattering portraits of Ronald Reagan. Nor are the wives of presidents left unblemished. Nancy Reagan is written about by Kitty Kelley with something less than warmth. Even Barbara Bush, wife of President Bush, is taken to task because she appears "to enjoy her dogs more than her children." But the subjects of exposés are not only politicians and their spouses. Newer biographies of Frank Lloyd Wright point out that favorable ones have often been falsified.

Even the inner workings of the United States Supreme Court, workings traditionally kept in strictest confidence, are being revealed, and somewhat unflatteringly, by former Justice William Brennan. [8]

Albert Goldman's biographies of Elvis Presley and John Lennon and Kitty Kelley's biographies of Frank Sinatra and Johnny Carson, among others, were hardly designed to sustain the heroic images of their subjects. Neither are books by the children of celebrities castigating their famous mothers as, for example, the writings of Joan Crawford's and Marlene Dietrich's daughters. Perhaps most surprising of all was Ralph Abernathy's book that demeaned the memory of Martin Luther King, Jr. [9]

It seems obvious that Peter H. Gibbon is right: "We have traded exemplary lives and heroes for information, irony, and reality." At one time the hero was allowed to maintain his privacy, and with his privacy he was able to maintain an illusion. Both are necessary for the hero and the media allow neither to exist today. We have knowledge and we have scandal and we have cynicism. Why bother with heroes?[10]

This effect of the mass media is suggested by a quotation from Georg W. F. Hegel's *Philosophy of History*:

"No man is a hero to his valet" is a well-known proverb. I have added—and Goethe repeated it ten years later: "But it is not because the former is no hero, rather because the latter is a valet." He takes off the hero's boots, assists him to bed, knows that he prefers champagne, etc. Historical personages waited upon . . . by . . . valets come poorly off. They are brought down by . . . their attendants, to a level with—or rather a few degrees below—the morality of such exquisite critics of the human spirit.

What Hegel is saying, in his usual ponderous way, is that when we get close to someone, we see their faults. This diminishes the stature of the person or thing we're seeing.

Jonathan Swift also offers an illustration of this point, perhaps more effectively than Hegel. In *Gulliver's Travels*, Swift has Gulliver in the land of the Lilliputians, a group of tiny, mean-spirited, nasty people. Yet they are beautiful, with soft unblemished skin and lovely features. The Brobdingnags, on the other hand, are a kind and gentle people, but they are massive and all of their unappealing physical characteristics are visible to Gulliver. Their warts are huge mesas; their pimples, repulsive mountains. Stature is not the issue here: ugliness contingent upon stature is the issue, or, rather, ugliness contingent upon closeness is the issue. The size of the Lilliputians prevents Gulliver from noticing any of their physical flaws, and he is overcome by their beauty; the massiveness of the Brobdingnags forces

Gulliver to notice every one of their flaws, each massive and grotesque blemish, and he is repulsed by them.

Unless someone or some thing is perfect, the closer we are to it, the closer we examine it, the more likely we are to discover its flaws. By similar reasoning, the closer we get to any hero, the more he seems to be a human being, with marvelous qualities in one or two areas, perhaps, but a human being nonetheless, and consequently someone with failings. Today, it seems, the mass media concentrate on failings rather than successes, weaknesses rather than strengths. Journalists, writers, and the electronic media detail the errors, sins, and foolish behaviors of famous people; and, as noted, some of the children and "friends" of some of these people do the same thing. This, obviously, can destroy any aura of heroism that might surround any of the subjects of the literary efforts.

Intense scrutiny of people, heroes and nonheroes, is possible in part because of modern technology. Nixon, for example, in speaking of the willingness of the press to ignore President Roosevelt's handicap, suggests that they could not do so today even if they wanted to "because of the television cameras that follow a President everywhere." This is one reason why Jon Margolis argues that "the latest technology all but eliminates greatness." He also suggests that "intrusive reporters" today would gladly report both Roosevelt's physical limitations and John F. Kennedy's physical ailments. The reason for this, as noted earlier, is that one does not become a celebrity journalist because of what one does not print. And Michael Kernan, a veteran newsman, points out that because of journalism's extreme "financial rewards" today, it cannot be surprising that "people are tempted to rummage in celebrities' garbage." [11]

In the past, information regarding a specific person was limited. It took time for the stories of both failings and noble exploits to reach across the country. Today information is available to the public by the mass media generally, and radio and television in particular, in time measured by the speed of light. It took a full two weeks for the news of President Lincoln's assassination to reach London. The news of the assassination of President Kennedy reached London in seconds. Richard Reeves points out that this is an "age of instantaneous communication." Instantaneous communication diminishes romantic embellishment and, therefore, illusion, a critical part of the creation of heroes.[12]

A second part of this story is that until recently few people knew what their heroes really looked like. The famous were hidden from view save for occasional and generally flattering sketches of them in the magazines that told of their exploits. In the accompanying articles they were invariably described as tall, good-looking, and strongly built. It was something like listening to a voice on the radio and attaching a face to the voice in one's imagination. The reality of the face that went with the voice may be disappointing, but only if one actually saw the face, and with radio one did not have to encounter reality.

One did encounter reality, or something approaching reality, when the voices on radio became images on television. Just as a number of silent movie stars—generally but not only those with accents—were out of jobs when the talkies came in, some people could not make the transition from radio to television because of their physical appearance. And it need hardly be mentioned here that television will be with us forevermore. In response to this new burst of reality, adjustments have been made. "Pure" media events are not entirely a thing of the past, but they are increasingly harder to find; stage-managed events are not yet an absolute part of our lives, but can anyone doubt that they will be? A quarter of a century ago Robert Lewis Shayon noted that television cameras will accompany future space explorers, who will, in effect, be actors; they will make their "exits and entrances for the benefit of multiplanetary audiences." Can anyone doubt that he is correct? [13]

We live in a world that increasingly plays to the camera. Tales of greatness were spread in the past, of course, but not with the same intensity or purpose as today. Today we live in what Louis Kronenberger calls an "Age of Publicity," and he isn't wrong. Perhaps nothing demonstrates the difference between past tales of greatness and current ones more clearly than the fact that today, in this "Age of Publicity," there exists those whose job it is to spread that publicity, public relations people. And public relations people are, almost by definition, concerned with image more than with truth. In a stage-managed world the genuine article is at a disadvantage; in an age of publicity the genuine hero will disappear. Everyone knows that the world has become a stage. Everyone knows that "fantasies seep into facts. Entertainment and journalism drift back and forth across the borders." Does it have to be pointed out that, in consequence, heroic illusion is destroyed and cynicism is increased? [14]

One final effect of modern technology and especially television might be noted here, the intimacy that people seem to feel between the celebrity-hero and themselves. We tend to believe that we know the people we see regularly on television. The same thing happens in the movies and sports arenas, but not as often or with the same intensity. Tabloids tell the absurd stories of movie stars and news magazines pretend to sympathize with the sports personalities they interview, but television creates a bond between the viewer and the celebrity. Besides, movie stars and sports personalities often appear on television, and it is then that we really get to "know" them. This works to create false heroes, to reveal and simultaneously hide the personality of the celebrity.

This is the argument of Jonathan Alter: The "false intimacy of TV . . . [is] truly damaging to public life." It relies on appearance, deftness, the slick commercial that is the anchor of the television industry. The media, not only television but especially television, substitute fancy for fact and damage the American hero in that way. And when the media tire of the old hero or discover a new (and inevitably temporary) one, they publicize the illusion that created the old hero.[15]

The argument could be made that we want to see the warts of the famous. After all, there wouldn't be this type of television, journalism, or biographical writing if there wasn't a market for it. It is possible that when all is said and done we want to see our heroes stripped of their glory. Perhaps we enjoy the idea that they are more like us than their images suggest or perhaps we entertain the fantasy that, given their failings, we are not really that far from being like them. This could explain the constant barrage of books, articles, print and electronic media revelations about (and generally unflattering toward) the famous and powerful, America's celebrities and icons.

It might also be noted that in one sense none of this is new. Gossip has been around for a long time, after all. What is new is the degree and the intensity of it. Gossip has become a full-blown industry. Certainly William A. Henry III is right, gossip is everywhere and doing quite well everywhere: "on television, in magazines, in nonfiction books, in docudrama TV movies and mini-series." There is no escaping it.[16]

It is probably true that one cannot fault the media for simply giving the public what they seem to want so very much. The companies that make up the media are businesses, and as businesses do, they try to satisfy their customers. It may be true that the media provided us with endless information about the Harding/Kerrigan case, for example. But it is also true that the American public wanted the information, that "Tonya and Nancy held our fascination for weeks." Some don't fault the public either. Thomas Kerr, an associate professor of business ethics, condemns neither the public nor the media for craving "titillating gossip" or satisfying the craving, respectively. He is not alone in this view. [17]

All of this has consequences, and in the context of this book, one of the consequences of examining people in public and pointing to their failings—indeed, often emphasizing their failings—is that our regard for them must diminish and their heroic stature must fade. If we require our heroes to be perfect—and we do; or at least we want our heroes to seem to approach perfection—we must be willing to allow an image of their perfection to be propagated; we must be willing not to examine the subject too closely. The hero needs to be distanced from his admirers, but that does not and cannot happen today. Because of our interest in the weaknesses of our potential heroes, because the means to satisfy that interest is readily available, because there are people happy to satisfy our interest, the hero is no longer separated from the rest of us.

Equally significant, one can make the argument that satisfying America's craving for gossip is not all that difficult because the subjects willingly offer themselves up to public scrutiny. Recall, for example, the celebrated cover of *Vanity Fair* magazine picturing a very pregnant and very nude Demi Moore. Recall that while years ago Joe DiMaggio wrote a book called *Lucky to Be a Yankee*, ballplayers today write books telling everyone how terrible they have it and why they can't stay away from drugs, liquor, and women. Talk show hosts regularly probe into the private lives of the famous and not so famous, who happily reveal and explain away their intimate secrets. Roger Rosenblatt is correct: "Privacy in our time has not only been invaded; it's been surrendered." [18]

Finally, as suggested above, the media has enhanced the significance of heroic appearance. When we didn't know what our heroes looked like, sounded like, acted like, when they weren't being heroes, writers of the stories of America's heroes had carte blanche. Daniel Boone became a "tall man of powerful frame." But he was of average height, 5'8", and weighed about 175 pounds. Kirk Douglas is handsome and solidly built, as was Victor Mature. Both men portrayed Doc Holliday on the screen. But the dentist had tuberculosis—it would eventually kill him—and was painfully thin because of the illness. Kit Carson was short, plain-featured, pigeon-toed, and unable to read or write. In the media he undergoes a metamorphosis: he grows taller, becomes handsome, and is literate. In the case of the screen version of Bonnie and Clyde, to take an extreme example, there was fabrication to the point of hilarity. Warren Beatty (Clyde) is handsome and tall, perhaps 6'2", and Faye Dunaway (Bonnie) is a beautiful, statuesque woman. Clyde Barrow was slightly built and at 5'6" under average height, while Bonnie Parker was just 5' tall and weighed about 90 pounds. [19]

It is almost impossible to underestimate the significance of physical appearance in the United States today, which may be one reason why there is so much fabrication in descriptions of the physical characteristics of America's heroes. Americans do not like their heroes or anti-heroes to be skinny, and they certainly don't like them to be fat. But most especially they don't like them to be short.

A *New York Times* article discussing the height of the 1992 presidential candidates notes what Ian Fleming had to say about James Bond's thoughts on height, or lack thereof: "Bond had always mistrusted short men. They grew up from childhood with an inferiority complex. All their lives, they would strive to be bigger than others who had teased them as a child. Napoleon had been short. And Hitler. It was the short men that created all the trouble in the world."[20]

Americans tend to feel as Bond does. In fact, their attitude toward people who are short, especially men who are short, can be harsher than 007's. Consider what novelist Pat Conroy has Colonel Bull Meecham say about short men: "Give me a guy less than five feet eight . . . and I'll give you a real bastard nine times out of ten. . . . I always keep my eye out for a little guy because I know he's down there low with his hands around my nuts waiting for a chance to give me the big squeeze." The American hero is handsome and powerfully built and, most important, he is tall.[21]

The consequences of the stress on physical appearance specifically and on public persona generally might be looked at in this way. Abraham Lincoln was one of the best presidents that this country has ever produced. Some may have equaled him, but none was better. He had the heart to know what should be done, the brains to see how to accomplish the task before him, and the courage to go ahead and do it. And he would never be elected to the presidency today.

Yes, he was tall, but the man was unattractive, awkward looking, and his taste in clothes was awful (although awful taste may have been in style in the mid-nineteenth century). His physical appearance—gaunt, homely, gangling—would be an enormous handicap and so would his speech. Abraham Lincoln spoke brilliantly, but only if you listened to what he said and ignored his mispronunciations. It is hardly likely that people today would accept English such as "thar's a bar over thar." His speech patterns, along with his appearance, would never work on television today. They would alienate as many voters as his heart, brilliance, and courage would attract. Of course, if Lincoln were projected into the late twentieth century, he would undoubtedly change; he would adjust to modern circumstances, to the modern media. The point here is that if he did not or could not adjust, he would be unelectable and the United States would have lost one of its greatest leaders.[22]

Among the effects of the mass media on American society, then, is the need for physical attractiveness. Good looks were always an asset. They are now a requirement.

The media has had a profound effect on the American hero, both in fomenting the illusion of the hero and in fomenting the people's disillusion with the hero. The media has created the hero by creating illusion. Extraordinarily sophisticated techniques are used in various media to manufacture images; the media enhance the visual and auditory impact of people who present us with ideas, and who by their feats make the world a magical place. Because of this and because the mass media reaches everywhere and everyone, it can and does turn some people into superbeings, into heroes.

But the media has also helped to destroy the American hero by destroying the illusion of the hero. It has done this by probing too deeply into areas once regarded as private, by exposing the failings of heroes and potential heroes, by satisfying the inquisitiveness of the public. It has fostered and strengthened the notion that appearance and image are more important than character and depth.

The media alone did not destroy the American hero; other factors, both social and nonsocial, contributed to the hero's disappearance, and one cannot blame the media for this as one cannot blame the media for all of society's ills. The media didn't do it all, but it did make a critical contribution.

The hero exists by virtue of public recognition; there cannot be an "unsung hero," the use of that popular phrase notwithstanding. But if there cannot be an unsung hero, if the accomplishments of the hero have to be known, then there must be someone or something to sing the hero's praises, to tell the public that there is, indeed, a hero. If the media is an evil, it is a necessary one, then, and the best that can be hoped for is voluntary restraint on the part of those who do distribute information to the public. It's not going to happen.

Chapter 15

In Conclusion: Americans and the American Hero at the End of the Twentieth Century

INTRODUCTION

"We can't all be heroes," Will Rogers once commented, "because somebody has to sit on the curb and clap as they go by." The problem is that in America today everybody is sitting on the curb. We don't have anyone to clap for as "they go by"; there's no one in the parade, and numerous factors—both social and nonsocial—have contributed to this situation.

From a sociological point of view, our social structure and social values no longer permit the existence of the hero as they once did. We've organized the system and created a culture that has eliminated the possibility of heroes. Bureaucracies demand team effort rather than individual effort, or at least team approval at the higher levels (thereby avoiding the unpleasant issue of individual responsibility), and human relationships in western societies have become the sort that sociologists call "secondary." They are based in the main on rational calculation, not feelings; they are pragmatic, not emotional. However, the hero evokes emotion, often intense emotion; thus, the existence of a hero is diminished in an unemotional system.

The hero is also an individual, and when the system works to minimize the individual, when the group is stressed and the members of the group are lost within the mass, the hero is also lost within the mass. There can be no doubt that the United States is an organized society, and no doubt that when we organized a few things, it was just a matter of time before we would organize all things. There can also be no doubt as to the unhappy consequences for individuality and, therefore, for heroes as a result of this organization. The United States has suffered the processes of rationality and organization, just as Max Weber predicted. And, again as Weber predicted, the cost of those processes—capsulized in bureaucracies—have been our sense of self, of freedom and individuality. The hero is often defined by his freedom and his individuality, and so the hero is again diminished.[1]

We live today within a system where accomplishing virtually anything that is noteworthy in the mind of the public invariably yields extraordinary economic rewards. It is rarely disputed that the modern reward system—for entertainment heroes, for example, but not only for entertainment heroes—is extreme. And who would refuse the rewards if they were proffered? Today the "purity" of heroism, if that is not too absurd a term, is tarnished by excessive rewards. In the United States we measure our current heroes manqué in terms of their success at achieving rewards; the rewards have become the measure of the deed, not the other way around.

Further, social science generally, and sociology and psychology specifically, analyzes human actions. In consequence, the ambitious man becomes a workaholic; the woman who is careful and precise has evolved into a compulsive. And the courageous man, the hero, has a death wish. Equally important, the social sciences (along with assorted talk shows, legal strategies, and self-help books) have contributed to the notion that no one is responsible for anything he may have done, for anything he is doing at the moment, or for anything that he may do in the future. We are all victims of circumstances beyond our control.

But heroes aren't victims. Heroes don't complain about adversity; they overcome it. That isn't the way things are done today, however. "Grin and bear it" has been replaced by "the squeaky wheel gets the grease." It is difficult today to find anyone who isn't a victim. As long as no one is responsible for his actions, as long as everyone has a legitimate (or at least an acceptable) excuse, as long as we're all victims, we're none of us heroes. We have psychological or sociological explanations for everyone and everything, and no one is responsible for his actions. Even the villain has become a victim. Again, there are truly ill and needy people, but there are also sadistic murderers and rapists, and the two categories ought not to be bound together by a single description termed "victim." The transformation of the villain into a victim has also contributed to the disappearance of the hero.

The media prohibit illusion except by design. Yet in these deceptions the media are often merely pandering to public taste. The public seems not at all interested in people's kindliness but, rather, in their lack of virtue and especially in the lack of virtue of potential heroes. In the past the stress was on glamor and dignity; efforts were made to hide scandals, and if they became known, efforts were made to salvage whatever heroic images remained. When heroes did something that was less than socially accept-able, they generally did it in private and it remained private; and the media often, though not always, acted with discretion. This contributed to the heroic stature of the movie idols of the past, for example.

Perhaps this is because in the past—in the 1930s, as an obvious case in point—the desire for reality wasn't very intense. Perhaps few people wanted reality during the Great Depression when reality was so horrible. They were happy to accept the image of goodness and innocence. Today, on the other hand, one has to work hard to present an image to the public that is faultless. Today there is a lot of reality, and that has its bad points as well as its good points. When everything comes out in the open, both mystery and glamor are lost; and both are needed if the hero isn't to fade from view.

There are heroes in all eras, but especially during eras when the role of hero supersedes the fact of the hero. The hero existed best when no one looked too closely at who he really was. When no one examines the hero too closely, his status is most secure, his existence most readily permitted.

The hero is an abstraction who exists only insofar as social structure and culture, and insofar as social values, permit him to exist. There are some structural and cultural standards and some values that last, which is why some heroes remain heroes as, for example, George Washington and Babe Ruth. Other social standards change as society changes. Some of these changes are dramatic, especially if the society goes through momentous social revolutions, as the United States has done in the past several decades.

Logically, then, as we change, as our society is altered structurally and culturally, our heroes change as well. Different times call for different attitudes and skills among leaders, as Kellerman suggests; extending this thought, different times call for different heroes.[2]

Because Americans are enthralled by change, we are forever puttering around with new ideas, new social systems, and new technologies. One consequence of this is that each succeeding generation has sought its own identity, especially since the time of the baby-boom generation. New generations are often encouraged to want their own generationally specific symbols. Recall that we have given over popular culture to the youth of the country. This is one of the key cultural changes that helped bring about the disappearance of national heroes in the United States. Because we lost our heroes in the 1960s, many older people (here defined as baby boomers and pre–baby boomers) want to go back to the pre-Kennedy days. But because we lost our heroes in the 1960s, it is hard for the youth of the 1970s, 1980s, and 1990s to understand the concept except in the abstract. They've never known a true American hero. They cannot know how heroes other than entertainment heroes are developed and sustained.

ON THE NECESSITY OF HEROES

Perhaps the high point of the era of American heroes occurred in the 1920s, as Roberts and Olsen argue, but that wasn't their final decade. To note this again, it wasn't until the conclusion of the Second World War that the hero began to disappear in the United States. We enjoy celebrating our heroes, as does every society. Yet the last truly full-blown ticker-tape parade for an individual hero in New York City, traditionally the symbol of the nation's love for one of its heroes, was the parade for astronaut John Glenn in 1962. We haven't had a major ticker-tape parade for an individual hero in well over thirty years. We may have seen the last of them.[3]

And that is a problem. But it is only a problem if society generally and American society in particular really need heroes, if society in general and American society in particular require some people to accept the status of hero and to fulfill the role appropriate to that status. There is no agreement on this point. Tolstoy not only thought that society did not need heroes, he thought that there weren't any heroes in the first place: "Heroes—that's a lie and invention: there are simply people, people and nothing else." And Jonathan Swift reduced the hero to an object of envy: "Who'er excels in what we prize/Appears a hero in our eyes."

Some twentieth-century Americans agree. Tom Wolfe has it that a hero is not appreciably more than a ready-made symbol, "[someone] a whole lot of people or class of people can identify with." And Barbara Kellerman thinks that Americans neither like nor want heroes: Americans do not lean toward hero-worship. Kellerman is speaking here specifically about politics, but the sentiment clearly applies to all other areas (save sports and entertainment).[4]

Yet we seem unable to avoid a need for heroes. Even Kellerman acknowledges Americans' "desire" for heroes, "even political heroes (especially during hard times)." And a great many scholars agree, supporting the view of the necessity of heroes, arguing that cultural heroes make up important references. We require heroes to lead us. It doesn't matter which social forces are at work, "a need will [always] be felt for a hero to initiate, organize, and lead." Moreover, that need stays with us: "There is a perennial interest in heroes even when we outgrow the hero worship of youth." From the perspective of the individual, Joseph Campbell's view may be correct: the hero reflects our inner being. [5]

From the perspective of the society, Hegel's view seems to be correct: the hero "actualizes his age." Tom W. Smith puts it this way: "Society's heroes both reflect social norms and shape them." In selecting heroes, people select "individuals who exemplify and personify virtues valued by the society." On a personal level, "the heroes become standards of excellence that people can identify with and . . . strive to emulate." It seems that for numerous people the hero is a necessary, even critical, part of the society. He benefits both the individual and the whole, he nourishes our personal essence, and he clarifies our national purpose. Georgie Anne Geyer is amazed, but she acknowledges that "there still are people who need to believe in great helmsmen."[6]

Heroes serve purposes in society. They permit standards to exist, they encourage excellence and effort, they explain the need for sacrifice and dedication without saying so specifically. William J. Goode notes that the hero puts "group interests ahead of one's own," and does so not for gain but for the sake of others. This, of course, is a reminder of a quality found in Weber's charismatic figure. According to Goode, the hero offers "an extraordinary free gift of the self, made with little thought of reward." Although the action that the hero takes may be dangerous and "the knowledge of survival is chancy," that does not prevent him from undertaking the effort for the good of society. [7]

There seems to be a general agreement on this point: the hero serves the society. William O. Beeman suggests that "our greatest cultural heroes are extreme individualists who served the public good." Warren I. Susman concurs: The hero takes "the responsibility of man for his fellow man." He is his "brother's keeper." More than this, the hero is a representative of the metaphysical ideal of the people. Norman Mailer argues that "a hero embodies the fantasy and so allows each private mind the liberty to consider its fantasy and find a way to grow."[8]

The traditional hero is a reflection of the critical definition of a society. He demonstrates to society, occasionally by word but more often by action, what is and is not important. The hero reinforces values that might otherwise be forgotten or disregarded. The hero inspires and leads, clarifies the often confused distinction between right and wrong, and inspires others to strive to go beyond their normal abilities. Tales of the heroes of America's past provide the youth of the nation with a sense of past glories, with a sense of history—even if this history is distorted on occasion. Sidney Hook notes this point: heroes help to educate the nation's young people. Nor is it only the young who are impressed with or who try to emulate the nation's heroes.[9]

Heroes, then, are a social necessity. In setting standards and establishing and reinforcing values, they not only provide leadership and direction, they provide the society with a sense of purpose, inspire social change, and determine the direction and intensity of social movements. Heroes today act as role models, guiding the young (and often the not so young). Joseph Epstein, writing in the *New York Times*, argues that we should do away with role models and embrace "heroes, who have more to teach us." But the latter do not exist even if we need them, and the former do even if they deny it.[10]

A while ago the Phoenix Sun's basketball star Charles Barkley went on television and announced that he wasn't a role model. His job, he said, was "to wreck havoc on the basketball court," not to raise "your children." But Barkley doesn't get to choose whether or not he'll be a role model. Neither does anyone else. The people do. Karl Malone, another basketball star, has it exactly: "I don't think it's [Barkley's] decision to make. We don't *choose* to be role models, we are *chosen*." The job of role model is not voluntary, but it surely exists.[11]

But the issue goes beyond that of role models. If William James was correct, the existence of a hero is critical for the nation. James, an American philosopher and psychologist, argued "that no significant social change has ever come about which is not the work of great men, and that the 'receptivities' of today which make that work possible are the result of the acts or examples of the outstanding individuals of yesterday." James exaggerated the issue. Significant social change has occurred in recent years, and without the "great men" (or women) James thought necessary for that change. Perhaps the "great man theory" was valid in the past, when an individual, Napoleon for example, could dominate the earth, but it no longer is today. Yet if social change has occurred without great leaders to command it, it is also true that great leaders expedite social change and point to the direction of the change. If they are not the critical element of social change, they are surely facilitators of it. If nothing else, they can ease the pain that social change inevitably brings to some.

On a loftier plane, heroes represent good in the fight against evil, they help in the countless mini-battles occurring within society, battles of virtue in arenas close to us; they help us visualize, seek, and occasionally obtain justice. This is often the hero's role in popular culture. He has been the victim of or witness to an outrage, and he seeks revenge in the name of ethics and honor. We seek justice and fight against systems that deny it to us, and in that the hero is critical. He leads society in this fight, in the battle for what is right. More than the battle, however, the hero is a manifestation of the unspoken faith in the good, in the idea that "evil men ... [will be] subdued by a hero." The hero succeeds in the name of good or dies trying.[12]

Of course heroes can evoke conflict within society. They can be negative role models, for example, or they can provoke class antagonism and general rebellion. In the United States ethnic heroes have provoked both violent and nonviolent strife, rioting and interethnic competition. Because different ethnic groups may have competing goals and their own heroes to help secure those goals, ethnic strife may be exacerbated by different ethnic heroes. Still and all, it appears clear that heroes are necessary for and beneficial to society.

Any question about whether or not society needs heroes becomes moot when we consider that every nation has its heroes (in whatever form) as does every city, state, and county, and as does every gang and softball team and association of sales personnel. The fact to begin with, the point to recognize, is that there are heroes and always have been heroes in American society. They are in and of American society as they are in and of every society. All nations both want and need heroes. In his *The Living and the Dead: A Study of the Symbolic Life of Americans*, W. Lloyd Warner put it this way: "Heroes and hero-worshipers are integral parts of any complex, changing society; which is to say that heroes must always be present in the culture of nations and civilizations, whether ancient or contemporary." It is safe to assume that there always will be heroes regardless of the form that the hero takes or the quality of the individual who occupies the status.

Nations create monuments to people deemed worthy of respect; these are seen in every city in the world. Parades honor heroes, postage stamps commemorate their glories and their persons. Even if some are denigrated in time, others arise, in marble, on posters, in new ceremonies. Among other things, we name streets, airports, ball fields, and buildings in honor of our heroes. Titles are given, medals handed out, and trophies awarded. Faces appear in portraits and occasionally on the sides of mountains. The list of ways in which we celebrate our heroes does not appear to be finite. All of this would seem to suggest that heroes are not only welcomed and celebrated in society, it would seem to suggest that they are needed.

In *The Elementary Forms of Religious Life*, Emile Durkheim argues that "it is an essential postulate of sociology that a human institution cannot rest upon an error and a lie, without which it could not exist. If it were not founded in the nature of things, it would have encountered in the facts a resistance over which it could never have triumphed." Durkheim is speaking here of religion. He is saying that because religion exists everywhere it must be accepted that, regardless of the validity of the particular tenets of any specific religion, religion itself serves a purpose, it fulfills a social need. By the same reasoning, as heroes exist in all societies, as they are found everywhere and desired by most social institutions, they too must fill a social need.

More than national (official) recognition with ceremonial honors and more than the social need for role models and more than the academic need for a tool through which the nation's heritage can be passed to future generations, people seem to need heroes in their day-to-day lives. People search for someone to admire, for someone to look up to and try to emulate. More than any other reason, that is why there are heroes.

The mayors of various cities, bright and perceptive men and women, battle each other furiously for the right to locate a professional football or baseball franchise within their city. Part of these battles is surely based on economics. A major league baseball, football, or basketball team in a city means increased tax revenue, jobs, tourism, and other financial benefits. But while this explains why businesspeople and politicians want a professional sports franchise in their city, it does not explain why so many fans so intensely, so passionately, want a team to support. The players rarely come from the area they are representing in athletic competition. Yet the cities, the taxpayers, will happily spend millions to attract and maintain a sports franchise, to assure that they have something, a team or a player, to root for. If professional teams aren't available to provide the fans with something to cheer for, the local teams—semiprofessional, college, and high school—act as substitutes, and they do so quite well. [13]

It seems clear that people need someone to admire, a person on a ball field, someone waving to people from a float in a parade, or an image on a strip of film—today, most especially, an image on a strip of film.

Initially movie studios tried to hide the identity of their actors, but it didn't work. By "1910 . . . the idea of the movie star was born." What is significant here is that the idea did not come from the fertile imaginations of the heads of the studios (they really did battle furiously against the idea of movie celebrities and stars). The idea of the movie star came from the public. William Goldman describes how in the early years of the motion picture industry the studios would get letters from fans addressed to movie stars. If the fans didn't know the actors' names the studios would get mail addressed to " 'The Butler with the Mustache' or 'The Girl with the Curly Blonde Hair.'" They kept pouring in from the public, from people who wanted someone to admire. This was around the turn of the century and things haven't changed all that much in the hundred years since.[14]

There are between 1200 and 1500 fan clubs in the United States. Some of them are big businesses, large and well organized and supporting very famous individuals. Others are made up of small numbers of people who admire athletes or entertainers who aren't as yet especially well-established. But large or small, the fan clubs are a clear indication of people's need for heroes and the fact, perhaps the necessity of, hero worship. Nor is it only the current matinee idol or rock star who is the object of the fans' adoration. Yes Brad Pitt and Madonna have their admirers, but so do Elvis and James Dean. And Custer and Billy the Kid and Dillinger too.[15]

As fans spend astonishing amounts of money for team merchandise—jackets, caps, sweatshirts—they spend an equally astonishing amount of money for celebrity clothing. Even the United States government recognizes the value of the possessions of the celebrity-hero. The leather jacket and brown fedora worn by Harrison Ford as Indiana Jones during his several *Crusades* have been placed in the Smithsonian Institution. His jacket is there, according to curator Charlie McGovern, because "heroism, as embodied by [Indiana Jones], is not a matter of defying all odds bravely and almost in a comic manner. This is not camp," McGovern argues. "This is very much an informed, psychologically complex heroism of both the big gesture under physical danger and the everyday life."[16]

McGovern may be exaggerating, but you'd never know that by the people who visit the exhibit. The objects are there, McGovern says, because they are the sort of thing that a lot of people want to see. Included in the Smithsonian Institution collection of heroic clothing are the military insignia worn by Tom Selleck as Thomas Magnum, P.I., some of Frank Sinatra's bow ties, and a dress Dustin Hoffman wore in *Tootsie*.

Heroes serve one final purpose in society generally and in the United States in particular: The existence of heroes is a business. It is not only a question of the money paid to entertainers—show people and athletes. It goes well beyond that. Museums are designated to celebrate heroes and attract customers, towns battle over the birthplace and, more important, the burial place of the hero. The burial place is more important because more tourists come to visit the cemeteries than the birthplaces of heroes. Places where heroes lived and worked are designated as landmarks to attract (paying) visitors. Can anyone deny the power of "Graceland"?

Beyond this, and beyond the income of various sports and entertainment heroes, is their wider economic impact. The individual hero often supports a group of people—attorneys and agents, secretaries and assistants—in addition to the inevitable hangers-on. (Some athletes are called "the franchise," an unnecessary reminder that the success of the team, financial and otherwise, depends on them.) In other words, the individual American celebrity-hero is today often an individual American industry.

THE SOCIAL CONSEQUENCES OF THE DISAPPEARANCE OF THE AMERICAN HERO

The lack of a contemporary American hero has consequences for society. First, the nation keeps reaching back to its past to recapture some of the glories of the heroes of legend, those who were heroes before the media probed into their sex lives and before bureaucracy and technology helped crush individual accomplishment, before the acute awareness of ethnicity made different groups celebrate different and often antagonistic peoples, and before the youth culture and geographical (cultural) divisions shut off some heroes to specific Americans. That is, the nation consistently reaches back to a time before the social system disallowed true heroes.

The Lindbergh story will forever be a part of American legend as will the bravery and daring of Amelia Earhart, the former in part because of the tragedy of the kidnapping and murder of his son, the latter in part because of her untimely and mysterious death, and both because of the courage of their deeds. Babe Ruth, along with other specific athletes, will continue as an American hero; and if the heroes of the glorious tales of the West have been tarnished a bit today by closer examinations of history and by revisionism, those tales and those heroes surely will return, if perhaps somewhat altered to accommodate contemporary standards.

The deeds of American adventurers, of Lewis and Clark and of Peary and Henson, for example, will continue to be regarded as heroic. So will the efforts of various scientists of the past and the contributions of some politicians, intellectuals, and business leaders. The nation will always remember fondly the imaginative tales of John Dillinger and Pretty Boy Floyd. And as long as history books glorify the famous battles of the past, military leaders and a number of soldiers will be heroes so entwined within American history as to be inseparable from it.

With the disappearance of the traditional American hero, contemporary American society will have to take its heroes where it can find them. Douglas Foster tells of his son, Jake, responding to his question about heroes, about political leaders he admires: "Jake says flatly: 'Except for sports, nobody. I don't think there are any people like that left any more.'" Jake is right. Contemporary American society is forced to find its heroes in the capacious arena of triviality—in rock concerts and television shows, in the movies and on assorted athletic fields. We go so far as to make up new sports and athletic events—arena football, for example—in order to create new heroes. And that, again, is because we need them. George Vecsey says that sports commentator "Red Smith used to apologize for 'godding up' the celebrities he covered." But Vecsey also notes that "usually that's exactly what the public wants." Can anyone doubt that he is correct?[17]

The criterion of being famous for being famous—in the context of this book of being a celebrity for being a celebrity, of being a hero for being a hero—is effected by Gresham's Law. Those who are celebrated because they are truly heroic will be ignored as those who are celebrated for being celebrated will achieve increasing, if temporary, popularity. As there are by definition few true heroes and an apparently endless number of people who seek fame for the sake of fame, the genuine hero will be destroyed by the sheer number of nonheroes, and the willingness of other nonheroes to replace those currently in vogue.

Even in the world of the celebrity, those with unusual abilities may be pushed out of the spotlight by those who are less gifted but more aggressive. The true artist who cannot or will not be involved in self-promotion will vanish in the glare of the less talented—or untalented—individual who, through slick promotion or media hyperbole, can successfully establish himself as one who is worthy of attention, for whatever reason. The alternative is for the truly gifted to behave in a less than heroic manner so as to gain the attention given to the less talented individual. This necessarily diminishes his heroic stature.

The idealism of the 1960s hippie movement was perhaps naive, but it did give direction to some of the youth of the time. It gave a portion of

America's young people a shared sense of responsibility, a collective sense of purpose. These are necessary or at least beneficial for the young. Without them, youth can easily become lost, and that is a dangerous situation. It is dangerous because it creates a state that Emile Durkheim called "anomie," normlessness, a social situation in which there are few rules, in which one is no longer guided by social requirements, because there is no one admired enough to give direction, guidance, a sense of purpose. The hero fulfills this need. The hero sets standards, establishes goals, and gives meaning to existence, something people generally and the young in particular need in their lives.

If the hero does not exist, people—again, especially the young—behave without focus; consequently they may seek out (potentially) antisocial goals on their own. They act without guidance. Currently in the United States one such goal takes the form of the ethnic awareness that has contributed to the historical revisionism noted earlier. Other goals, however, and other forms of behavior are less idealistic and more dangerous; they include violence (sometimes based on ethnic considerations, sometimes not), gang membership, and drug use. In this sense, the rock, sports, and movie stars who are the heroes of the youth, the celebrity-hero who does nothing but be a celebrity, can be an important safety valve for society at large. If we have seen the last of America's traditional national heroes, the institutionalization of the celebrity-hero may be a critical factor in adding stability to the lives of America's youth and, consequently, to American society as a whole.

Celebrities may live well if they are clever enough to recognize their weaknesses and the brevity of their fame and if they prepare for the future. They may indeed displace more gifted people whose talents deserve but do not receive the attention of the public. Ultimately, however, celebrities do little harm to anything save perhaps popular culture and, as noted, they may even do some good. What is worrisome is not the celebrity-hero, but the false hero, who diminishes us as the true hero would elevate us: the populist politician who appeals to callousness and emotion rather than reason and moderation; the scientist who focuses on attaining the prize instead of scientific integrity; the business executive who sees tomorrow and cannot see next year.

The lack of heroes presents a danger. Given the need for heroes, there is a real possibility that if the right person doesn't come along to fulfill that status the wrong person will. Recognizing that heroes are required but that numerous forces—structural and cultural, geographical, historical, and technical—have caused the true national hero to disappear in the United States, we are forced to make do with substitute heroes. Hobsbawn notes that society truly needs heroes and that there is danger inherent in that need: "such is the need for heroes and champions, that if there are no real ones, unsuitable candidates are pressed into service." This was the concern of George Bernard Shaw, who noted that the problem was not the search for a Nietzschean Superman. That search predates Nietzsche. The problem is, as always, "what kind of person is this Superman to be?"[18]

Because society needs heroes, it will create them. The danger is that it may create the wrong heroes. If those who reflect society's values, who inspire people to reach beyond themselves for greater accomplishment, who establish higher standards for the human condition, are not regarded as heroes, others—people of lesser qualities and with lesser goals—may be.

If things go well, those others will continue to be trivialities, celebrities in the Boorstinian sense of having achieved fame because they achieved fame. If things do not go well, there may be a very different kind of hero. The individual to worry about, the "hero" to which a nation without heroes is susceptible, is the false hero, the one who appears to have the qualities of the true hero but in fact distorts, exaggerates, lies.

In all probability, these concerns are not especially realistic, although they should not be discounted. The probability is that the future will be mundane. The local hero will become a permanent fixture in American society, as a regionally, ethnically, generationally specific, or gender-based idol. A second type of hero will come into being: the temporary hero, who for example risks his life to save someone else's, receives a great deal of attention because of that demonstration of courage, and returns rather quickly to obscurity. We are evolving into a nation of three specific types of heroes: the trivial celebrity-hero—the sports star, movie star, rock hero; the local hero who appeals to a particular group of people; and the transitory hero who performs a marvelous feat, gets (and deserves) praise, and is never heard from again.

Marshall McLuhan thought that new heroes, equal in importance to those of the past, would develop. That is a highly optimistic view. Yet in a way McLuhan is correct. We will continue to develop heroes because the society continues to need heroes, and in the sense that they are accepted as heroes they will be as important as past heroes. But they will not be of the same quality, endurance, or breadth of appeal as past heroes.[19]

If we allow that heroes exist today, they are different than the heroes of the past (excepting sports and entertainment heroes), not only in actions but in form. The nature of heroism today is different from the nature of heroism past. Heroism fades quickly these days. Emerson's assertion "Every hero becomes a bore at last" has never been more accurate. Because of the number of changes and the rate of those changes within American culture these days, should a miracle occur and the nation come to accept a hero, he is surely going to become a bore, and rather quickly. That is one of the conveniences of having celebrity-heroes; they are easily replaceable. They change whenever a new generation alters the tastes of the previous generation and therefore defines its own (new) celebrity-heroes.

Emerson helps to explain the hero worship of actors and athletes, people whose celebrity is notorious for quick rises and quick falls, people who go in and out of style almost overnight. If heroes are needed and if they get old fast, then they must be replaced and rapidly. Perhaps this is because they haven't really done much that is truly heroic or perhaps it is because everyone does recognize that all they've done is to act in a movie or sing a song or play in a ball game. Perhaps we all know that all they've done at last is trivial. Perhaps we really do recognize and understand the nature of the celebrity-hero.

SOCIAL CONDITIONS NECESSARY FOR HEROES TO EXIST

Soon after Ralph Abernathy revealed in his autobiography that Martin Luther King, Jr., had had frequent affairs while married to Coretta Scott King, Don Wycliff wondered why, more than two decades after his assassination, it was still "important to maintain an image of Martin Luther King as faultless." Noting that Achilles, the Greek hero had a vulnerable spot in his heel and that King David, "as great a hero as there is in the Bible," had a lusty nature, Wycliff asserts that "Heroes are only human" and that "the greatest human is no god." P. L. Travers agrees that "the hero is not a god, nor even a saint." Because the hero "has a human heart," he necessarily has some weaknesses, some potential for failure.[20]

But Wycliff and Travers are mistaken. American heroes are gods, or at least they were "fashioned" by God, as Søren Kierkegaard has it. That's how they've traditionally been regarded in the United States and why we've had them until recent decades and why we no longer have them. People can have failings, but heroes cannot. At best, at the American public's most generous, heroes can have human faults, but they can never have human weaknesses. America's heroes can stumble, but they cannot fall. The errors that they commit must be either conspicuously forgivable or immediately redeemable. American heroes may be human, but they cannot act as humans act; they cannot be weak as humans are weak. In a very real sense the traditional demand is that the American hero maintain a god-like illusion.

Thus, the hero existed in the United States when the image of the hero as god was accepted and sustained by society; as long as the American people allowed their imaginations to permit the hero-as-perfection, the American hero was secure. The image and the hero were destroyed when, for a variety of structural and cultural reasons, the people demanded and the media offered a realistic examination of the hero. Reality supplanted imagery, and reality destroys heroes.

As changes in America's social system increasingly prohibited the existence of a traditional national hero, the American people began to accept the idea that the typical American hero now would be a celebrity-hero. To bring back the heroes of the past, America's present social system would have to be altered; it would have to be made to accommodate the type of heroes we once had. If we only admire heroes of the past, we will have only images of fading icons. To create and sustain modern heroes, social conditions—our culture and social structure—must be changed. The question is, then, what changes must be made to find these new heroes? What social conditions must be met if heroes who measure up to past heroes are found and permitted to exist in the United States today?

First among these conditions is the opportunity to do something the nation recognizes as truly heroic. By "nation" here is meant not only a substantial number of people, but a reasonable sampling from every ethnic and economic group, from every part of the country and from every age group, and from both sexes. In a word, the American hero must truly represent the people who make up the United States. Included within the people's recognition of someone who is truly heroic is the ability of the hero to grow with the memory of the heroic act and the willingness of the public to permit this.

Second, the requirement that the hero appeal to the nation at large implies that the nation must recognize and agree upon a specific set of values and goals, and recognize and agree also that the hero has uniquely and courageously manifested those values in order to achieve those goals. In the United States that generally means that the hero has taken a risk, demonstrated an extraordinary degree of bravery, and has done so selflessly.

It also means that the people within the nation agree that the goal was worthy of heroic effort as, for example, the saving of lives at the risk of one's own life.

The agreed upon set of values and goals within society can be taken to represent the purpose of the nation, its ideology, its meaning. Only with a unified sense of purpose, a common moral view evident in universally accepted values and goals, can nationally accepted heroism be manifest. Only with a unified sense of purpose can the nation rally around an action and regard it as heroic.

As a corollary here, it should be acknowledged that a fair effort counts for something. The "winning is all" attitude has its place in American society, and reasonably. What is less reasonable is that the "winning is all" permits—encourages—an abandonment of the rules and regulations that permit social systems to exist. The nation is better off respecting the person or team that played by the rules and came in second than adoring the person or team that came in first but dishonestly. In a word, we should restore a degree of integrity to our standards (or reinvent it).

Third, there must be a willingness on the part of the public to allow the hero some indiscretions, some failings, and still accept him as a hero. Society, that is, must be willing to either ignore any unpleasant qualities the hero may manifest or, better yet, avoid learning about them. It is a sociological axiom that people do not respond to the truth, they respond to what they believe to be true. If unhappy characteristics of a hero can be kept from the public—arrogance, mean-spiritedness, silliness—they will be irrelevant insofar as his heroic status is concerned. If his undesirable qualities are hidden his image and, consequently, his possible position as hero, are secure. There must also be an exaggeration of the hero's exploits and a willingness on the part of the media and the public to accept that exaggeration. There must be a minimum of attention to the rewards that inevitably follow recognition as a hero, or at least a degree of discretion concerning the rewards.

Fourth, the media must be willing to acknowledge the hero as a hero and accept the conditions that he not be examined too closely. The further we are from a hero, the more hero-like he is perceived to be; conversely, the closer we are to a hero, the more human the hero becomes and the more obvious are the hero's failings. If we get too close we see those failings, and even if they are forgiven they may not be forgotten. In any case he is diminished as a hero. For a hero to exist, the detailed examinations of his failings and the attempts to get close enough to him to see his flaws, two characteristics deeply ingrained in American culture today, must stop. One of the self-imposed jobs of the media today—and the media are very good at this job—is to bring the hero's weaknesses out into the open. For the hero to continue to exist, the nature of this self-imposed job must change.

The media must stress the hero's actions and refrain from exploiting the fact that many people are interested in the man and want to know more about him. Roderick Nash argues that heroism "depends on achievement but even more on recognition," a point that has been noted throughout this book. That recognition, however, must be selective. Some parts of the hero's life must be known—indeed, well publicized; other parts of the hero's life must be kept from public view. In the past the media helped to produce and sustain heroes quite deliberately, by publicizing some but not all of the hero's story. Perhaps it was in the interests of the media to do so then (and perhaps it is in the interest of the media today to do exactly the opposite). But once the heroes of the past were established as heroes they were generally respected; they remained heroes through the efforts of the media long enough to be remembered that way. For heroes to return to America, similar efforts by the media are necessary, although that possibility seems improbable at best. [21]

To be a hero one must look like a hero and act as a hero. But these can happen only if we allow heroes to look like heroes, which we do, and only if we allow heroes to behave as heroes, which we no longer do.

The people must be willing to allow the hero to maintain his heroic status, and this can only occur if they do not examine him too closely. The media must cooperate by avoiding publication of embarrassing tales of the potential hero. And the public must restrain its curiosity. The action that the hero undertook to achieve that status must be taken to represent a collective national ideal and the action must be accepted as having been deliberate. We must be willing to exaggerate the positive aspects of the individual and his heroic gestures, and we must we willing to ignore the negative aspects of the individual and of any of his unheroic (but not illegal) gestures. The issue of reward must be muted. The hero must be seen as a representative of the people. The hero must be an inspiration. Every man, woman, and child must be able to see in the hero a reflection of what we all want to be, what we all should be. The traditional American hero can exist once more if and only if American society permits all of this.

It is unlikely to happen. Americans are contented with their celebrity-heroes, their temporary heroes, and their local heroes. More than this contentment, Americans will never allow their curiosity about heroic individuals to remain unsatisfied, and the media will not stop pandering to

Notes

ABBREVIATIONS

NYT - *New York Times*
NYTM - *New York Times Magazine*
NYTBR - *New York Times Book Review*
NYRB - *New York Review of Books*
BES - *The (Baltimore) Evening Sun*
TBS - *The Baltimore Sun*

CHAPTER 1

1. *NYT*, October 6, 1991, p. H 2; *Insight*, October 21, 1991, pp. 11–17. *NYTM*, October 31, 1993, p. 33 and *Newsweek*, July 26, 1993, p. 44. *NYT*, March 29, 1994, p. A 10. *NYTM*, October 31, 1993, p. 33. *Newsweek*, July 26, 1993, p. 44.

2. Schlesinger, "The Decline of Heroes," in *Heroes and Anti-Heroes*, ed. Harold Lubin (Scranton, Pa.: Chandler Publishing, 1968), p. 341; ibid., p. 322. Clark is cited in Don Wycliff, "Where Have All the Heroes Gone?" *NYTM*, July 31, 1985, p. 23; Boorstin, "From Hero to Celebrity," in Lubin, p. 327; Nachman, "Thoughts on Heroism," *The World and I*, February 1988, p. 547. McQuaid, *The Anxious Years: America in the Vietnam-Watergate Era* (New York: Basic Books, 1989), p. ix.

3. Wolfe, in *Time* magazine, February 13, 1989, p. 90; Mailer, in Richard Schickel, *Intimate Strangers: The Culture of Celebrity* (New York: Doubleday & Company, 1985), p. 172. Royko, in *BES*, July 2, 1993, p. 2 A; *The UTNE Reader*, May/June, 1993, p. 95; President Carter, in Peter N. Carrol, *It Seemed Like Nothing Happened* (New York: Holt, Rinehart and Winston, 1982), p. 172. *See also Newsweek* magazine, January 18, 1993; the quote from the Shepard play is given in an article by Marilyn Stasio, *NYTBR*, October 14, 1990, p. 1. Bill Buford, in *The New Yorker*, June 26/July 3, 1995, p. 12.

4. Hoagland, in *NYTM*, March 10, 1984; Meyrowitz, in *Psychology Today*, July 1984; Wycliff, in *NYTM*, July 1, 1985; Walden, "Life in America," *USA Today*, January 1986.

5. *Time* magazine, May 9, 1988, p. 46 and *Time* magazine, July 16, 1990, p. 23. James Patterson and Peter Kim, *The Day America Told the Truth: What People Really Believe about Everything That Really Matters* (Englewood Cliffs, N.J.: Prentice-Hall, 1991) p. 207.

6. Schlesinger, in Lubin, p. 343. *Parade* magazine, March 15, 1992, p. 6 and February 25, 1990; *Newsweek* magazine, February 17, 1992, p. 27.

7. The quote explaining the criteria for awards from the Carnegie Hero Fund comes from their 1991 *Annual Report*; data on the Giraffe Project from *The Giraffe Gazette*, vol. 2, no. 1 (Winter 1991).

8. Tuchman is quoted in Patterson and Kim, p. 207.

9. See *The World Almanac*, 1992; *Psychology Today*, December 1988, p. 52; *Parade* magazine, May 2, 1993, p. 18; *NYT*, May 9, 1993, p. A 1 and November 6, 1988, p. E 9.

10. Boorstin, in Lubin, p. 334. Peter Shaffer, *Amadeus* (New York: Harper & Row, 1981) p. 93.

11. Greer, "Hero Today and Gone Tomorrow," *The World and I*, February 1988, p. 595.

12. Dee Brown, *The Year of the Century: 1876* (New York: Charles Scribner's Sons, 1966), p. 197. Also see Boorstin, in Lubin, p. 336.

13. *The Ladies Home Journal*, June-July, 1984; Goldman, in *Newsweek* magazine, Summer 1986, Collector's Edition, Special Issue. The *Washington Post Magazine*, December 24, 1989. *Modern Maturity*, June-July, 1990.

14. Berkowitz, *Local Heroes* (Lexington, Mass.: Lexington Books, 1987). Hentoff, *American Heroes: In and Out of School* (New York: Delacorte Press, 1987). Stark, in *Psychology Today*, May 1986; McGinley is quoted in Berkowitz (p. 170), who notes that her view "reduces heroism to nothingness."

15. Goldman, *The Season: A Candid Look at Broadway* (New York: Bantam Books, 1970). Holden's book is *Big Deal: A Year as a Professional Poker Player* (New York: Viking Press, 1990). See also *NYT*, May 5, 1993, p. E 2 and *The Washington Post*, August 13, 1993, p. D 16.

16. On Chessman as a Reichian hero, see Frederick F. Siegel, *Troubled Journey* (New York: Hill and Wang, 1989), p. 182.

17. Mailer is cited by Marshall Fishwick, "Prologue," in *Heroes of Popular Culture*, eds. Ray B. Browne, Marshall Fishwick, and Michael T. Marsden (Bowling Green, Ohio: Bowling Green University Popular Press, 1972), p. 7.

18. Ian Frazier, *Great Plains* (New York: Penguin Books, 1989), pp. 171, 176.

19. Eksteins, *Rites of Spring: The Great War and the Birth of the Modern Age* (Boston: Houghton Mifflin Company, 1989), pp. 183, 217; Pfaff, *The New Yorker*, May 8, 1989, pp. 105–6.

20. Erik Barnouw, *Tube of Plenty: The Evolution of American Television*, rev. ed. (New York: Oxford University Press, 1982), pp. 472–3.

21. McLuhan, "The Popular Hero and the Anti-Hero," in Browne, Fishwick, and Marsden, p. 136. Johnson, *Modern Times: The World from the Twenties to the Eighties* (New York: Harper Colophon Books, 1983), p. 10. Lubin, pp. 305, 315.

22. Laqueur, *Europe since Hitler* (New York: Penguin Books, 1982), p. 279.

23. Fishwick, in Browne, Fishwick, and Marsden, " p. 3. William Manchester, *The Glory and the Dream* (New York: Bantam Books, 1975), pp. 726–29.

24. Hoagland, "Where Have All the Heroes Gone?" *NYTM*, March 10, 1984. Lubin, p. 305.

25. Martin's comments are in Edmund Fawcett and Tony Thomas, *America and the Americans* (Glasgow, Scotland: Fontana and Collins, 1983), p. 376.

26. Joe McGinniss, *Heroes* (New York: Pocket Books, 1977).

CHAPTER 2

1. *NYT*, March 3, 1991, p. A 1 and *Time* magazine January 28, 1991, p. 18; *BES*, March 10, 1991, p. 4 E. Estimates of the number of Iraqis killed were sharply lowered in time. *BES*, March 9, 1993, p. 8 A.

2. See Browne, *NYTM*, March 3, 1991, p. 29. Tilford, in *Newsweek*, January 20, 1992, p. 20.

3. Surveys are cited in *Newsweek*, March 11, 1991, p. 43 and *Time* magazine, March 18, 1991, p. 28 and June 17, 1991, p. 61.

4. On the media during the Gulf War, see Browne, *NYTM*, March 3, 1991, p. 29; Walter Cronkite, in *Newsweek*, February 25, 1991, p. 43; Frank Starr, in *TBS*, March 10, 1991, p. 13; Norman Solomon, *NYT*, May 24, 1991, p. A 31.

5. Will, in *Newsweek*, March 11, 1991, p. 78.

6. *NYT*, June 11, 1991, p. A 16. Stanley, *Army Times*, June 24, 1991, p. 25. Tom Wicker, in *NYT*, February 27, 1991, p. A 27.

7. Baer is quoted in *TBS*, June 23, 1991, p. 3.

8. *Time* magazine, May 6, 1991, p. 26.

CHAPTER 3

1. See P. L. Travers, "The World of the Hero," in *Parabola: Myth and the Quest for Meaning*, vol. 1, no. 1 (Winter 1976), pp. 42–48. Campbell's most noteworthy books on this subject are *The Hero with a Thousand Faces* and *The Power of Myth*. See Robert A. Segal, *Joseph Campbell: An Introduction*, rev. ed. (New York: Mentor Books, 1990).

2. See Charles I. Glicksberg, "The Tragic Hero," in Lubin, pp. 356–66.

3. Steckmesser, *The Western Hero in History and Legend* (Norman: University of Oklahoma Press, 1965), p. 255. Hook, *The Hero in History* (Boston: Beacon Press, 1943), p. 184; ibid., p. 175.

4. Kissinger, *Diplomacy* (New York: Simon and Schuster, 1994). Wright, *The Atlantic Monthly*, July 1994. Rothstein; *NYT*, December 18, 1994, p. H 39.

5. On Norman's analysis, see Carol Pearson and Katherine Pope, *The Female Hero in American and British Literature* (New York: R. R. Bowker, 1981), p. 3. Also see Carl Jung, *Man and His Symbols* (New York: Dell Publishing, 1968).

6. Pearson and Pope, p. 3.

7. Stephen Jay Gould, *NYT*, April 26, 1992, p. H 15.

8. Boorstin, in Lubin, p. 329; Hook, p. 152.

9. See Berger, *Invitation to Sociology* (New York: Doubleday Anchor, 1963), p. 110.

10. See Manchester, *The Glory and the Dream*, pp. 537–56 on General MacArthur and, especially, Manchester, *American Caesar: Douglas MacArthur, 1880–1964* (Boston: Little, Brown and Company, 1978). See also Michael Schaller, *Douglas MacArthur: The Far Eastern General* (New York: Oxford University Press, 1989). In 1990 the Congress of the

United States paid "tribute to Dwight D. Eisenhower as a hero of war, an architect of peace and a no-nonsense Kansas farm boy affectionately known to millions of Americans simply as 'Ike' " (*NYT*, March 28, 1990, p. A 18). But see Margaret Truman, ed., *Where the Buck Stops: The Personal and Private Writings of Harry S. Truman* (New York: Warner Books, 1989), p. 62.

11. See Stephen Hunter, *TBS*, April 12, 1992, p. 6. *NYT*, January 12, 1992, p. E 7 and May 4, 1992, p. C 4.

12. Will, *Men at Work* (New York: Macmillan Publishers, 1990), p. 305.

13. Rafferty, in *The New Yorker*, December 5, 1994, pp. 132–33. Maslin, in *NYT*, December 2, 1994, p. C 8.

14. Bob Feller, with Bill Gilbert, *Now Pitching, Bob Feller* (New York: Birch Lane Press, 1990), p. 83. Greenberg shares this record with Jimmy Foxx.

15. See Warren I. Susman, *Culture as History: The Transformation of America in the Twentieth Century* (New York: Pantheon Books, 1984), pp. 145–47. Also see Leverett T. Smith, Jr., "Ty Cobb, Babe Ruth and the Changing Image of the Athletic Hero," in Browne, Fishwick, and Marsden, pp. 73–85. Feller, with Gilbert, p. 83. Hank Greenberg, *The Story of My Life* (New York: Times Books, 1989), p. 116.

16. Greenberg, pp. 43, 111.

17. John Steadman, *BES*, August 16, 1988, p. 2 C.

18. See *Newsweek*, May 5, 1994, p. 43. See also William Goldman and Mike Lupica, *Wait till Next Year* (New York: Bantam Books, 1989), p. 277.

19. Fromm is quoted in Alvin Toffler, *The Third Wave* (New York: Bantam Books, 1981), pp. 381–82. See Barbara Kellerman, *The Political Presidency* (New York: Oxford University Press, 1984), p. 4. Hook, p. 169.

20. For Max Weber's analysis of charisma, see H. H. Gerth and C. Wright Mills, eds., *From Max Weber: Essays in Sociology* (New York: Oxford University Press, 1958), especially chapter 9.

21. Nachman, p. 555.

INTRODUCTION TO PART II

1. Lubin, p. 9.

CHAPTER 4

1. See *TBS*, August 15, 1993, p. 5 J.

2. Baskir and Strauss, "The Wounded Generation: The Twenty-Seven Million Men of Vietnam," *American Heritage*, April/May 1978, vol. 29, no. 3, p. 27.

3. See *Newsweek*, April 4, 1994, p. 41; *Time* magazine, October 18, 1993, p. 38; *NYT*, October 8, 1994, p. A 1 and October 25, 1993, p. A 1.

4. See Fawcett and Thomas, p. 51.

5. David H. Hackworth, in *Newsweek* magazine, January 20, 1992, p. 29. See also Howard Fineman, in *Newsweek*, April 1, 1991, p. 24.

6. Lubin, p. 12. Also see Loren Baritz, *Backfire* (New York: Ballantine Books, 1986).

7. Turkel, *"The Good War"* (New York: Ballantine Books, 1984). Fussell's article is in *The Atlantic Monthly*, August 1989. Also see *Insight*, November 13, 1989, p. 58.

8. Goode, *The Celebration of Heroes: Prestige as a Control System* (Berkeley: University of California Press, 1978), p. 170.

9. Ibid., p. 170. Also see David Wallechinsky, Irving Wallace, and Amy Wallace, *The Book of Lists* (New York: Bantam Books, 1978), pp. 39–40.

10. See, for example, *NYT*, January 1, 1992, p. A 26 and *TBS*, January 16, 1994, p. 15 E. See also *NYT*, June 11, 1991, p. A 16.

11. O'Grady's picture was on numerous magazine covers and he did the talk show circuit; however, O'Grady called the rescuers the heroes. See *BES*, June 9, 1995, p. 1 A. The quote is from Lena Williams's commentary in *NYT*, June 18, 1995, p. E 5. The December 25, 1995/January 1, 1996 issue of *Time* magazine labeled O'Grady a future Trivial Pursuit answer (p. 164).

CHAPTER 5

1. "The Age of Play" originally printed in *The Independent*, December 20, 1924, reprinted in George E. Mowry, ed., *The Twenties: Fords, Flappers & Fanatics* (Englewood Cliffs, N.J.: Prentice-Hall, 1963), p. 44.

2. Ibid., p. 82.

3. Quoted in Susman, p. 142.

4. *BES*, June 26, 1991, p. 1 B.

5. O'Connor, "Where Have You Gone, Joe DiMaggio?" in Browne, Fishwick, and Marsden, p. 88.

6. *NYT*, September 20, 1994, p. A 23 and October 30, 1994, p. F 9; and see *BES*, September 21, 1994, p. 14 A. See also *Newsweek*, December 12, 1994, p. 83 and August 22, 1994, pp. 47–56. On the troubles in the NBA, see *NYT*, July 1, 1995, p. C 1.

7. *NYT*, April 10, 1991, p. C 6 and April 7, 1988, p. C 3. See also *BES*, October 31, 1994, p. 1 C. As this is being written, players' incomes and owners' profits continue to increase.

8. Susman, p. 141. See *Time* magazine, August 22, 1994, p. 72, for an analysis of the salaries of both past and modern athletes.

9. *Insight*, December 18, 1989, p. 55. *TBS*, November 3, 1994, p. 5 C.

10. Larry Merchant, *Ringside Seat at the Circus* (New York: Holt, Rinehart and Winston, 1976), pp. 10–11.

11. *Time* magazine, November 4, 1991, p. 53. *BES*, September 7, 1992, p. 24. Also see *Newsweek*, November 11, 1991, p. 53. See Susman, p. 142.

12. *NYT*, June 25, 1989, p. E 27.

13. *NYT*, June 25, 1989, p. E 7. And see *NYT*, July 14, 1995 p. D 1. Also see *Time* magazine, May 15, 1989, p. 78, on athletes selling their autographs. José Canseco's 900-number and Reggie Jackson selling his canceled checks were noted in a *NYT* editorial reprinted in *BES*, October 31, 1989, p. 6 A.

14. *NYT*, August 20, 1987, p. A 1.

15. *NYTM*, September 18, 1994, p. 46. Also see *Time* magazine, April 12, 1993, p. 60 and September 26, 1994, p. 71.

16. See, for example, Murray Sperber, *College Sports, Inc.: The Athletic Department vs. the University* (New York: Henry Holt and Company, 1990). On the movie *Hoop Dreams*, see Ira Berkow, *NYT*, October 9, 1994, p. H 1.

17. See, for example, H. G. Bissinger, *Friday Night Lights: A Town, a Team, and a Dream* (New York: HarperPerennial, 1991). Also see McMillen, with Coggins, *Out of*

Bounds: How the American Sports Establishment is Being Driven by Greed and Hypocrisy and What Needs to Be Done About It (New York: Simon and Schuster, 1992).

18. Bensman and Lilienfeld, *Craft and Consciousness* (New York: John Wiley & Sons, 1973), pp. 71, 75.

19. See, for example, Gerald O'Connor, p. 89.

20. Roderick Nash, "The Mood of the People," Randy Roberts and James S. Olson, eds., *American Experiences*, vol. 2, *1877 to the Present* (Glenview, Ill.: Scott, Foresman and Company, 1986), p. 141.

21. *BES*, July 13, 1993, p. 10 D. Lipsyte, "The Emasculation of Sports," *NYTM*, April 2, 1995, pp. 51–56.

22. *BES*, June 18, 1991, p. 14 A.

23. *NYT*, March 9, 1992, p. C 2.

24. See Dave Anderson, *NYT*, December 21, 1995, p. 15.

CHAPTER 6

1. Barbara Kellerman, *The Political Presidency* (New York: Oxford University Press, 1984), p. 8.

2. Etzioni quoted in *Time* magazine, May 6, 1991, p. 37.

3. Fawcett and Thomas, p. 163. Also see *American Heritage* magazine, July-August 1994, p. 59.

4. The *Philadelphia Daily News* quoted in *BES*, November 3, 1989, p. 14 A.

5. Fawcett and Thomas, p. 133.

6. See Schlesinger, *The Cycles of American History* (Boston: Houghton Mifflin, 1986), p. 277.

7. Paul Johnson, *Modern Times: The World from the Twenties to the Eighties* (New York: Harper & Row, 1983), p. 259.

8. See, for example, Manchester, *The Glory and the Dream*, especially chapters 2 and 4; Ted Morgan, *FDR: A Biography* (New York: Simon and Schuster, 1985); William E. Leuchtenburg, *Franklin D. Roosevelt and the New Deal* (New York: Harper Books, 1963); James MacGregor Burns, *Roosevelt: The Lion and the Fox* (New York: Harcourt, Brace & World, 1956); Richard Hofstadter, *The American Political Tradition* (New York: Vintage Books, 1974).

9. *NYT*, November 21, 1993, p. E 1.

10. *NYT*, November 22, 1988, p. A 27.

11. Hodgson, *America in Our Time* (New York: Vintage Books, 1978), p. 165; Johnson, p. 614.

12. Roberts and Olson, p. 270; Burns is quoted in Kellerman, p. 80; Schlesinger, p. 405.

13. Kellerman, p. 87; Roberts and Olson, p. 272.

14. Fawcett and Thomas, p. 140; Kellerman, p. 24.

CHAPTER 7

1. *NYT*, October 22, 1989, p. H 1. In 1995, Demi Moore signed a contract with a film studio that paid her $12 million. Tom Hanks reportedly earned $45 million from *Forrest Gump*.

2. *Insight*, August 5, 1991, pp. 40–41.

3. Wallechinsky, Wallace, and Wallace, pp. 186–87. One can use statistics to argue the level of athletes' skills, but judgments of theatrical performances are purely subjective.

4. See May, "You are the Star: Evolution of the Theater Palace, 1908–1929," in Roberts and Olson, pp. 154, 158. Emphasis in original. See also Susman, p. xxvii.

5. See William Goldman, *The Season*, especially chapter 35. See *NYT*, April 3, 1995, p. B 1, for recent figures on Broadway theater attendance.

6. Neil Offen, *God Save the Players* (Chicago: Playboy Press, 1975), p. 159.

7. *NYT*, July 1, 1994, p. C 1. *Time* magazine, June 29, 1989, pp. 76–82 and July 17, 1989, p. 16. *NYT*, May 13, 1990, p. H 17.

8. See *Time* magazine, February 8, 1988, p. 70.

9. See David Puttnam, in *Time* magazine May 1, 1989, pp. 62–63.

10. Canby here is speaking about *Die Hard*, *NYT*, July 31, 1988, p. H 19.

11. Morris, *A Time of Passion: America 1960–1980* (New York: Penguin Books, 1986), p. 291.

12. Goldman and Lupica, p. 240. Jones is cited by Ed Sanders, *NYTBR*, December 13, 1987, p. 14.

13. Sanders, p. 13. Also see William Goldman, *Adventures in the Screen Trade: A Personal View of Hollywood and Screenwriting* (New York: Warner Books, 1983), pp. 4–38. In 1992, Madonna signed a $60 million deal. *NYT*, April 20, 1992, p. C 11.

14. See Husock, "Popular Song," *The Wilson Quarterly*, Summer 1988, pp. 51–52.

15. See Manchester, *The Glory and the Dream*, pp. 308, 725. Daniel Dotter, "Growing Up Is Hard to Do: Rock and Roll Performers as Cultural Heroes," *Sociological Spectrum*, vol 7, no. 1 (1987), pp. 25–44.

16. Derek Taylor, *It Was Twenty Years Ago Today* (New York: Simon and Schuster, 1987), p. 18.

17. Irving Wallace, Amy Wallace, David Wallechinsky, and Sylvia Wallace, *The Intimate Sex Lives of Famous People* (New York: Dell, 1981), pp. 31–32, 39.

18. Manchester, *The Glory and the Dream*, p. 592. See also Jim Koch, "Gone to Their Reward," *NYT*, June 5, 1994, p. V 1, on the effects of stars' deaths on people's memory of them.

19. Wallace, Wallace, Wallechinsky, and Wallace, p. 568.

20. Prose, "Timeless Marilyn, the Movies' Mona Lisa," *NYT*, July 26, 1992, p. H 1. Also see *BES*, August 5, 1992, p. 2 C. See *NYT*, September 12, 1993, p. H 45, on *Marilyn* as an opera.

21. See Denise Farran, "Heroines and Victims: Some Thoughts on the Biographies of Marilyn Monroe and Ruth Ellis," *Studies in Sexual Politics*, 1986; pp. 13–14, 73–93.

22. *BES*, June 8, 1988, p. 1 B; *NYT*, October 10, 1994, p. C 11. See also Viki Goldberg on Elvis and Marilyn, "A Pair of Saints Who Refuse to Stay Dead," *NYT*, December 18, 1994, p. H 49. At least one college course was taught about Elvis Presley (at the University of Iowa); see *Insight*, February 17, 1992, p. 29. On questions regarding Elvis's death, see *USA Today*, September 30, 1994, p. 3 A. See Andrew Leckey, in *BES*, July 8, 1994, p. 12 C, on the prices of Elvis memorabilia.

23. See Roberts and Olson, p. 302. Also see *Time* magazine, July 20, 1987, p. 78.

24. *Time* magazine, October 10, 1988, p. 91.

CHAPTER 8

1. Potter, "American Individualism in the Twentieth Century," in *Individualism: Man in Modern Society*; ed. Ronald Gross and Paul Osterman (New York: Dell, 1971), pp.

57–58. See also Lubin, pp. 305–6. On the official closing of the frontier, see Ronald Takaki, *A Different Mirror* (New York: Little Brown and Company, 1993), p. 225.

2. Potter, p. 57. See also *NYT*, July 9, 1989, p. A 23.

3. See Brown, p. 180.

4. See Roberts and Olson, p. 3.

5. See Nash, p. 146.

6. See Steckmesser, p. 246; Brown, pp. 22–24.

7. Jake Barnes, "A New Look at the Outlaws of the Old West," in *The American West*, ed. Raymond Friday Locke (Los Angeles: Mankind Publishing, 1971), p. 246.

8. Steckmesser, pp. 105–157 (quote p. 105).

9. Ibid., p. 4.

10. Brown, pp. 27–28.

11. Steckmesser, pp. 13–53.

12. Among the most famous African-American cowboys were Nat Love, Ben Hodges, and Bill Pickett.

13. Eric Hobsbawm. *Bandits* (New York: Dell Paperback, 1971), p. 13.

14. Quoted in Leo Gurko, *Heroes, Highbrows and the Popular Mind* (New York: The Bobbs-Merrill Co., 1953), p. 184. Towns in New Mexico and Texas have both claimed that Billy is buried there. Missouri has a Jesse James Museum.

15. Steckmesser, especially Part 2. Burns, "The Kid," in Lubin, pp. 243, 245. Brown, p. 195. Barnes, pp. 228–30. Hobsbawm, p. 38.

16. Brown, p. 195. Michael Wallis, *Pretty Boy: The Life and Times of Charles Arthur Floyd* (New York: St. Martin's Press, 1992), p. 227.

17. Steckmesser, p. 98. Burns, p. 244. Virtually all of the movies and television shows about Billy the Kid are sympathetic to him and most are at best cool to Garrett.

18. Hobsbawm, p. 38. Barnes, p. 228. Also see F. Bruce Lamb, *Kid Curry: The Life and Times of Harvey Logan and the Wild Bunch, An Old West Narrative* (Boulder, Colo.: Johnson Books, 1991). Lamb notes the ease with which outlaws of the day traveled around the country.

19. Barnes, p. 228. Wallis, pp. 53–54.

20. Hobsbawm, p. 36.

21. The 1934 book was Frederick F. Van de Water's *Glory Hunter: A Life of General Custer*.

22. *USA Today*, June 10, 1991, p. 1 A.

23. Brown, p. 178.

24. Ibid., pp. 196–97.

25. Ibid., p. 171.

26. See, for example, Virgil E. Baugh, *Rendezvous at the Alamo* (Lincoln: University of Nebraska Press, 1960). Both Baugh and Lamb consistently refer to the influence of lawyers in the West. See also *Insight*, February 4, 1991, p. 58, for a similar analysis of the West.

27. Quoted in *Insight*, February 4, 1991, p. 61.

CHAPTER 9

1. Goldman and Lupica, p. 49.

2. Kenneth C. Davis, *Don't Know Much about History* (New York: Avon Books, 1990), p. 180. Also see Gwynne Dyer, *War* (New York: Crown Publishers, 1985).

3. Gurko, p. 176.

4. Nash, p. 141; Fawcett and Thomas, pp. 59–60.

5. Roberts and Olson, pp. 30–31.

6. Susman, p. 132.

7. Johnson, p. 259. Michael Mehlman "Hero of the 30's—The Tenant Farmer," in Browne, Fishwick, and Marsden, p. 61.

8. Johnson, p. 402.

9. This point is wonderfully detailed in George Ritzer, *The McDonaldization of Society* (Newbury Park, Calif.: Pine Forge Press, 1993).

10. Riesman's thesis is discussed in *The Lonely Crowd* (New Haven, Conn.: Yale University Press, 1950). See also Kellerman, pp. 28–29.

11. See Kellerman, p. 29. Norman Mailer, "Perspective from the Biltmore Balcony," in Lubin, p. 374.

12. Susman, pp. 126, 131.

13. *Atlantic Monthly*, June 1990, p. 117.

14. See Baugh. Also see Evan S. Connell, *A Long Desire* (New York: H. Holt & Company, 1980).

15. Wecter, "Charles Lindbergh," in Lubin, p. 75. See Tom Wolfe, *The Right Stuff* (New York: Bantam Books, 1979).

16. Steiner, *The Waning of the West* (New York: St. Martin's Press, 1989).

17. Davis, p. 266.

18. See, for example, Herbert Asbury, *The Gangs of New York* (New York: Capricorn Books, 1970). (Originally published in 1927.)

19. Haller, "Organized Crime in Urban Society: Chicago in the Twentieth Century," in Roberts and Olson, p. 171. Also see Nicholas Pileggi, *Wiseguy: A Life in a Mafia Family* (New York: Simon and Schuster, 1985).

20. Lacey, *Little Man: Meyer Lansky and the Gangster Life* (Boston: Little, Brown and Company, 1991), p. 444; ibid., p. 369.

21. Roberts and Olson, p. 161.

22. Gurko, p. 185.

23. *NYT*, February 19, 1990, p. B 1.

24. See Hobsbawm, p. 29.

25. Michael Wallis. *Pretty Boy: The Life and Times of Charles Arthur Floyd* (New York: St. Martin's Press, 1992). Also see Nash, pp. 199-203.

26. Hobsbawm, p. 83. Nash, pp. 39–45.

27. Gurko, p. 184.

28. See Manchester, *The Glory and the Dream*, p. 94.

CHAPTER 10

1. George Bernard Shaw's tribute to Einstein is reprinted in the *NYT*, March 14, 1991, p. A 25. See *NYTM*, October 30, 1994, p. 23 and *NYT*, August 26, 1994, p. B 5. See André Millard, "Thomas Edison and the Theory and Practice of Innovation," *Business and Economic History*, Fall 1991.

2. Regina Markell Morantz, "The Scientist as Sex Crusader: Alfred C. Kinsey and American Culture," in Roberts and Olson, p. 232. See also David Halberstam, *The Fifties* (New York: Villard Books, 1993), pp. 272–81.

3. See Roberts and Olson, p. 197.

4. *BES*, January 29, 1992, p. 12 A.

5. Ibid.

6. See, for example, Bruce Nussbaum, *Good Intentions* (New York: The Atlantic Monthly Press, (1990).

7. See *NYT*, March 27, 1992, p. A 16 and April 26, 1994, p. C 3. Also see *The New York Times Education Life*, August 2, 1992, pp. 26–27 and *BES*, July 14, 1992, p. 2 A. Ehrenreich, in *Time* magazine, May 21, 1991, p. 66.

8. *Time* magazine, July 3, 1995, p. 63. Greenberg, in *NYT*, July 4, 1995, p. 31. Also see *Newsweek*, July 3, 1995, p. 48 and *NYT*, June 24, 1995, p. A 1.

9. *NYTM*, June 7, 1992, p. 42. Also see *NYT*, June 14, 1994, p. C 19.

10. *The Atlantic Monthly*, April 1992, p. 59.

11. See Robert F. Kennedy, *Thirteen Days* (New York: Mentor, 1969). Fussell, *BAD, or the Dumbing of America* (New York: Simon and Schuster, 1991), p. 34. Tuchman, "A Nation in Decline," *NYTM*, September 20, 1987, p. 23.

12. Honan, in *NYT*, January 28, 1990, p. 6. Bell, "The Cultural Wars: American Intellectual Life, 1965–1992," *The Wilson Quarterly*, Summer, 1992, pp. 74–107.

13. Mark Crispin Miller, "Out of Mind," a review of Jacoby's *The Last Intellectuals*, *Atlantic Monthly*, October 1987. See also Hodgson, p. 96.

14. *NYT*, June 21, 1992, p. E 2. On a recent biography of Carl Sandburg, see *Insight*, September 9, 1991, p. 46.

15. Fishwick, "Heroic Style in America," in Browne, Fishwick, and Marsden, p. 17.

16. *Time* magazine, June 16, 1986, p. 63.

17. See *Newsweek*, October 3, 1994, p. 42; *NYT*, August 7, 1994, p. 22; March 3, 1987, p. A 1; and February 16, 1987, p. A 1.

18. See *BES*, November 15, 1994, p. 1 A. See *TBS*, September 9, 1990, p. 12 A. Pat Robertson has denied any wrongdoing; see his letter to *Newsweek*, October 31, 1994, p. 12. On Oral Roberts, see *Time* magazine, January 26, 1987, p. 63, and on Jimmy Swaggart, *NYT*, February 25, 1988, p. A 16. It might be noted that Billy Graham, at this writing the most famous American clergyman, has never been accused of impropriety.

ADDENDUM TO PART II

1. Sommers, *Who Stole Feminism?* (New York: Simon and Schuster, 1994), pp. 56–57.

2. *NYT*, November 2, 1994, p. A 16.

3. *TBS*, September 23, 1994, p. 3 D. *NYT*, June 14, 1993, p. A 15 and November 18, 1994, p. B 1. *BES*, September 10, 1993, p. 2 A. *USA Today*, September 3, 1993, p. D 1.

4. See a review by Larry Engelmann of Lichtenstein's *The Goddess and the American Girl*, *NYTBR*, June 12, 1988, p. 13.

5. Holland, *Hail to the Chiefs* (New York: Ballantine Books, 1990), p. 248. On tributes offered to Jacqueline Kennedy Onassis, see *NYT*, May 22, 1994, p. 29.

6. See Malcolm Forbes, with Jeff Bloch, *Women Who Made a Difference* (New York: Simon and Schuster, 1990).

7. Segal, pp. 34, 125.

8. Richard Louis Thomas, *Linn's Who's Who on U.S. Stamps* (Sidney, Ohio: Amos Press, 1991). Sherr and Kazickas, *NYT*, June 14, 1993, p. A 15.

9. Barnes, p. 232. Also see Even S. Connell, *Son of Morning Star* (New York: Harper, 1991).

10. Nellie Cashman, for example, is included in the "Legends of the West" series of stamps issued by the U. S. Post Office in 1994. So are Annie Oakley and Sacagawea.

11. The *NYT*, December 11, 1992, p. D 19, notes the passing away of Helen C. St. Aubin, the woman who inspired the film.

12. *BES*, October 12, 1994, p. 2 A. *NYT*, October 7, 1994, p. B 14. See also A. Fausto-Sterling, *Myths of Gender: Biological Theories about Men and Women* (New York: Basic Books, 1985) and Ralph Keyes, *The Height of Your Life* (New York: Warner Books, 1980).

13. See Richard Rabicoff, *BES*, September 25, 1989, p. 7 A.

14. Cited in *NYTBR*, September 7, 1986, p. 12. See also *The Atlantic Monthly*, March 1988, pp. 71, 74.

INTRODUCTION TO PART III

1. Hodgson, p. 14.

2. Roberts and Olson, p. 223; Toffler, p. 407.

3. Kael, in Turkel, *"The Good War,"* p. 122; Hodgson, p. 14.

4. Hodgson, p. 68.

5. Toffler, p. 294.

6. Morris, pp. 104–5.

7. Boorstin, p. 332.

CHAPTER 11

1. Williams, *American Society: A Sociological Interpretation*, 3d ed. (New York: Alfred A. Knopf, 1970).

2. Steckmesser, p. 255.

3. Manchester, *The Glory and the Dream*, p. 283. Also see Turkel, *"The Good War."*

4. Baskir and Strauss, p. 26. Manchester, *The Glory and the Dream*, p. 283.

5. Richard S. Tedlow, "Intellect on Television: The Quiz Show Scandals of the 1950s," *American Quarterly*, vol. 27, no. 4 (Fall 1976) p. 492.

6. Morris, p. 5.

7. Gurko, p. 198. See also *Time* magazine, June 13, 1994, p. 14 on the number of "Congressmen Facing Criminal Charges." Also see Suzanne Garment, *Scandal: The Culture of Mistrust in American Politics* (New York: Anchor/Doubleday, 1992).

8. Tedlow, p. 255.

9. Gabler in *TBS*, June 21, 1992, p. 5 L.

10. Fawcett and Thomas, pp. 1, 7.

11. Mark Haller, "Organized Crime in Urban Society: Chicago in the Twentieth Century," in Roberts and Olson, p. 165.

12. *BES*, July 24, 1992, p. 11 A.

13. *NYT*, April 26, 1991, p. A 29. On the studies, see *TBS*, November 12, 1992, p. 5 A.

14. *NYRB*, November 19, 1987.

15. William Goldman, *Butch Cassidy and the Sundance Kid* (New York: Bantam Books, 1969), pp. 22–27.

16. Manchester, *The Glory and the Dream*, p. 850. Tedlow, p. 486, quoting Eric Goldman.

17. Tedlow, p. 488, and Manchester, *The Glory and the Dream*, pp. 850–52.

18. See Lawrence S. Hall's comment, in Tedlow, p. 491. For examinations and criticisms of the movie, see *Time* magazine, October 12, 1994, p. 91; *NYTM*, October 9, 1994, p. 32; *NYT*, September 4, 1994, p. 20 H.

19. Murray Kempton, "The Family Business," *NYRB*, November 19, 1987, p. 16 and J. Anthony Lukas, *NYTBR*, October 11, 1987, p. 8. Both Kempton and Lukas are here reviewing Howard Blum's book *I Pledge Allegiance* (New York: Simon and Schuster, 1987).

20. Manchester, *The Glory and the Dream*, p. 868.

21. See *NYTM*, July 10, 1994. p. 28. See also Ilene Philipson, *Ethel Rosenberg: Beyond the Myths* (New York: Franklin Watts, 1988). Philipson argues that the Rosenbergs were innocent. Recently revealed documents seem to refute this.

22. See J. Anthony Lukas, in *NYTM*, July 10, 1994, p. 29.

23. *NYTM*, July 31, 1994, pp. 16–19. *NYT*, July 28, 1994, p. A 1. *Newsweek*, March 7, 1994, p. 34 and *Time* magazine, August 8, 1994, p. 42. See also the *NYT* editorial, April 5, 1987, p. E 26.

24. See *NYT*, April 5, 1992, p. 30. Also see *Time* magazine, March 16, 1992, p. 32 and *TBS*, September 27, 1994, p. 58.

25. See a review of "The Blame Game," *NYT*, October 26, 1994, p. C 18. The quote is from Robert Hughes, in *Time* magazine, February 3, 1992, p. 45.

26. *NYTM*, June 3, 1991, p. 26. See *TBS*, May 5, 1992, p. 2 A and August 7, 1994, p. 1 J. Stevenson is quoted in *NYT*, October 11, 1994, p. A 21.

27. The comment by Rosenbaum is in *NYTM*, July 7, 1994, p. 50. The commentary on bad writing as a mental disorder by Kirk and Kutchins, in *NYT*, June 20, 1994, p. A 17. See Susan Estrich, in *BES*, October 27, 1993, p. 15 A. See also *NYT*, December 6, 1992, p. E 4 and *Time* magazine August 12, 1991, pp. 14–18. See *New York* magazine, June 3, 1991.

CHAPTER 12

1. Gross and Osterman, p. xxiii.

2. Ibid., p. xix. Manchester, *The Glory and the Dream*, p. 778.

3. Kellerman, p. 29. Potter, p. 59.

4. Potter, p. 52. Schlesinger, *The Cycles of American History*, p. 40. Susman, p. 168.

5. Reisman, "Individualism Reconsidered," in Gross and Osterman, p. 71. Susman, p. 168. Potter, p. 59.

6. Samuels, "The Age of Conspiracy and Conformity: Invasion of the Body Snatchers," in Roberts and Olson, p. 265.

7. Ibid., p. 263. Also see Susman, p. xxii.

8. Samuels, p. 265.

9. Finley, *The Dictionary of the History of Ideas*, vol.4 (New York: Charles Scribner's Sons, 1973), p. 365.

10. Johnson, p. 10.

11. Quoted in Barnouw, pp. 174–75. Morris, p. 66.

12. Susman, p. 200.

13. Schlesinger, "The Decline of Heroes," in Lubin, p. 344.

14. Wecter, "Charles Lindbergh," in Lubin, p. 76.

15. Lubin, pp. 121, 307.

16. O'Faolain, *The Vanishing Hero* (Cutchogue, N.Y.: Buccaneer Books, 1991).

CHAPTER 13

1. Robert Hughes, in *Time* magazine, February 3, 1992, p. 44.

2. Ibid. Susman, p. 54.

3. William M. Kephart, *Extraordinary Groups*, 2d ed. (New York: St. Martin's Press, 1982), p. 1. Emphasis in the original.

4. See, for example, R. B. Jones, in *BES*, May 5, 1992, p. 11 A on Malcolm X. On Custer, see *BES*, December 22, 1991, p. 3 J. On Indigenous Peoples' Day, see *Time* magazine, January 27, 1992, p. 25. Also see *Time* magazine October 7, 1991, p. 52 and the commentary by Tim Giago, "I Hope the Redskins Lose," in *Newsweek*, January 27, 1992, p. 8. See also Hobsbawm, p. 56 and Charles E. Silberman, *Criminal Violence, Criminal Justice* (New York: Vintage Books, 1978), pp. 198–201. On African-American comic book heroes, see *Newsweek*, August 16, 1993, p. 58 and *NYT*, September 13, 1992, p. F 8. See also *Newsweek*, January 27, 1992, p. 49 and *NYT*, July 24, 1994, p. E 7.

5. Susman, p. 212.

6. See, for example, *Time* magazine, July 8, 1991, p. 12.

7. Morantz, p. 235.

8. Fawcett and Thomas, p. 33.

9. It might be noted that a *Newsweek* poll taken the week of June 19–25, 1995, reports that more than one quarter of whites and nearly half of all blacks polled think that the United States will not exist as one nation "100 years from today." *Newsweek*, July 10, 1995, p. 26.

10. On revisionism, see Michael Kammen, *Mystic Chords of Memory* (New York: Knopf, 1991). On African-American soldiers, see *TBS*, July 26, 1992, p. 11 A and *NYT*, July 26, 1992, p. A 16. See Fishwick, in Browne, Fishwick, and Marsden, p. 4; *TBS*, October 13, 1991, p. 2 A; *NYT*, October 11, 1992, p. 18. See Cynthia Orozco, in *NYT*, March 29, 1994, p. A 16. See also *BES*, January 20, 1992, p. 2 A and *TBS*, September 8, 1994, p. 10 A.

11. Richard Bernstein, in *NYT*, December 17, 1989, p. E 5. See Schlesinger's comments in *Time* magazine July 8, 1991, p. 21 and Will's comments in *Newsweek*, November 14, 1994, p. 84.

12. Goode, p. 152. Emphasis in the original.

13. Ibid., p. 181. Boorstin, p. 339. On the number of science awards, see Robert J. Samuelson, in *Newsweek*, December 21, 1992, p. 45.

14. *BES*, March 24, 1992, p. 2 A; January 13, 1993, p. 2 A; February 5, 1993, p. 2 A.

15. *TBS*, May 2, 1993, p. 17 A.

16. Robert J. Samuelson, in *Newsweek*, August 1, 1994, p. 44. See also *NYT*, July 4, 1995, p. 8.

17. Paul Dickson, *Timelines* (New York: Addison-Wesley, 1991), p. 272.

ADDENDUM TO PART III

1. Manchester, *The Glory and the Dream*, pp. 242, 577.
2. See Barnouw, pp. 102, 132, 170. Fawcett and Thomas, p. 448 on America and the "Norm of Youth." Also see Morris, p. 78.
3. *NYT*, July 3, 1994, p. H 1. See Manchester, *The Glory and the Dream*, p. 1100, for the quote from *Life* magazine; also see ibid., p. 591. Morris, pp. 70–71. See also Halberstam, *The Fifties*, pp. 463–71.
4. Manchester, *The Glory and the Dream*, p. 429.
5. *NYT*, April 24, 1994, p. E 7. Morris, pp. 72–73. Manchester, *The Glory and the Dream*, p. 724.
6. Morris, p. 72.
7. Ibid., p. 238.
8. See *Newsweek*, December 28, 1992, p. 67.
9. Morris, p. 239. See also *NYT*, July 17, 1995, p. D 1.
10. See, for example, Stephanie Coontz, *The Way We Never Were* (New York: Basic Books, 1992). See also Karl Zinsmeister, "Growing Up Scared," in *The Atlantic Monthly*, June 1990.

CHAPTER 14

1. Kellerman, pp. 24, 37.
2. Stringer, in *BES*, October 3, 1991, p. 17 A.
3. See *Time* magazine, October 12, 1987, p. 57.
4. Susman, p. 147; Nash, p. 140.
5. Louis Howe had an "iron rule . . . that [FDR] never be carried in public"; from *In the Arena* (New York: Simon and Schuster, 1990), quoted in *Time* magazine, April 12, 1990, p. 36. See also Bernard Asbell, "F.D.R.'s Extra Burden," in Roberts and Olson, pp. 180, 182.
6. Rosenblatt, in *NYT*, January 31, 1993, p. 26.
7. Boorstin, p. 331.
8. A PBS television show aired in April 1994 dealt unfavorably with FDR and the Holocaust. Also see Arthur Schlesinger, Jr.'s rebuttal in *Newsweek*, April 18, 1994, p. 14. On Eisenhower and Summersby, see *BES*, June 6, 1991, p. 3 A. On the attack on Barbara Bush, see *Newsweek*, September 28, 1992, p. 10, noting Marjorie Peroff's commentary in *The New Republic*.
9. See, for example, James Atlas, *NYT*, November 6, 1988, p. 40. On Martin Luther King, Jr., see the commentary by Gregory P. Kane, in *BES*, November 20, 1989, p. 7 A. See also the review in *NYTBR* by Henry Hampton, October 29, 1989, p. 32. On Marlene Dietrich, see *BES*, January 17, 1992, p. A 3. The book about Joan Crawford is, of course, the well-publicized *Mommy Dearest*.
10. Gibbon, in *Newsweek*, January 18, 1993, p. 9.
11. *Time* magazine, April 2, 1990, p. 43. Margolis, in *BES*, October 16, 1992, p. 16 A; Kernan, in a letter to *NYTM*, July 17, 1994, p. 9.
12. Reeves, in *TBS*, September 27, 1987, p. 15 A.
13. Barnouw, p. 428, quotes Shayon from *The Saturday Review*, August 9, 1969. See also *NYT*, November 9, 1988, p. C 1.

14. Manchester, *The Glory and the Dream*, p. 1259; ibid., p. 593. Lance Morrow, in *Time* magazine, September 21, 1992, p. 50. Ian Mitroff is quoted in *Insight*, November 27, 1989, p. 47.

15. Alter, in *Newsweek*, June 27, 1994, p. 25.

16. *Time* magazine, March 5, 1990, p. 46. See also Elizabeth Kolbert, in *NYT*, July 17, 1994, p. E 3. She argues that television has created a "global front stoop" rather than a global village. Also see the essay by Lance Morrow, in *Time* magazine, October 26, 1981, p. 98.

17. Richard Corliss, in *Time* magazine, July 18, 1994, p. 36. Kerr is quoted in *Time* magazine, October 12, 1987, p. 65.

18. Rosenblatt, in *NYTM*, January 31, 1993, p. 24.

19. Steckmesser, pp. 6, 13. Barnes, pp. 243–44.

20. *NYT*, June 21, 1992, p. V 1. Italics in original.

21. Conroy, *The Great Santini* (Boston: Houghton Mifflin, 1976), pp. 165–66.

22. See Stephen B. Oates, *With Malice toward None* (New York: Mentor Books, 1977), pp. 13, 21, 265–66. Also see Robert McCrum, William Cran, and Robert MacNeil, *The Story of English* (New York: Penguin Books, 1986), p. 36: "Lincoln spoke . . . 'with a wilderness air and a log-cabin smack.' "

CHAPTER 15

1. Gross and Osterman, pp. xii–xiii, xix.

2. Kellerman, p. x.

3. Roberts and Olson, p. 137.

4. From Wolfe, *The Kandy Colored Tangerine-Flake Streamline Baby* (New York: Farrar, Straus, and Giroux, 1967). Kellerman, p. 3.

5. Kellerman, p. 10. Hook, *The Hero in History*, p. 13; ibid., p. 3. Also see A. McEvoy and E. Erickson, *Sociological Forces*, vol. 14, no. 2 (April 1981), pp. 111–122.

6. Tom W. Smith "The Polls: The Most Admired Man and Woman," *Public Opinion Quarterly*, vol. 50 (Winter 1986) pp. 573–83. Geyer, in *BES*, October 7, 1994, p. 21 A.

7. Goode, pp. 344–45.

8. Beeman, in *TBS*, August 12, 1990, p. 4 E. Susman, pp. 88–89. Mailer, p. 337.

9. Hook, p. 8. This can have undesired consequences. See, for example, *NYT*, August 18, 1991, p. E 3.

10. *NYT*, April 23, 1991, p. A 21. One might distinguish between "hero" and "role model," but the line separating them is thin at best. The terms are generally used interchangeably today, Esptein notwithstanding.

11. *Newsweek*, May 24, 1993, pp. 64–65. Malone, in *Newsweek*, June 28, 1993, p. 56. Emphasis in the original.

12. Barnouw, p. 215. Ivan Olbracht, in Hobsbawm, p. 115.

13. See Kenneth Lasson, in *BES*, July 8, 1993, p. 13 A. Also see *TBS*, October 24, 1993, p. 1 A and October 24, 1993, p. 1 E.

14. Susman, p. 282. Goldman, *Adventures in the Screen Trade*, p. 5.

15. See *NYT*, November 4, 1990, p. H 20 and *Newsweek*, February 1, 1993, p. 66 and April 22, 1991, p. 62.

16. *NYT*, January 31, 1993, p. F 7 and November 9, 1988, p. C 16. *BES*, June 5, 1989, pp. 1 D and 3 D.

17. Foster, in *NYTM*, May 23, 1993, p. 16. Vecsey, in *NYT*, February 12, 1992, p. B 9.
18. Hobsbawm, p. 34. Shaw's quote is from *Man and Superman*.
19. See Lubin, p. 308.
20. Wycliff, in *NYT*, November 14, 1989, p. A 22. Travers, pp. 46–47.
21. Nash, p. 138. There were, of course, exceptions. These usually took the form of political scandals or sexual improprieties, as in the case of the Reverend Henry Ward Beecher.

Bibliography

Asbury, Herbert. *The Gangs of New York*. New York: Capricorn Books, 1970.

Baritz, Loren. *Backfire*. New York: Ballantine Books, 1986.

Barnouw, Erik. *Tube of Plenty: The Evolution of American Television*. Rev. ed. New York: Oxford University Press, 1982.

Baugh, Virgil E. *Rendezvous at the Alamo*. Lincoln: University of Nebraska Press, 1960.

Bender, David L., ed. *American Values: Opposing Viewpoints*. 2d ed. St. Paul: Greenhaven Press, 1984.

Bensman, Joseph, and Robert Lilienfeld. *Craft and Consciousness*. New York: John Wiley & Sons, 1973.

Berger, Peter. *Invitation to Sociology*. New York: Doubleday Anchor, 1963.

Berkowitz, Bill. *Local Heroes*. Lexington, Mass.: Lexington Books, 1987.

Bissinger, H. G. *Friday Night Lights: A Town, a Team, and a Dream*. New York: HarperPerennial, 1991.

Brown, Dee. *The Year of the Century: 1876*. New York: Charles Scribner's Sons, 1966.

Browne, Ray B., Marshall Fishwick, and Michael T. Marsden, eds. *Heroes of Popular Culture*. Bowling Green, Ohio: Bowling Green University Popular Press, 1972.

Carrol, Peter N. *It Seemed Like Nothing Happened*. New York: Holt, Rinehart and Winston, 1982.

Connell, Evan S. *A Long Desire*. New York: H. Holt & Company, 1980.

_____. *Son of Morning Star*. New York: Harper, 1991.

Davis, Kenneth C. *Don't Know Much about History*. New York: Avon Books, 1990.

de Tocqueville, Alexis. *Democracy in America*. Edited by J. P. Mayer. New York: Doubleday & Co., 1969.

Dickson, Paul. *Timelines*. New York: Addison-Wesley, 1991.

Durkheim, Emile. *The Elementary Forms of Religious Life*. New York: The Free Press, 1954.

Dyer, Gwynne. *War*. New York: Crown Publishers, 1985.

Eksteins, Modris. *Rites of Spring: The Great War and the Birth of the Modern Age*. Boston: Houghton Mifflin Company, 1989.

Erdoes, Richard. *Tales from the American Frontier*. New York: Pantheon Books, 1991.

Fausto-Sterling, A. *Myths of Gender: Biological Theories about Men and Women*. New York: Basic Books, 1985.

Fawcett, Edmund, and Tony Thomas. *America and the Americans*. Glasgow, Scotland: Fontana and Collins, 1983.

Feller, Bob, with Bill Gilbert. *Now Pitching, Bob Feller*. New York: Birch Lane Press, 1990.

Forbes, Malcolm, with Jeff Bloch. *Women Who Made a Difference* New York: Simon and Schuster, 1990.

Frazier, Ian. *Great Plains*. New York: Penguin Books, 1989.

Fussell, Paul. *BAD, or the Dumbing of America*. New York: Simon and Schuster, 1991.

Gerth, H. H., and C. Wright Mills, eds. *From Max Weber: Essays in Sociology*. New York: Oxford University Press, 1958.

Goldman, William. *Adventures in the Screen Trade: A Personal View of Hollywood and Screenwriting*. New York: Warner Books, 1983.

————. *Butch Cassidy and the Sundance Kid*. New York: Bantam Books, 1969.

————. *The Season: A Candid Look at Broadway*. New York: Bantam Books, 1970.

Goldman, William, and Mike Lupica. *Wait till Next Year*. New York: Bantam Books, 1989.

Goode, William J. *The Celebration of Heroes: Prestige as a Control System*. Berkeley: University of California Press, 1978.

Greenberg, Hank. *The Story of My Life*. New York: Times Books, 1989.

Gross, Ronald, and Paul Osterman, eds. *Individualism: Man in Modern Society*. New York: Dell, 1971.

Gurko, Leo. *Heroes, Highbrows and the Popular Mind*. New York: The Bobbs-Merrill Co., 1953.

Halberstam, David. *The Fifties*. New York: Villard Books, 1993.

Harper, Charles L. *Exploring Social Change*. 2d ed. Englewood Cliffs, N.J.: Prentice-Hall, 1993.

Hentoff, Nat. *American Heroes: In and Out of School*. New York: Delacorte Press, 1987.

Hobsbawm, Eric. *Bandits*. New York: Dell Paperback, 1971.

Hodgson, Godfrey. *America in Our Time*. New York: Vintage Books, 1978.

Holland, Barbara. *Hail to the Chiefs*. New York: Ballantine Books, 1990.

Hook, Sidney. *The Hero in History*. Boston: Beacon Press, 1943.

Johnson, Paul. *Modern Times: The World from the Twenties to the Eighties*. New York: Harper & Row, 1983.

Kael, Pauline. *Taking It All In*. New York: Holt, Rinehart and Winston, 1984.

Kellerman, Barbara. *The Political Presidency*. New York: Oxford University Press, 1984.

Kennedy, Robert F. *Thirteen Days*. New York: Mentor, 1969.

Kephart, William. *Extraordinary Groups*. 2d ed. New York: St. Martin's Press, 1982.

Keyes, Ralph. *The Height of Your Life*. New York: Warner Books, 1980.

Kissinger, Henry. *Diplomacy*. New York: Simon and Schuster, 1994.

Lacey, Robert. *Little Man: Meyer Lansky and the Gangster Life*. Boston: Little, Brown and Company, 1991.

Lamb, F. Bruce. *Kid Curry: The Life and Times of Harvey Logan and the Wild Bunch, An Old West Narrative*. Boulder, Colo. Johnson Books, 1991.

Laqueur, Walter. *Europe since Hitler*. New York: Penguin Books, 1982.

Locke, Raymond F., ed. *The American West: Selected Readings from Mankind Magazine*. Los Angeles: Mankind Publishing Company, 1971.

Louv, Richard. *America II*. New York: Penguin Books, 1985.

Lubin, Harold, ed. *Heroes and Anti-Heroes*. Scranton, Pa: Chandler Publishing Company, 1968.

Manchester, William. *American Caesar: Douglas MacArthur 1880–1964*. Boston: Little, Brown and Company, 1978.

———. *The Glory and the Dream*. New York: Bantam Books, 1975.

McCrum, Robert, William Cran, and Robert MacNeil. *The Story of English*. New York: Penguin Books, 1986.

McGinniss, Joe. *Heroes*. New York: Pocket Books, 1977.

McGrath, Roger. *Gunfighters, Highwaymen & Vigilantes: Violence on the Frontier*. Berkeley: University of California Press, 1984.

McMillen, Tom, with Paul Coggins. *Out of Bounds: How the American Sports Establishment Is Being Driven by Greed and Hypocrisy and What Needs to Be Done about It*. NewYork: Simon and Schuster, 1992.

McQuaid, Kim. *The Anxious Years: America in the Vietnam-Watergate Era*. New York: Basic Books, 1989.

Merchant, Larry. *Ringside Seat at the Circus*. New York: Holt, Rinehart and Winston, 1976.

Morris, Charles R. *A Time of Passion: America 1960–1980*. New York: Penguin Books, 1986.

Mowry, George E., ed. *The Twenties: Fords, Flappers & Fanatics*. Englewood Cliffs, N.J.: Prentice-Hall, 1963.

Nash, Jay Robert. *Bloodletters and Badmen: A Narrative Encyclopedia of American Criminals from the Pilgrims to the Present*. New York: M. Evans and Company, 1973.

Nolan, Frederick. *The Lincoln County War: A Documentary History*. Norman: University of Oklahoma Press, 1992.

Noonan, Peggy. *What I Saw at the Revolution*. New York: Ivy Books, 1990.

Oates, Stephen B. *With Malice toward None*. New York: Mentor Books, 1977.

O'Faolain, Sean. *The Vanishing Hero*. Cutchogue, N.Y.: Buccaneer Books, 1991.

Offen, Neil. *God Save the Players*. Chicago: Playboy Press, 1975.

Patterson, James, and Peter Kim. *The Day America Told the Truth: What People Really Believe about Everything That Really Matters*. Englewood Cliffs, N.J.: Prentice-Hall, 1991.

Pearson, Carol, and Katherine Pope. *The Female Hero in American and British Literature*. New York: R. R. Bowker, 1981.

Pileggi, Nicholas. *Wiseguy: A Life in a Mafia Family*. New York: Simon and Schuster, 1985.

Reisman, David. *The Lonely Crowd*. Abridged ed. New Haven, Conn.: Yale University Press, 1971.

Ritzer, George. *The McDonaldization of Society*. Newbury Park, Calif.: Pine Forge Press, 1993.

Roberts, Randy, and James S. Olson, eds. *American Experiences*. Vol. 2, *1877 to the Present*. Glenview, Ill.: Scott, Foresman and Company, 1986.

Roche, George. *A World without Heroes: The Modern Tragedy*. California: Hillside College Press, 1987.

Roemer, William F., Jr. *The Enforcer. Spilotro: The Chicago Mob's Man Over Las Vegas*. New York: Ivy Books, 1994.

Rosenberg, Bernard, and David Manning White. *Mass Culture: The Popular Arts in America*. New York: The Free Press, 1957.

Rossiter, Margaret. *Women Scientists in America*. Baltimore: The Johns Hopkins Press, 1984.

Schickel, Richard. *Intimate Strangers: The Culture of Celebrity*. New York: Doubleday & Company, 1985.

Schlesinger, Arthur M., Jr., *The Cycles of American History*. Boston: Houghton Mifflin, 1986.

Segal, Robert A. *Joseph Campbell: An Introduction*. Rev. ed. New York: Mentor Books, 1990.

Siegel, Frederick F. *Troubled Journey: From Pearl Harbor to Ronald Reagan*. New York: Hill and Wang: 1989.

Slotkin, Richard. *Gunfighter Nation: The Myth of the Frontier in Twentieth-Century America*. New York: HarperPerennial, 1993.

Sommers, Christina Hoff. *Who Stole Feminism?: How Women Have Betrayed Women*. New York: Simon and Schuster, 1994.

Sperber, A. M. *Murrow: His Life and Times*. New York: Freundlich Books, 1986.

Sperber, Murray. *College Sports, Inc.: The Athletic Department vs. the University*. New York: Henry Holt and Company, 1990.

Steckmesser, Kent Ladd. *The Western Hero in History and Legend*. Norman: University of Oklahoma Press, 1965.

Steiner, Stan. *The Waning of the West*. New York: St. Martin's Press, 1989.

Susman, Warren I., *Culture as History: The Transformation of American Society in the Twentieth Century*. New York: Pantheon Books, 1984.

Takaki, Ronald. *A Different Mirror: A History of Multicultural America*. Boston: Little, Brown and Company, 1993.

Taub, Richard P., with Doris L. Taub. *American Society in Tocqueville's Time and Today*. Chicago: Rand McNally, 1974.

Taylor, Derek. *It Was Twenty Years Ago Today*. New York: Simon and Schuster, 1987.

Terkel, Studs. *"The Good War."* New York: Ballantine Books, 1984.

Thomas, Richard Louis. *Linn's Who's Who on U.S. Stamps*. Sidney, Ohio: Amos Press, 1991.

Toffler, Alvin. *The Third Wave*. New York: Bantam Books, 1981.

Wallace, Amy, David Wallechinsky, and Irving Wallace. *The Book of Lists #3*. New York: Bantam Books, 1983.

Wallace, Irving, Amy Wallace, David Wallechinsky, and Sylvia Wallace. *The Intimate Sex Lives of Famous People*. New York: Dell, 1981.

Wallechinsky, David, Irving Wallace, and Amy Wallace. *The Book of Lists*. New York: Bantam Books, 1978.

Wallis, Michael. *Pretty Boy: The Life and Times of Charles Arthur Floyd*. New York: St. Martin's Press, 1992.

Warner, W. Lloyd. *The Living and the Dead: A Study of the Symbolic Life of Americans*. New Haven, Conn.: Yale University Press, 1965.

White, John Kenneth. *The New Politics of Old Values*. Hanover, N.H.: The University Press of New England, 1988.

White, Richard. *It's Your Misfortune and None of My Own*. Norman: University of Oklahoma Press, 1993.

Will, George F. *Men at Work*. New York: HarperPerennial, 1990.

Wolfe, Tom. *The Right Stuff*. New York: Bantam Books, 1979.

Williams, Robin M., Jr. *American Society: A Sociological Interpretation*. 3d ed. New York: Alfred A. Knopf, 1970.

Index

About the Author

ALAN EDELSTEIN is Associate Professor of Sociology at Towson State University and the author of *An Unacknowledged Harmony: Philo-Semitism and the Survival of European Jewry* (Greenwood, 1982).